POLITICAL CULTURE
IN SPANISH AMERICA,
1500–1830

Political Culture
in Spanish America,
1500–1830

JAIME E. RODRÍGUEZ O.

University of Nebraska Press
Lincoln and London

Library of Congress Cataloging-in-Publication Data

Names: Rodríguez O., Jaime E., 1940– author.
Title: Political culture in Spanish America,
1500–1830 / Jaime E. Rodríguez O.
Description: Lincoln: University of Nebraska
Press, 2018. | Includes bibliographical
references and index. |
Identifiers: LCCN 2017033948 (print)
LCCN 2017035047 (ebook)
ISBN 9781496204684 (epub)
ISBN 9781496204691 (mobi)
ISBN 9781496204707 (pdf)
ISBN 9781496200884 (hardback: alk. paper)
Subjects: LCSH: Political culture—
Latin America—History—Case studies. |
Spain—Colonies—America. |
BISAC: HISTORY / Latin America / General. |
HISTORY / Latin America / South America.
Classification: LCC F1410 (ebook) |
LCC F1410 .R56 2018 (print) | DDC
306.20946/09031—dc23 LC record
available at https://lccn.loc.gov/2017033948

Set in Arno Pro by Mikala R Kolander.

Dedicated to
WILLIAM F. SATER
distinguished colleague
and the best of friends

CONTENTS

TABLES

PREFACE

During my career I have published numerous articles and book chapters in Europe and the Western Hemisphere. Although the majority of these publications are in Spanish, they are not widely known outside of the country of publication. Since my work focuses primarily on Mexico, I know a number of scholars in that country. Some of these colleagues have noted that many of my articles and book chapters are not available to scholars and to students. José Antonio Serrano Ortega, then professor and now president at El Colegio de Michoacán, a distinguished center for graduate studies and research, proposed that his institution publish a select group of my essays dealing with political culture. Mariana Terán Fuentes, an eminent scholar at the Universidad Autónoma de Zacatecas, read the manuscript and recommended it for publication. As a result, nineteen essays were published in 2015 in two volumes entitled *"Lo político" en el mundo Hispánico*. I received advance copies in time to take two sets to the Rocky Mountain Conference on Latin American Studies (RMCLAS). Various colleagues suggested that a smaller English version be published. Bill Beezley encouraged me to prepare a book that discussed aspects of Hispanic political culture that are not well known in the Anglophone world. I am grateful for his encouragement. Bridget Barry, acquisitions editor for history, geography and environmental studies of the University of Nebraska Press, expressed an interest in the project and sent it out for review. I am also grateful to the two anonymous scholars who read the manuscript and offered valuable suggestions for improving the work. I did not always take their advice but I considered it seriously. My greatest debt is to my colleague, friend, and wife, Linda Alexander Rodríguez. She read the present work in all its versions and offered valuable suggestions that helped clarify and enrich my analysis of political culture in the Hispanic world.

Eight essays were published, including one in English: 1) "La natu-raleza de la representación en la Nueva España y México" in *Secuencia: Revista de historia y ciencias sociales*, núm. 61 (enero-abril 2005): 6–32; 2) "Los Orígenes de la Revolución de 1809 en Quito" in *Soberanía, lealtad e igualdad: Las respuestas americanas a la crisis imperial hispana, 1808–1810*, edited by Ana Buriano and Johanna von Grafenstein, 199–227 (Mexico City: Instituto Mora, 2008); 3) "La cultura política clerical en el Reino de Quito y Ecuador" in *Religiosidad y Clero en América Latina: La época de las Revoluciones Atlánticas (1767–1850)*, 285–306 (Cologne: Böhlau-Verlag, 2011); 4) "Ciudadanos de la Nación Española: Los indígenas y las elecciones constitucionales en el Reino de Quito" in *La mirada esquiva. Reflexiones históricas sobre la interacción del Estado y la ciudadanía en los Andes (Bolivia, Ecuador y Perú), Siglo XIX*, edited by Marta Iroruzqui, 41–64 (Madrid: Consejo Superior de Investigaciones Científicas, 2005); 5) "The Emancipation of America" in *American Historical Review* 105, no. 1 (February 2000): 131–52; 6) "Sobre la supuesta influencia de la independencia de los Estados Unidos en la independencia de His-panoamerica" in *Revista de Indias* 70, no. 250 (septiembre-diciembre 2010): 691–714; 7) "Los caudillos y los historiadores: Riego, Iturbide y Santa Anna" in *La construcción del héroe en España y México, 1789–1847*, edited by Manuel Chust and Víctor Minguez, 309–55 (Valencia: Universitat de Valencia, 2003). The eighth article, "Nuevos caminos; viejas preguntas" was presented at the Coloquio Internacional "Los caminos de la democracia en América Latina: Revisión y balance de la 'nueva historia política' del siglo xix" held at El Colegio de México on November 26–28, 2003. It was not published in Spanish until 2015 in *"Lo político" en el mundo Hispánico* by Jaime E. Rodríguez O. (Zamora: El Colegio de Michoacán, 2015), 1:123–35.

During the years that I have worked on these essays, I have been for-tunate in receiving financial aid from the Academic Senate Committee on Research of the University of California, Irvine, the Research of Travel Committee of the School of Humanities at UCI, the University of California Institute for Mexico and the United States (UC MEXUS), the Social Science Research Council, two from the Fulbright Foundation, and the president of the University of California in the form of a President's Humanities Fellowship. I am also grateful to the Rockefeller Foundation for its invitation to reside five weeks in its Study and Conference Center in Bellagio, Italy, which afforded me the opportunity to read, think, and discuss my ideas and theirs with Linda Alexander Rodríguez, Christon I. Archer, and Virginia Guedea as well as other scholars then resident in the Center.

A NOTE ON USAGE

Cristóbal Colón (Christopher Columbus) had been en route to India when he tripped over the islands of the Caribbean; therefore the inhabitants of the Western Hemisphere came to be called *indios* (Indians) and their lands *las indias* (the Indies). In the eighteenth century, however, the continent was renamed *América* and its inhabitants, *americanos*. Since America is the name of the Western Hemisphere, all peoples from Canada to Argentina may correctly be called *Americans*. This was a concern that vexed Spanish Americans even before independence.

The Mexican political theorist Servando Teresa de Mier identified the problem during a visit to the United States in 1820. He explained:

> Since the Europeans believe there is no other America than the one their nation possesses, an erroneous nomenclature has formed in each nation. . . . In France, generally, when one speaks of America one means Santo Domingo [Haiti]; in Portugal, Brazil. The English call their islands in the Caribbean Archipelago, our Indies or the West Indies; and for the English there is no other North America than the United States. All Spanish North America is to them South America, even though the largest part of the region is in the north. The people of the United States follow that usage and they are offended when we, in order to distinguish them, call them Anglo Americans. They wish to be the only Americans or North Americans even though neither name is totally appropriate. Americans of the United States is too long. In the end, they will have to be content with the name *guasintones*, from their capital Washington (the w is pronounced *gu* [in English]), just as they call us Mexicans, from the name of our capital.

xiii

In this book, I refer to Spanish America as *America;* the people of Spanish America, the subject of this work, are called *Americans.* This seems to me entirely appropriate because those terms were used formally and informally in the Hispanic world during the period examined in this work and because they continue to be used today.

Introduction

"The people of ... [Spanish] America are the most ignorant, the most bigoted, the most superstitious of all Roman Catholics in Christendom. . . . No Catholics on earth were so abjectly devoted to their priests, as blindly superstitious as themselves. . . . Was it probable, was it possible, that ... a free government ... should be introduced and established among such a people ... ? It appeared to me ... as absurd as ... [it] would be to establish democracies among the birds, beasts, and fishes."

JOHN ADAMS, Quincy, March 27, 1815

John Adams is not the only one to have believed the Hispanic world incapable of self-government. Many scholars then and now believe that constitutional representative government is alien and unsuited to the supposedly conservative society of the Hispanic world.[1] They erroneously believe that the Spanish Monarchy was highly centralized, they confuse absolute with autocratic rule, and they equate the modern concept of colony with pre-nineteenth-century governing practices. As a result they are certain that the representative political structures established in the post-independence period were alien systems imported from Great Britain, the United States, and France. These scholars are unaware of the broad body of scholarship that demonstrates that Spain played a central role in the development of ideas that were embraced by fifteenth-century intellectuals and refined over subsequent centuries. To understand the nature of Spanish American political culture it is necessary to dispel misperceptions about the political system of the Spanish Monarchy and the theory and practice that sustained it.

A SHARED POLITICAL CULTURE

Western political culture originated in ancient Greece and Rome. As Paul Cartlege states: "Much of our political terminology is Greek in etymology: aristocracy, democracy, monarchy, oligarchy, plutocracy, tyranny, to take just the most obvious examples, besides politics itself

1

and its derivatives. Most of the remainder—citizens, constitution, dictatorship, people, republic and state—have an alternative ancient derivation, from the Latin."[2] The government of the Roman Republic (509–27 BC) influenced political theorists in the West over the centuries. Most contemporary regimes are modeled on the Roman Republic, which is considered a mixed government because it included the rulers (two consuls), an aristocratic elite (the senate), and the people (the assembly). Indeed, it provided the United States with virtually all its political concepts, such as the two members of the executive branch (president and vice president), the senate, and the assembly (House of Representatives), as well as separation of powers, term limits, regularly scheduled elections, checks and balances, quorum requirements, vetoes, block voting, and dilatory tactics known as the filibuster.[3] Many of these principles appear in the charters of other Western nations because they share the Greco-Roman heritage.

During the Middle Ages, Western Europe developed a common political culture. The works of scholars, who created a Western legal and political culture, circulated throughout Europe. Writing in Latin, the language of erudition, facilitated intellectual interchange. Some of these treatises advanced the theory of a mixed government.

Based upon the political cultures of ancient Greece, Rome, late medieval Europe, and the Italian Renaissance, city-states embraced the concept of mixed government, a regime in which all shared sovereignty: the one, the ruler; the few, the prelates and the nobles; and the many, the people. Mixed governments were considered the best and most lasting because they limited the arbitrary or tyrannical power of the king, the nobles, and the people.[4]

During the twelfth to fifteenth centuries, cities and commerce expanded in Western Europe, creating a new class who were neither vassals nor nobles. These urban residents emerged as significant political actors in twelfth-century Iberia. The cities and towns gained power and influence in León-Castile because their financial and physical resources—particularly their militias—proved crucial to the Crown during the *Reconquista* (the reconquest of territory from the Muslims).[5]

In 1188 King Alfonso IX convened the *Cortes,* the first congress in Europe that included the three estates: the clergy, the nobility, and the cities. Although the English Magna Carta of 1215 is often considered the foundation of representative government, the first true English parliament, which included the representatives of cities, met in 1275; and although regions of France created *parlements* (autonomous courts), the first true French congress, the States-General, met in 1302. Subsequently, other areas of Europe also established representative assemblies. All of those bodies convened randomly when the ruler required counsel and, especially, when he sought tax increases.[6]

This heritage and three events in the sixteenth century transformed the nature of Hispanic political thought. A great political revolution, the Rebelión de las Comunidades de Castilla (the rebellion of the cities of Castile), erupted in the Iberian Peninsula during the years 1517 to 1521. Taking advantage of the coronation of King Carlos I, who was raised in Flanders and had few direct ties with Spain, the representatives of the cities of Castile attempted to assume power and establish a new constitutional order. They formed a Junta General de las Comunidades de Castilla (a general assembly of the cities of Castile), which insisted that the cities represented the *patria,* that the king was their servant, that they possessed the right to elect the Cortes on a regular basis, and that they could defend their liberties with force if necessary. They maintained that the will of the people and the consent of the governed had to be recognized, insisting not only on liberty but also on democracy. The forces of the Crown defeated this movement, which has been called the first modern revolution, in the Battle of Villalar on April 23, 1521. Thereafter, the Cortes continued to function in a traditional form. Nevertheless, the *rebelión* became the foundational myth for the revolutionaries in the Cortes of Cádiz three centuries later.[7]

The Protestant Reformation also contributed to the expansion of the concept of popular sovereignty among Hispanic political theorists. When Martin Luther advanced the principle of the divine right of princes, in order to reject similar papal claims, the Catholic theorists of the School of Salamanca responded to Luther's arguments by advancing the principle of *potestas populi* (sovereignty of the people). Francisco Suárez directly refuted Luther's claims of the divine right of princes. He and other authors, such as Francisco de Vitoria, Diego de Covarrubias, Domingo de Soto, Luis de Molina, Juan de Mariana, and, most important, Fernando Vázquez de Menchaca, "helped to lay the foundations for the so-called 'social contract' theories of the seventeenth century .... [Moreover, the] Jesuit Mariana ... [advanced] a theory of popular sovereignty which, while scholastic in origins and Calvinist in its later developments, was in essence independent of either religious creed, and was thus available to be used by both parties."[8] As the English historian Quintin Skinner shows, the Hispanic neo-scholastic theorists provided "a large arsenal of ideological weapons available to be exploited by the revolutionaries" of later periods.[9]

The seven northern provinces or states of the Low Countries— Brabant, Gelderland, Flanders, Holland, Zeeland, Friesland, Mechlin, and Utrecht—relied on these and other political theories to challenge the authority of the Spanish monarch, Felipe II. In 1579 they signed the Union of Utrecht, thereby becoming *united states*, and agreed to cooperate with each other in their opposition to higher taxes, the persecution of Protestants, and the elimination of their medieval representative governing structures. Two years later they issued the Act of Abjuration, their declaration of independence from Felipe II.[10] Then in 1588 they established the Dutch Republic. Naturally, those insurgents justified their revolt against the king to whom they owed allegiance in numerous treatises defending their right to self-determination, religious freedom, and representative government.[11] According to the Dutch historian Martin van Gelderen, the insurgents relied principally on works of the Hispanic neo-scholastics, particularly Vázquez de Menchaca.[12]

Ideas of the Hispanic theorists established "a vocabulary of concepts and an accompanying pattern of political arguments that Grotius, Hobbes, Pufendorf and their successors all adopted and developed in building up the classic version of the natural-law theory of the State in the course of the following century."[13] Vázquez de Menchaca's arguments influenced English and French thinkers and other well-known theorists such as Johannes Althusius, Hugo Grotius, Thomas Hobbes, John Locke, and others.[14] The political theories Enlightenment thinkers advanced were essentially refined versions of previous works. The revolutions that erupted at the end of the eighteenth and the beginning of the nineteenth centuries relied on earlier concepts and practices. According to Skinner, "the concepts in terms of which Locke and his successors developed their views on popular sovereignty and the right of revolution had already been largely articulated and refined over a century."[15] Thus, it is not surprising that the leaders of Spanish American independence, both on the royalist and insurgent sides, relied heavily on the writings of the Hispanic neo-scholastics and on Hispanic legal traditions.

The Spanish Americans of the *antiguo régimen* (Old Regime) knew that their lands were kingdoms and not colonies because they shared the same legal foundations as the kingdoms of southern Castile after they had been retaken from the Muslims.[16] For example, most of the *audiencias* (high courts with administrative authority) that were introduced early into the New World were founded on the Ordenanzas de Monzón de Aragón of 1563.[17] As late as 1808, the Peninsula was divided into *capitanías generales* (captaincies general) administered by *capitanes generales* (captain generals) similar to those exercised by *virreyes* (viceroys) in America.[18] The overseas realms were divided into viceroyalties and regions subject to external attack, captaincies generals. Similarly, Bourbon improvements such as the intendancies and the municipal reforms of 1776, the church and army reforms, and free trade, were introduced first in Spain and later in America.

As Servando Teresa de Mier, one of the most distinguished advocates of the thesis of American rights, declared:

> Our kings, far from having considered establishing in our Americas the modern system of colonies of other nations, not only made our [kingdoms] the equals of Spain but also granted us the best [institutions] she possessed. [And he maintained:] in conclusion it is evident that under the constitutions granted by the kings of

Spain to the Americas, these lands are kingdoms independent of her [Spain] without any other link than the king, . . . who, according to political theorists, must govern us as though he were the king of each one of them [the American realms].[19]

Today there is an extensive debate about the nature of the overseas realms. The term colony is difficult to define. Many historians no longer use this term but instead utilize *antiguo régimen*. The French historian Annick Lempériere, for example, argued that historians should not use the concept *colony* because it is misleading.[20] The United States was a colony but few discuss its *postcolonial* status. Scholars do not consider the former as a postcolonial nation because it lacks the characteristics that most attribute to postcolonialism: limited economic and political success. They do not consider the United States a postcolonial nation because its economy continued to flourish and they erroneously believe it immediately consolidated its political system.

In Spanish America the term "colony" is often associated with the *Leyenda Negra* (black legend), which holds that virtually everything that is bad, brutal, and evil comes from Spain. No Leyenda Negra exists about England despite the fact that it conquered Scotland and Ireland with great brutality and virtually exterminated the natives of North America.[21] On the contrary, scholars attribute the success of the United States, to a significant extent, to its English heritage. The opposite is true for the Spanish American nations. The supposedly backward, repressive, and obscurantist Spanish heritage is generally blamed for the area's limited economic and political success.

The appellation *absolutism* is generally associated with the antiguo régimen. One of the most important advocates of this term is Perry Anderson, whose *Lineages of the Absolutist State* essentially maintains that the absolute monarch exercised total power over the land. Other scholars, such as William Bouwsma and Roger Mettan, disagree. According to Bouwsma: "Nothing so clearly indicates the limits of royal power as the fact that governments were perennially in financial trouble, unable to tap the wealth of those most able to pay, and likely to stir up a costly revolt whenever they attempted to develop adequate income."[22] This is also a perfect description of how the French Revolution began. Moreover, a group of European historians published a volume entitled *Der Absolutismus-ein Mythos* in 1996 in which they demonstrate that no western European monarch had possessed total power over his or her kingdom.[23]

THE *ANTIGUO RÉGIMEN*

The Spanish possessions in America constituted a part of the worldwide Spanish Monarchy—a confederation of disparate kingdoms and lands that extended throughout portions of Europe, Africa, America, and Asia. The Catholic faith played a fundamental role in uniting the Spanish Monarchy. Although the people of its various realms retained their languages, laws, and customs, they all had to be Catholics. The "one true faith" defined Hispanic society. In the Hispanic world, however, the Catholic Church was not autonomous: Spanish rulers had administrative control over the church. Clergymen held numerous government posts, including the position of viceroy. When acting as government officials, churchmen represented the king, not the pope. Ecclesiastics in their nonclerical capacity were virtually indistinguishable from their secular counterparts since they were educated at the same institutions. Many were distinguished scholars and scientists who addressed topics that today we consider secular.[24] Clergymen as well as seculars developed Hispanic political theory in a parallel fashion to political thought in Italy, France, and the Protestant countries. As a major segment of Occidental civilization, the Hispanic world shared a common Western European culture. The intellectuals of the Spanish Monarchy based their political ideas on ancient classical thought, on Catholic theories, and on the writings of a group of sixteenth- and seventeenth-century Hispanic theorists.

Spanish Americans traced their right to representation to their Hispanic heritage and to the unique governing relationship that developed during the Spanish settlement. Cities and the *Cortes* became the principal venues for representation in Castilian politics during the period of the conquest and settlement of the New World. From the outset the settlers of the New World insisted not only on representation at the court but also in the parliament of Castile.

Neither the independence of the United States nor the French Revolution convinced the people of Spanish America to sever ties with the Spanish Monarchy. Instead, an unexpected upheaval transformed the Hispanic world. In 1808 the French invaded Spain. Emperor Napoleon Bonaparte lured the royal family into France, compelled them to abdicate in his favor, and then granted the Spanish Monarchy to his brother, José. The Spanish people did not accept the usurper king, José I, because he represented the "atheist" French whose actions threatened the very foundations of Hispanic society—God's representative on earth, the church, and the representative of Hispanic rights and liberties, the legitimate king, Fernando VII. Moreover, unlike previous dynastic changes, no Cortes confirmed the transfer of power as the law required.

The people of Spanish America responded to the 1808 monarchical crisis with great patriotism and determination. Americans of all races and classes unanimously expressed their fidelity to Fernando VII, their opposition to Napoleon, and their determination to defend their faith and their patrias from French domination.[25]

The collapse of the Spanish Monarchy triggered a series of events that culminated in the establishment of representative government in the Spanish world. A political revolution erupted that sought to change the worldwide Spanish Monarchy into a modern nation-state with a representative government for all parts of the *Spanish Nation*, as the Spanish Monarchy was now called. The initial step in that process was the formation of local governing juntas in Spain and America that invoked the Hispanic legal principle that in the absence of the king, sovereignty reverted to the people. Ultimately this process resulted in the creation of a Hispanic parliament, the Cortes. Ayuntamientos throughout Spain, Spanish America and the Philippines held elections for deputies to the Cortes.[26] Approximately 220 deputies, including 65 Americans and 2 Filipinos, eventually participated in the General and Extraordinary Cortes that met in Cádiz in September 1810. The delegation from New Spain, for example, included 14 ecclesiastics, 3 government officials, 2 military men, and 2 merchants. The deputies from the New World played a central role in the parliament, serving as presidents, vice president, and secretaries of the Cortes and participating in important committees. Five Americans served on the commission to prepare the project of the constitution.[27]

The constitution promulgated in March 1812 was not a Spanish document; it was a charter for the Hispanic world. Indeed, the Constitution of Cádiz would not have taken the form it did without the participation of the New World representatives. The Constitution of 1812, the most radical charter of the nineteenth century, abolished seigniorial institutions, Indian tribute, and forced labor, and it asserted the state's control of the church. It created a unitary state with equal laws for all parts of the Spanish Monarchy, substantially restricted the king's authority, and entrusted the legislature with decisive power. The Charter of 1812 also dramatically increased the scope of political activity by establishing representative government at three levels: the city or town with a thousand or more inhabitants (constitutional ayuntamiento), the province (provincial deputation), and the monarchy (Cortes). Political power was transferred from the center to localities, incorporating large numbers of people into the political process for the first time. When it enfranchised all adult men except those of African ancestry, without requiring either literacy or property qualifications, the Constitution of 1812 surpassed all existing representative governments, such as Great Britain, the United States, and France, in providing political rights to the vast majority of the male population. An analysis of the 1813 election census in Mexico City, for example, concludes that 93 percent of its adult male population possessed the right to vote.[28]

The Cortes entrusted the provincial deputation with overall responsibility for its province. The new institution, with the *jefe político superior* (superior political chief) presiding and with the intendant as a member, consisted of seven elected deputies. Although the constitution abolished the office of viceroy, the chief officials of the former viceregal capitals retained broad military authority in the kingdoms as *capitanes generales* and *jefes políticos superiores*. The Cortes established nineteen provincial deputations for the overseas territories: New Spain, New Galicia, Yucatán, San Luis Potosí, Provincias Internas de Oriente, Provincias Internas de Occidente, Guatemala, Nicaragua, Cuba with the two Floridas, Santo Domingo and Puerto Rico, New Granada, Venezuela, Quito, Peru, Cuzco, Charcas (present-day Bolivia), Chile, Río de la Plata, and the Philippines. Autonomists controlled Chile and Río de la Plata and therefore they did not recognize the Constitution of Cádiz or hold elections. Nothing is known about the Philippines.

The second home-rule institution that the Cortes created, the constitutional ayuntamiento, substituted popularly elected officials for the hereditary elites, who had heretofore controlled city government. For the first time local populations directly elected the officials who administered important aspects of their lives. Citizens of the Hispanic world exercised an unprecedented level of authority within their communities. This right included inhabitants of indigenous villages. Although the Constitution of Cádiz excluded from suffrage men of African ancestry, recent studies demonstrate that in many instances men of African ancestry in fact voted and, in some cases, the electorate chose them as officials in New Spain, Guatemala, Guayaquil, and Peru.[29]

The crisis of 1808 and the Constitution of 1812 provided an opportunity for laymen and ecclesiastics to enter politics in new arenas. Churchmen became some of the most active politicians, participating at all levels from the parish and the province to the monarchy. Like their secular brethren, they came from a variety of social and economic backgrounds and held a variety of political views. The post-1808 clerical politicians did not represent the interests of the church as an institution. Indeed, some of the most virulently anticlerical politicians were churchmen.

The new system required the development of new procedures such as population and electoral censuses and entities such as electoral officials to hold and determine the validity of elections. Since completing these tasks was more difficult in some regions than in others, the pace of implementing the new system varied throughout the Hispanic world. During the first constitutional period (1812–1814) two American kingdoms, New Spain and Quito, fully established the new constitutional order. Although fewer scholarly studies exist, Guatemala and Peru also appear to have implemented the constitutional structure fully. However, in most regions researchers have found only fragmentary evidence concerning the number of constitutional ayuntamientos. Other areas, such as Puerto Rico, Cuba with the two Floridas, Santo Domingo, Venezuela, New Granada and Charcas, introduced the reforms partially.

The constitutional elections from 1812 to 1814 were the first popular elections held in the former Kingdom of New Spain. Nearly one thousand constitutional ayuntamientos were established, the vast majority of them in Indian towns. In some areas, cities and towns held three successive ayuntamiento elections from 1812 to1814. Five regions created provincial deputations. Novohispanos (persons of New Spain) elected forty-one deputies to the 1813–1814 ordinary Cortes that met in Madrid and a comparable number for the 1815–1816 congress. The scope of political participation was extraordinary. Hundreds of thousands of citizens, including Indians, mestizos, castas (persons of racial mixture that included blacks) and blacks participated in elections and in government at the local, provincial, and monarchy-wide levels.[30]

The Constitution of Cádiz divided the former Kingdom of Guatemala into two provincial deputations, Guatemala and Nicaragua. The preparatory junta determined that with a population of 840,000 inhabitants, Central America had the right to elect twelve deputies. Although the documentation is vague, residents appear to have established more than a hundred constitutional ayuntamientos in the two provincial deputations, including indigenes (natives) and castas. Only one elected deputy served in the Ordinary Cortes of 1813–1814 in Madrid. However, many Central Americans who had been deputies to the Cortes of Cádiz served as *suplentes* (substitute deputies) in the Cortes of Madrid.[31]

In South America, an armed struggle to maintain autonomy complicated the electoral process. Civil wars ravaged the former Kingdom of Venezuela from 1810 to 1814. Royalists and insurgents gained and subsequently lost control of various provinces. In this unstable situation the six provinces that escaped most of the conflict—Maracaibo, Valencia, Coro, Barcelona, Cumaná and Margarita—elected constitutional ayuntamientos. Although Caracas attempted to hold elections for deputies to the Cortes of 1813–1814 and the Provincial Deputation of Venezuela when the royalists were in power, researchers have found no evidence indicating that such elections were held.[32]

The former Kingdom of New Granada also endured civil wars among the centralist State of Cundinamarca headed by Santa Fé de Bogotá, the confederate United Provinces of New Granada directed by Cartagena de las Indias, and the royalist forces of the provinces of Santa Marta and Panama. The capitals of the royalist provinces formed constitutional ayuntamientos. The small towns of those two provinces likely also established constitutional ayuntamientos but no information has been found to substantiate that elections took place.[33]

It is striking that popular elections occurred in royalist areas in the midst of a violent insurgency. The 1813–1814 elections in the Provincial Deputation of Quito provide an example. Royalist forces under the command of General Toribio Montes crushed the second junta of Quito at the end of 1812, leaving much of northern New Granada in autonomist hands. As required by the Hispanic constitution, however, General Montes initiated the process of holding popular elections. After months of effort, the electoral census of the Provincial Deputation of Quito—which included the highland provinces from Pasto and Popayán in the north to Loja in the south, Marañon, Mainas, and Jaén de Bracamoros in the eastern jungles, and the northern coastal provinces of Barbacoas and Esmeraldas—was completed in June 1813.[34] More than thirty constitutional ayuntamientos had formed during the months from September 1813 to January 1814. Since some regions were "currently occupied by the enemy," the authorities determined that the Provincial Deputation of Quito had the right to elect six proprietary deputies and two suplentes. The election of deputies to the Cortes and the provincial deputation in the former Kingdom of Quito proved to be lengthy and complicated. Finally, eighteen representatives met in Quito from August 24 through 26, 1814, to elect the six deputies to the Cortes, the two suplentes, and the seven deputies to the provincial deputation. As occurred in other areas of the New World, the quiteños (people from Quito) selected Americans rather than peninsulares (persons from Spain) to represent them. Significantly, what they had been unable to win by force, the quiteños accomplished through the ballot.[35]

The Constitution of Cádiz divided the former Kingdom of Peru into two provincial deputations, Peru and Cuzco. The preparatory junta determined in February 1813 that with a population of 1,180,669 inhabitants, Peru had the right to elect twenty-two deputies to the Cortes.[36] However, only eight deputies managed to attend the Cortes of Madrid. The provincial deputation was formally established on April 30, 1813; it functioned only until October 1814, when news arrived that Fernando VII had restored the antiguo régimen. Although communities throughout the Provincial Deputation of Peru formed constitutional ayuntamientos, scholars only have carried out detailed studies of events in Lima.[37]

The Constitution of 1812 had a far-reaching impact in Cuzco. There the provincial deputation functioned from September 1813 to November 1814. The provincial government held elections for its seven deputies to the Cortes in April 1813. None of the deputies arrived in Madrid to participate in the first ordinary session of the legislature. At the local level, residents held elections for constitutional ayuntamientos in the entire provincial deputation. However, scholars base their conclusion on events in Cuzco and Puno, where the populace recognized the importance of the opportunities provided by the new system to defend the interests of areas independent from Lima. Instead of returning to the antiguo régimen as the restored King Fernando VII ordered, local leaders established an autonomous junta.[38]

The situation of Charcas is not clear. Professional historians are only now beginning to study the political and constitutional processes here. Invaded by armies from Buenos Aires and royalist forces from Peru, the region endured continuous warfare. No evidence has emerged to indicate that residents formed the Provincial Deputation of Charcas. Although some researchers allege that elections for deputies to the Cortes were organized in 1812, given insufficient time and political stability, elections seem improbable. Moreover, only the name of one deputy who was in Cádiz as a suplente receives mention. Local populations did, however, hold elections for constitutional ayuntamientos.[39] Scholars of the region are engaged in research that will expand our understanding of events in this area and in other Andean regions.

The Constitution of Cádiz divided the Caribbean into three provincial deputations: Cuba with the two Floridas, Puerto Rico, and Santo Domingo. Residents of towns and villages in the first two provincial deputations held elections for constitutional ayuntamientos. It also appears that there were elections for the Cortes and the provincial deputation.[40] Scholars have only begun to study this period in Santo Domingo.

Had all the provinces of America eligible to elect deputies exercised that right, 149 delegates would have represented the New World, just a few less than the number from Spain. However, circumstances in America prevented many elections from taking place. Sixty-five deputies from the New World participated in the ordinary Cortes of October 1, 1813 to May 10, 1814. Only 23 were elected under the new constitutional system; the other 42 were suplentes. American deputies in the 1813–1814 Cortes represented the following provinces: Cuba had 3 representatives; the Floridas, 1; Puerto Rico, 1; Santo Domingo, 1; New Spain, 19; Guatemala, 7; Venezuela, 3; New Granada, 2; Panama, 1; Quito, 1; Guayaquil, 1; Peru, 18; Charcas, 1; Montevideo, 1; Río de la Plata, 3; and Chile, 1.[41]

INSURGENCY

Fear of domination by the French emperor Napoleon Bonaparte, widely known in the Spanish world as *el tirano* (the tyrant), strengthened the desire of many in America to govern at home. Because all areas of the Spanish Monarchy possessed the same political culture, all these movements, including the insurgencies, justified their actions on the same grounds and in virtually identical terms. They argued that since the French had imprisoned the king, sovereignty reverted to the people. The South American juntas initially consisted of both *peninsulares* and Americans. However, when it appeared that Spain was falling completely under French domination, more radical Americans took control, ousting the Europeans from power. In most cases, the governing juntas acted as though they were independent. Only a few eventually declared formal independence from the Crown. The vast majority of the politically active population of Spanish America desired to retain ties with the Spanish Monarchy. Thus, they remained open to negotiating with the Crown to achieve self-rule.

In 1809 movements for autonomy emerged in Charcas (present-day Bolivia) and Quito; they reappeared in 1810 in Venezuela, Río de la Plata, New Granada, New Spain, Chile, and Quito, all seeking to establish local juntas in the name of the imprisoned King Fernando VII. Historians generally have assumed that these movements invoked the name of Fernando VII to *mask* their real goal: independence. Strong evidence to the contrary exists, however. Not only did the leaders of the American juntas insist that they were acting in the name of the sovereign, they invited Fernando to come to America and govern.

The American juntas based their actions on the same juridical principle that their peninsular counterparts invoked: in the absence of the king, sovereignty reverted to the people. While that principle justified the formation of local governments in the name of Fernando VII, it did not support separation from the monarchy. Therefore those favoring autonomy grounded their arguments on the *unwritten* American constitution, the direct compact between the individual kingdoms and the monarch. According to their interpretation, the king, and only the king, possessed ties with the New World kingdoms. If that relationship changed, for whatever reason, the bond between any American kingdom and Spain or even among individual New World realms disappeared.

The authorities in Spain found such views unacceptable. The Council of Regency, which functioned as the executive, and the Cortes could not constitutionally accede to the separation of the New World kingdoms. Therefore, when reforms and negotiations failed to restore the American juntas to compliance with the government, the authorities in Spain resorted to force.

Several additional factors complicated the subsequent struggle. Some Spaniards and Americans in the New World who believed that the Council of Regency was, indeed, the legitimate government, opposed the formation of local juntas. While various provinces within the American kingdoms concluded that they also possessed the right to form their own local governments—a view that their capital cities rejected with force—in some regions, the elites were divided into factions that competed to control government posts and the formation and implementation of public policy. In other instances, conflict erupted between the cities and the countryside. Thus, civil wars engulfed large parts of the New World, pitting supporters of the Spanish government against the American juntas, the capitals against the provinces, the elites against one another, and urban against rural groups.

The nature of transportation and communication also influenced events. Normally, the two- to four-month delay in communications between Europe and America was inconsequential, but during emergencies it became very significant. The Atlantic ports were the first to learn of events in the Old World. Those on the Pacific received the news much later. In much of South America, geography and climate impeded transportation and communication between coastal cities and the interior; great distances, forests, mountains, heat, rain, and cold all affected communications. Highland cities such as Santa Fé de Bogotá, Quito, and La Paz, frequently were cut off from the coast for months during rainy season. Thus, it was not an accident that Caracas and Buenos Aires were among the first to respond to the crisis of the monarchy. Lima, on the other hand, often learned of events in Europe at the same time that it received news of reaction to those events by cities such as Caracas and Buenos Aires. In the North, better roads facilitated communication in the great Viceroyalty of New Spain.

When news of 1808 events in the Peninsula arrived, European Spaniards in Mexico City overthrew the viceroy in an effort to prevent the formation of a local junta to rule in the name of Fernando VII. They feared that Americans would dominate the junta. Most Spaniards and some Americans opposed this illegal usurpation of power. When they failed to topple the new government through peaceful means, some resorted to violence. Sporadic localized uprisings and conspiracies erupted into widespread rural insurgencies by the end of 1808. The royalists defeated the organized insurgencies in 1810, but the countryside continued to be plagued by banditry and localized uprisings.

South America experienced a very different political process in 1810. The kingdoms in the South, with the exception of Peru, established governing juntas that assumed authority to rule in the name of the imprisoned king and sought to dominate their respective regions. Many provinces, however, rejected their capitals' pretensions and, as a result, armed conflict engulfed most realms in South America. In some instances these civil wars occurred because some provinces supported the government in Spain while their capitals opposed it. But in others, such as New Granada, the conflict consisted primarily of regional power struggles.

The conflict in the New World waxed and waned during the first constitutional period, from 1810 to 1814. At times it appeared that the new Hispanic constitutional system might accommodate the insurgents. That situation changed when King Fernando VII returned; he abolished the constitution and the Cortes and restored the antiguo régimen. Initially autonomists in America believed the king would support moderate reforms, but ultimately the king opted to rely on force to restore royal order in America.

The Crown's repression prompted the minority of America's politically active population that favored independence to act decisively. Republicans renewed the struggle in Venezuela in 1817, and by 1819 the tide had turned against the monarchy when a combined force of *neogranadinos* (people from New Granada) and Venezuelans defeated the royalists at Boyacá, forcing the viceroy of New Granada and other officials to flee from Bogotá. In the South, José de San Martín won a decisive victory in Chile in April 1818.

The renewed conflict in South America enhanced the power of military men. Self-proclaimed generals like Simón Bolívar and former professional soldiers such as José de San Martín gained immense power and prestige as leaders of the bloody struggles to win independence. Although civilian and clerical institutions—ayuntamientos, courts, parishes, cathedral chapters—continued to function, and although new governments were formed and congresses elected, military power predominated. Colombia provides the clearest example. The Congress of Angostura that Bolívar convened in February 1819 legitimized his power and in December created the Republic of Colombia, incorporating Venezuela, New Granada, and Quito. Although Venezuela and New Granada had some representation, Quito had none. Most representatives were military men who served as suplentes.[42]

THE CONSTITUTION OF CÁDIZ RESTORED

Spanish and American liberals grew increasingly dissatisfied with the autocratic government of Fernando VII. In March 1820 liberals in Spain forced the king to restore the Constitution of Cádiz.[43] The return of constitutional order transformed the Hispanic political system for the third time in a decade.

The new liberal regime sought to end the conflict in America through conciliation. On April 11, 1820, it instructed the viceroys and captains general in the New World to publish the monarch's decree restoring the constitution and encouraging everyone, including the dissidents, to swear allegiance to the charter. The decree restored representative government and required authorities to hold immediate elections. Insurgent leaders were encouraged to acknowledge the constitution; even those refusing were allowed to retain their authority if they recognized the monarchy. The government ordered a ceasefire, an exchange of prisoners, and the initiation of negotiations. Finally, as they had done in 1809 and during the first constitutional period, the authorities in Spain appointed royal commissioners to resolve American grievances.[44]

The junta provisional in Madrid decided not to restore the old Cortes but to convene new elections. It issued a new convocatoria (convocation or call for elections) on March 22. The government convened the new Cortes before the arrival of proprietary deputies from the New World. Until the new deputies arrived, the authorities charged citizens from the overseas territories residing in the Peninsula to elect thirty suplentes chosen from individuals residing in the Peninsula. Americans in Spain, some of them recently released from confinement for opposing authoritarianism, vehemently protested that the number of suplentes allocated to the New World was inadequate. They insisted on doubling their representation, and some refused to participate in the election of suplentes unless the government acceded to their demands. Despite numerous protests, the junta provisional refused to modify its decision. It maintained that elections in America would provide the New World with parity in the new Cortes. The distinguished parliamentarian from Coahuila, New Spain, Father Ramos Arizpe, convinced the Americans that it was better to possess fewer representatives than none at all. The Americans ultimately agreed to participate, electing 29 suplentes, including 15 for America Septentrional: New Spain, 7; Guatemala, 2; Cuba, 2; Philippines, 2; Santo Domingo, 1; and Puerto Rico, 1. South America received 14 suplentes: Peru, 5; New Granada, 3; Buenos Aires, 3; Venezuela, 2; and Chile, 1.[45]

Although the royal authorities in the overseas territories, with varying degrees of enthusiasm, restored the constitutional order in those regions under their control, there was a considerable difference between North and South America. While the former experienced fully the new political system in its first and second periods, the latter did not. Autonomists, who did not implement the Spanish constitutional system, controlled large regions of South America. In 1820 the Río de la Plata, Chile, and parts of Venezuela and New Granada were in the hands of autonomist regimes unwilling to return to the monarchy, even under the Hispanic constitution. Some South American political leaders, however, still favored establishing independent kingdoms with European—preferably Spanish—rulers and retaining ties to the Spanish Crown in a federal system of monarchies. In that sense no region of Spanish America completely severed its links with the Spanish Monarchy.

The constitutional elections dominated the political life of most royalist areas, particularly in North America. Former Viceroy Apodaca distributed more than a thousand copies of the constitution to the cities and towns of New Spain, while Captain General Carlos Urrutia disseminated about five hundred copies in the Kingdom of Guatemala. In New Spain, for example, elections for its six provincial deputations occurred between August and October 1820. The provinces held two separate elections for deputies to the Cortes: one rapidly in the autumn of 1820 for the 1821–1822 parliament, and a second starting in December for the 1822–1823 session of the Cortes. In addition, local communities conducted more than a thousand elections in December for the constitutional ayuntamientos of 1821. Thus from June 1820 to March 1821, electioneering and elections preoccupied the politically active population of New Spain—perhaps numbering into the hundreds of thousands.[46] Similarly intense political participation occurred in the Kingdom of Guatemala, Cuba with the two Floridas, Puerto Rico and Santo Domingo. These areas not only held elections for constitutional ayuntamientos, but also for deputies to the Cortes of Madrid and to their provincial deputations.[47]

Extensive warfare in South America, however, restrained electoral politics. Quito's experience during the second constitutional period is illustrative of the conflicts and difficulties of holding elections at a time of widespread insurgency. In mid-1820 General Melchor Aymerich, president of the audiencia, faced insurgencies from Colombia in the north and Peru in the south. Only the coastal provinces in the west and the jungles on the eastern side of the cordillera appeared quiet. Fears of insurgent threats intensified in July and August as reports from Barbacoas and Guayaquil indicated widespread unrest along the coast. In an effort to maintain order, the audiencia imposed travel restrictions throughout the kingdom.[48]

In these tense circumstances, news reached Quito on August 27, 1820, that the constitution had been restored. After consulting the Audiencia and the Ayuntamiento of Quito, Aymerich instructed the cities and towns of the realm not to hold the elections scheduled for December 1820, but to extend the terms of their constitutional officials for another year. This emergency measure continued until the Province of Quito, as the realm was called under the constitution, was pacified. Nevertheless, Guayaquil, which had been restored to Quito, held constitutional ayuntamiento elections on September 29, 1820.[49]

Although the separatist movements in the north and south had accepted the crown's ceasefire, they used this period to prepare for a renewed offensive. As a result, the leaders of Guayaquil decided to protect the autonomy of the Kingdom of Quito. A junta of notables declared independence in the name of the people on October 9, 1820, as the first act in the establishment of the State of Quito. They elected their former deputy to the Cortes of Cádiz, José Joaquín Olmedo, president of the new government. The new regime informed Quito, Cuenca and other cities and towns of the former Kingdom of Quito of their actions and convened a constitutional congress to meet in Guayaquil on October 8, 1820. The government of Guayaquil also formed an army, the *División Protectora de Quito* (division to protect Quito), to liberate the rest of the realm.[50]

The highland cities and towns, however, preferred the restored Constitution of Cádiz and began electing constitutional ayuntamientos and deputies to the Cortes of Madrid and to the Provincial Deputation of Quito. The elections were lengthy and complicated. Some cities and towns found it difficult to hold elections "because of the political circumstances" of the day.[51] Authorities in Riobamba, for example, declared that a large proportion of the city's population so feared the insurgents that they had fled to the countryside. Cuenca officials expressed concern with subversives determined to open the city to the "rebels" from Guayaquil. Despite the growing power of the republican forces from Guayaquil, the constitutional order was in full operation in all royalist-held areas as 1822 began.[52]

Venezuela's experience was similar. On December 17, 1819, in Angostura, a congress that contained no representatives from Quito, very few from Nueva Granada, and only suplentes from most provinces of Venezuela—including the most populous, Caracas—established the Republic of Colombia. It named Simón Bolívar, an authoritarian leader who had awarded himself the title of "libertador," president. A few months later, the citizens of Spain restored the Constitution of Cádiz. The majority of the population of Venezuela, including Caracas, rejected the Constitution of Angostura and instead elected numerous constitutional ayuntamientos, deputies to the Cortes of Madrid and to the Diputación Provincial de Venezuela. As a result, Bolívar had to conquer Venezuela in order to liberate it.[53] In the years that followed, he subdued large parts of Nueva Granada, Quito, Peru, and Charcas because those kingdoms also preferred the Constitution of Cádiz.

The situation in Peru was equally complicated. After the restoration of the Constitution of Cádiz, Peru held elections for constitutional ayuntamientos, deputies to the Cortes, and Diputación Provincial del Peru. Shortly thereafter, José de San Martín arrived and forced the city of Lima to declare independence and abolished the diputación provincial.[54] When San Martín's forces occupied Lima, the royalists retreated to the highlands where they carried out the instructions of the Cortes. In 1821 they established a provincial deputation in Cuzco and new ones in Huamanga, Arequipa, Puno, and La Paz. The royalists governed a territory that contained heavily populated Indian communities, most of whom believed that the Constitution of Cádiz offered them the greatest opportunities, and therefore they overwhelmingly supported the Crown.[55]

When the Cortes convened in Madrid in July 1820, the American deputies, led by the North American contingent, again raised the "American Question." They demanded equal representation, free trade, and the abolition of monopolies. They also called for the installation of a provincial deputation in every New World intendancy. Because Spain was becoming embroiled in internal political conflicts between the moderate *doceañistas*, the men of the first constitutional period, and the *exaltados*, the younger and more radical men of 1820 who wanted rapid political change, the suplentes from America found it difficult to obtain a complete hearing of their proposals. Nevertheless, the Cortes considered projects for economic and institutional improvements in the New World. It also authorized the establishment of one new provincial deputation in Valladolid, New Spain before recessing at the end of 1820.

The arrival of the proprietary deputies in 1821 reinforced the American delegation. From February to June 1821, more than forty proprietary deputies arrived from New Spain, six from Guatemala, one from Cuba, one from Panama, and three from Venezuela. They and the suplentes, who remained in the new session, constituted a powerful coalition that continued to press the American Question and to criticize the government for failing to resolve the issues that had led to the conflict in the New World.[56]

SEPARATION

Political instability in Spain during the previous dozen years, however, had convinced many novohispanos that it was prudent to establish an autonomous government within the Spanish Monarchy. The autonomists, the members of the national elite who ultimately gained power after independence, opted for a constitutional monarchy. They pursued two courses of action. New Spain's deputies to the Cortes proposed a project for New World autonomy that would create three American kingdoms governed by Spanish princes allied with the Peninsula. The Spanish majority, however, rejected the proposal that would have granted Americans the home rule that they had been seeking since 1808. At the same time, New Spain's autonomists encouraged and supported the royalist Colonel Agustín de Iturbide, who accepted their plan for autonomy, which resembled the proposal that Americans had presented to the Cortes. Iturbide and his supporters won the backing of the majority of the royal army, assuring independence. Mexico achieved its independence not because the royal authorities lost on the battlefield but because the novohispanos no longer supported the Crown politically.

The newly independent Mexicans carefully followed the precedents of the Spanish constitutional system. Although they initially established an empire, they soon formed a federal republic in 1824. They modeled their new constitution on the Hispanic charter because it had been part of their recent experience. Like Mexico, the new Central American republic established a federation based on Hispanic constitutional practices.[57]

In South America the restoration of the Hispanic constitution provided those favoring independence the opportunity to liberate the continent. In contrast to New Spain, the South American insurgents defeated the royal authorities militarily. Two pincer movements, one from the south and the other from the north, eventually converged on Peru.

The separatists began to occupy Venezuela and New Granada in 1820. On October 9, 1820 Guayaquil declared independence, formed a republic, and attempted without success to free the highland provinces of the Kingdom of Quito. A mixed force consisting mainly of local troops, Colombians, and men from San Martín's army under the command of General Antonio José de Sucre finally defeated the royal forces in Quito on May 24, 1822, at the Battle of Pichincha. Simón Bolívar, who arrived from the north in June with more Colombian troops, incorporated the region into the republic of Colombia despite opposition from both Quito and Guayaquil. Subsequently, Bolívar imposed martial law in the former Kingdom of Quito, known as the South or Ecuador, to impress men as well as to requisition money and supplies for the struggle against the royalists in Peru, the last bastion of royal power in America.[58]

The southern forces led by San Martín landed in Lima in August 1820 with a liberating army composed of Chileans and *ríoplatences*. Although he controlled the coast, San Martín could not overcome the royalists in the highlands. The Spanish constitutionalists reorganized the royal army and nearly drove San Martín's forces from the coast. But divisions within the royalist ranks prevented them from defeating the forces of independence.

Unable to obtain the support he needed in Peru and abroad, San Martín ceded the honor of the final victory to Bolívar. Although the Colombians arrived in force in 1823, they made little progress. Divisions among Peruvians, shortage of supplies, and strong royalist armies kept them pinned down in the coast. However, the royalist armies were also divided. In Charcas, the absolutist general Pedro Antonio Olañeta opposed general Joaquín de la Serna and the *liberales*. After King Fernando VII again abolished the Hispanic Constitution, General Olañeta took up arms against the Spanish liberales on December 25, 1823. This internecine warfare contributed to the royalists' defeat. For nearly a year, while Bolívar and his men recovered, royalist constitutional and absolutist armies waged war in the highlands. Ultimately, General Sucre defeated the royalist constitutional army in the decisive battle of Ayacucho on December 9, 1824. Olañeta's absolutist forces, however, remained in control of Charcas. Political intrigue finally ended the struggle. The assassination of Olañeta in April 1825 marked the end of royal power in Charcas. Subsequently, General Sucre formed the new republic of Bolivia. By 1826 when the last royal forces surrendered, Bolívar dominated northern South America as president of Colombia, dictator of Peru, and ruler of Bolivia.

Two competing political traditions emerged during the independence period: one, forged in more than a decade of war, emphasized strong executive power; the other, based on civilian parliamentary experience, insisted on legislative dominance. They epitomized a fundamental conflict about the nature of government. New Spain, which achieved its independence through political compromise rather than by force of arms, is representative of the civil tradition. There, the Hispanic constitutional system triumphed and continued to evolve. Despite subsequent *golpes de estado (coups d'etat)* by military men, civilian politicians dominated Mexican politics.

In contrast, military force ultimately liberated northern South America. Unlike Mexico, in Colombia, Peru, and Bolivia, the men of arms dominated the men of law. The Hispanic constitutional experience exerted little influence in the region. In the north, the three newly independent South American nations established strong centralist governments with powerful executives and weak legislatures. In 1830 Colombia—sometimes called *Gran Colombia*—splintered into three countries: Venezuela, New Granada, and Ecuador. There the preponderance of militarism continued for decades.

In contrast, the Southern Cone, which also had won independence by force, did not fall under the control of military men. The region endured only limited warfare with royalist forces. Most of the armed conflicts occurred between and among provinces. Although Santiago and Buenos Aires toyed with federalism, Chile eventually established a highly centralized oligarchical republic, whereas in the Río de la Plata, the various provinces formed a loose confederation. Despite vast differences in the nature of their regimes, civilians dominated both nations.[59]

CASE STUDIES

The essays in this volume concentrate on politics and political processes or "the political," as the *Nouvelle Histoire Politique* calls it.[60] To understand the complex process that led to the creation of the Spanish American nations, we must place it within the context of the broader political transformation to representative government in the Hispanic world. Although the work focuses primarily on what some scholars call *high politics*, it does not assume that *low politics* did not exist. The urban and rural lower classes possessed their own interests and concerns. Researchers have examined some of these, primarily those of the rural groups. But many scholars fail to incorporate these finding into their analysis and assume that the *campesinos* (rural people) as well as the urban poor, either did not know, understand, or care about the pressing political issues of the day. That conclusion is incorrect. Urban and rural popular groups not only knew and understood the advantages and disadvantages of what has been called the *social compact* of the monarchy but also were keenly aware of the political change carried out by the Hispanic Cortes. The evidence indicates that poor people, whether urban or rural, were not only affected by high politics but also understood their interests and took action to defend them; that is, they engaged in politics. Some participated in autonomist and insurgent movements. Others took advantage of the upheavals to pursue their own goals. Many others joined members of the urban upper and middle classes who remained loyal to the Crown.[61] Their staunch defense of the Spanish Monarchy continued until independence, thirteen years after the crisis unleashed by the collapse of the monarchy in 1808.

The book consists of eight case studies that examine aspects of political culture in Spanish America during the three centuries in which the New World realms formed part of the worldwide Spanish Monarchy. Although four of the eight essays focus on New Spain and Quito, the topics considered in them are generally applicable to the rest of Spanish America.

Chapter 1 examines the nature of representation in the Kingdom of New Spain, the largest, most developed, and most populous realm in America. It demonstrates that the settlers of the New World possessed representation through their cities from the beginning of the sixteenth century. The Spanish Monarchy also considered granting the American realms, such as New Spain, the right to convene a cortes as well as representation in the Cortes of Castile. That did not occur because the American cities were satisfied with the representation they possessed. In the late eighteenth century, the Crown introduced municipal reforms to provide more ample representation in the cities. Finally, the French invasion of Spain in 1808 resulted in the uprising of the *people*, a new political actor, against the invaders that led to the establishment of constitutional government in the Spanish-speaking world.

Chapter 2 sustains that the 1809 Revolution of Quito was not a movement for independence. Rather, it was a local reaction to the crisis of the Spanish Monarchy. The Quito movement, like those in the Peninsula and the rest of America, sought to safeguard the Spanish Monarchy from the French usurpers. The essay focuses on the factors that led to the formation of the 1809 junta and its eventual demise. Quito's eighteenth-century economic and political decline and its failure to achieve autonomous status within the Spanish Monarchy shaped the 1809 movement. The crisis of the monarchy, however, provided the leaders of Quito an opportunity to form an autonomous government that would free it from the authority of New Granada and Peru. Their plan, which threatened the interests of the other provinces, led to a civil war that ended in Quito's defeat.

Chapter 3 examines the nature of clerical culture in the Kingdom of Quito. In the Spanish Monarchy the Catholic Church was not autonomous; it was subordinated to the kings who had obtained administrative control over the church through the *patronato real* (royal patronage), as a result of the papal donation of 1493 and the papal bulls of 1501 and 1508. In essence the Hispanic church responded to the king and became one of the monarchy's mainstays. The clergy, particularly the members of the regular orders, also dominated higher education and provided most social services. The city of Quito, which had several universities, became a center of learning, especially in the eighteenth century. Clergymen served as administrators as well as professors who taught courses ranging from science and law to the humanities. When the crisis of the Spanish Monarchy erupted in 1808, churchmen became important leaders of royalist and autonomist movements. They also participated in the Quito Revolution of 1809.

Chapter 4 analyzes the role of indigenes in the constitutional elections of 1813 to 1814 in the Kingdom of Quito. Contrary to the widely-held view of prominent historians that Indians were not interested and did not understand the political, economic, or social implications of the revolution in the Hispanic world, the essay demonstrates that the natives were not only interested, but also involved in the day's events.[62] It examines the many ways in which they participated in the political processes of the time. Indeed, they were central to the electoral process in the Province of Quito. They not only controlled their towns, they also formed coalitions with other groups to win elections in large cities, such as Cuenca and Loja in the south.

Chapter 5 demonstrates that the independence of the United States did not influence the Spanish Americans to separate from the Spanish

Monarchy. Their failure to act did not stem from ignorance. On the contrary, numerous printed works provided them with detailed information about events in North America. Since the Seven Years' War Spanish-language newspapers and publications had kept the Hispanic public informed about the discontent in the North American colonies, the process of independence, and the establishment of a republican government. Subsequently, an unprecedented event —the French invasion of the Iberian Peninsula—transformed the Hispanic world. The ouster of the Spanish king triggered a series of events that culminated in the establishment of representative government in that worldwide polity and eventually in the dissolution of the composite Spanish Monarchy. Thus, the independence of the United States and of Spanish America occurred not only at different times, but also under different circumstances.

Chapter 6 compares and contrasts the processes of independence of the United States, Haiti, and Spanish America. British America, aided by Spain and France, achieved its independence as part of an international war and through an international settlement, the Treaty of Paris of 1783. In Haiti the reaction by white residents to the French Revolution sparked a successful slave rebellion and revolution that totally transformed the colony. Napoleon's 1808 invasion of Spain triggered a political revolution that established a liberal representative government in the Spanish world. However, the emancipation of Spanish America did not merely consist of separation from the mother country, as in the case of the United States: it also destroyed a vast and responsive social, political, and economic system that had functioned well despite its many imperfections. In the post-independence era it became apparent that, individually, the former Spanish Monarchy's separate parts were at a comparative disadvantage in the new world order dominated by English-speaking countries. As a result, neither Spain nor the Spanish American nations managed to recover sufficiently to become developed nations in the nineteenth century.

Chapter 7 examines the tendency of scholars to rely on the concept of *caudillo*, which means *leader* in English, to explain the nature of politics during most of the nineteenth century in Spanish America. Their ignorance of representative government in Hispanic America leads them to explain Hispanic American political culture in terms of authoritarianism. As a result, they do not study the political institutions of Spanish America. The chapter demonstrates that three famous caudillos—Rafael Riego, Agustín de Iturbide, and Antonio López de Santa Anna—did not act alone. Rather, an analysis of the roles of Riego, Iturbide, and Santa Anna demonstrates that they did not impose their will upon a passive people. Instead, circumstances of the time and broad political forces shaped their actions. In the three instances, a wide variety of individuals and groups were responsible for the political transformations rather than the three leaders.

Chapter 8 considers the trends of Anglophone historiography during the last half century. It traces the movement away from political and institutional history to cultural and social approaches by most scholars and its impact on the field. The chapter evaluates the debates that emerged in the Anglophone world, particularly in the United States. It discusses the emergence of "postmodernist" cultural history and the decline of political and institutional history. It concludes with the extensive debates between the historians of Latin America who base their work on evidence and those who have adopted the jargon of postmodernism. Recently, scholars—particularly those in Spanish-speaking nations, "the new Latin American political historians"— are undertaking the detailed state, regional and political studies necessary to understanding the complex political, social, and economic relationships among the elites and the popular groups.

Future scholarly research will be required to achieve a profound understanding of the political culture of the Spanish American countries that emerged from the breakup of the composite monarchy. It is my hope that these essays will encourage historians of Spanish America to reexamine the political institutions and processes of those nations from a broad perspective.

1

The Nature of Representation in New Spain

As part of the worldwide Spanish Monarchy, the Viceroyalty of New Spain had a long tradition of representation that began during the Spanish settlement of America and reached its apogee with the Hispanic Constitution of 1812. The Spanish Monarchy, a major segment of Occidental civilization, drew upon a shared Western European culture that originated in the ancient classical world. The cities or *los pueblos*, and the *Cortes* were dominant venues for political participation or representative government in Castile during the period of the conquest and settlement of the New World.[1] They emerged as important political structures in the twelfth century, when Iberian rulers sought resources to retake the Muslim territories in the Peninsula. The political power of the cities gradually increased, reaching its zenith during the reign of the Catholic Kings—Isabel of Castile and Fernando of Aragon—who used these entities to pacify and unite the realm. The cities and *villas* (towns) gained power and influence in Castile-León because their financial and physical resources—particularly their militias—were crucial to the Crown during the Reconquista.[2]

In return for their support, the cities obtained *fueros* (privileges or liberties), granting them the right to administer both the urban settlements and their large rural hinterlands. They obtained a form of autonomy and self-government comparable to the city-states of northern Italy. By the end of the fourteenth century, the Crown began to appoint *corregidores* (magistrates) to the cities and towns with ayuntamientos. In this way the incorporation of these new political actors allowed the monarch to free himself from the power of the prelates and nobles.[3] The relationship between the king and the pueblos, particularly in the Cortes, constituted a form of mixed government. Political theorists identify it with the mixed constitutions of ancient Greece and Rome and with the Germanic warrior bands, the *comitatus,* who selected their rulers.[4]

The first settlers established cities and towns with their own governments in the islands of the Antilles because, within the Iberian system, those institutions provided them sovereignty and therefore, authority. In 1518 the governor of the island of Hispaniola convened a junta of the island's city and town *procuradores* (representatives); the ayuntamientos authorized their representatives to take whatever steps they considered appropriate to promote the common good. Later, the junta moved to Cuba, where it assembled annually in the city of Santiago to identify and inform the king of the island's most important needs and to request their fulfillment.[5] The Crown subsequently ratified these actions. According to José Betancourt, the Ayuntamiento of the Villa of Puerto Principe received a letter dated April 2, 1532, declaring: "His Majesty orders that every year in a timely fashion the procuradores of the *villas* (towns), meet every year in [the city of] Santiago and together with the procuradores of that city inform His Majesty of their most important needs."[6] The cities and pueblos also sent procuradores to the court in Castile to represent their interests. Thus, representation and mixed government were fundamental features of the Spanish conquest and settlement of the Indies and the rest of the New World.[7]

The conquest of Mexico exemplifies the application of both the theories of Saint Thomas Aquinas, which emphasize the right of *el pueblo* (the people) to rebel against a tyrant, and the authority and sovereignty of the Iberian municipality. Hernán Cortés launched his expedition in defiance of the governor of Cuba, Diego Velázquez, and secured authority for his actions by establishing a city. His men assumed the role of *vecinos* (citizens of the city) who established a *cabildo* (city government) in Villa Rica de Vera Cruz. They justified their actions on the ground that there was no formal authority. In such circumstances, according to Isadoro de Seville, the Siete Partidas, and Saint Thomas, sovereignty reverted to the people. The sovereign people of Vera Cruz appointed Cortés their leader and authorized the conquest of the land for the king.[8]

After the conquest, the first settlers founded a number of cities and towns, principal among them Mexico. In May 1529 the procuradores of the villas of Veracruz, Espiritu Santo, Colima, and San Luis convened in Mexico City "to discuss and agree upon what is convenient in service of God and of H.M. and for the well being and perpetuity of this land." The body named procuradores to travel to the court to protect the interests "of this New Spain." The following month, the representatives met again to approve the salaries of the procuradores. They also commissioned the procurador Dr. Ojeda "to request and negotiate with H.M. that this city of Mexico, in the name of New Spain, have voice and vote in the Cortes that H.M. or the kings who succeed him convene."[9] From the outset, the settlers of New Spain insisted not only on representation at the court, but also in the parliament of Castile. The request is particularly impressive when one considers that they were asking that the city of Mexico become the capital of its region in the same way that Burgos and Toledo regulated their regions in Castile.

Demetrio Ramos contends that in 1635 the Crown granted New Spain and Peru, the two great viceroyalties in the Indies, representation in the Cortes of Castile. He bases his assertion on a *cédula* (royal warrant) that proposed granting representation to the New World: "Among the recommendations proposed for the utility and well-being of those provinces [in the New World] it is convenient to my service to grant to the inhabitants of the audiencias of" those overseas territories representation in the Cortes of Castile. However, José Miranda, who examined the records of the Ayuntamiento of Mexico, found no indication that the residents of the Indies had accepted that privilege. It is likely that they were unwilling to fund the cost of sending deputies to the Cortes of Castile in part because they considered the existing system of representation sufficient.[10]

The nature and history of these New World assemblies has been the subject of much disagreement. Some historians argue that these juntas or congresses of cities functioned as true cortes. Others, such as Alfonso

García Gallo maintain that they were "mere congresses of cities, which considered matters of common interest . . . without aspiring to intervene in the higher politics of the state."[11] In either case, these assemblies are evidence of the early settlers' insistence upon representation and a mixed constitution. The subsequent history of these congresses is murky. José Betancourt, Rafael Altamira, and Jesús E. Casariego maintain that these cortes of the Indies continued to convene during the sixteenth and seventeenth centuries. The first two assert that as many as forty such congresses met during that time, while Casariego raises their number to fifty.[12] Unfortunately, these scholars do not offer precise citations. Betancourt declares simply that the minutes of these sessions are in the Archive of Simancas. Guillermo Lohmann Villena questions the assertions, arguing that no one else has found "references about such important events, which would have left traces in some other document."[13]

The issue is further complicated by the fact that proponents of the cortes *indianas* do not distinguish between New Spain and Peru when they assert that such congresses met during the first two centuries. We know that on various occasions during the sixteenth century, the authorities in South America discussed the possibility of introducing juntas or cortes in the Viceroyalty of Peru, which then included all of Spanish South America. Perhaps the most detailed analysis of the question took place in 1609 when the procuradores of the cities and towns of Peru requested permission from Viceroy Marqués de Montesclaros to hold periodic juntas. The viceroy's council, after weighing and considering the advantages and disadvantages of holding such congresses, ultimately recommended against them.[14]

The situation was different in New Spain. On June 25, 1530, Emperor Don Carlos and the Governing Empress issued the following cédula: "In consideration of the greatness and nobility of the city of Mexico . . . we order that it have the first vote of the cities and villas of New Spain, and the first place, after the judges, in the congresses that may be convened on our instructions; because without them it is not our intention or will that the cities and villas of the Indies meet."[15] The declaration clearly established the possibility that a true cortes—that is, a parliament convened by the king—assemble. However, it also clearly stated that such a body could meet only if the monarch convened it. Since Carlos I had diminished the role of the Cortes of Castile after the defeat of the *Comuneros* at Villalar in 1521, he was unlikely to permit the vecinos of New Spain to develop a potentially autonomous parliament.[16] There is no evidence of a request by Hispanic rulers to convene a congress of cities or cortes in New Spain. Nonetheless, Mexico City's right to preeminence in a congress of cities of New Spain represented an important step in the region's political evolution.

Some historians, such as Mario Góngora, contend that the Indies never fully accepted the concept of absolute royal power, which had emerged in Europe in the sixteenth century. This was certainly true in New Spain where, for example, in 1680 Carlos de Sigüenza y Góngora insisted on the primacy of the people over the ruler, relying on Fernando Vázquez de Menchaca's assertion that "The laws of a kingdom, even the positive ones, are not subject to the will of the prince. Therefore, he does not have the power to change them without the consent of the people because the prince is not the absolute lord of the laws but the guardian, servant, and executor of them. And that is how he is considered."[17] In addition, Castilian law required and the Crown acknowledged that authorities must refuse to implement laws that contravened the best interests of the community. Since 1379 the formula *se obedece pero no se cumple* (it is obeyed but not implemented) expressed that fact. In 1528 King Carlos I decreed that "the ministers and judges are to obey but not to enforce our warrants and dispatches tainted by the vices of *obrepción* and *subrepción* [laws based on false information provided to the royal authorities to derive personal gain or decisions that inadvertently harm the community]. And at the first opportunity they must notify us of the reason why they did not implement them."[18] Moreover, the settlers of the Indies insisted on the right to resist unjust laws, particularly taxes.

Resistance to royal authority—in effect, civil disobedience—was rampant during the sixteenth century. For example, the ayuntamiento led the 1592–1593 revolt of the *alcabala* (sales tax) in the city of Quito, declaring that it had already made sufficient contributions to the monarchy and that new taxes were unwarranted.[19] The people of the Indies claimed that they possessed rights that even the king could not abridge. A form of mixed government or a mixed constitution, in which the Crown and the people reached a consensus that did not require institutionalized consent, emerged in the New World. The Spanish population of the New World believed "that the 'unwritten constitution' provided that basic decisions were reached by informal consultation between the royal bureaucracy" and the king's subjects in the Americas. In fact this was the way the system functioned for three centuries; the parties constructed workable compromises that reconciled what the central authorities wanted with what local conditions and the residents would tolerate.[20]

Although a mixed constitution and representation were part of the experience of the first settlers and their descendants, the demand for representation in a cortes did not escalate. Instead, at the end of the sixteenth and the beginning of the seventeenth century, New World elites seem to have abandoned their efforts to obtain a local cortes. Instead, the cities became the leading representatives of their regions' interests, and the *venta de cargos* (the sale of offices) emerged as a significant mechanism of home rule, suppressing the desire for representation in a cortes. The criollos, who controlled the ayuntamientos or cabildos of the viceregal capitals, the capitals of audiencias, and the capitals of frontier regions, assumed the responsibility and the right to represent their areas. As John Elliott observes, those lands "were becoming Creole states."[21]

The ayuntamientos became the centers of power. Because we lack careful analyses of most of these municipal governments, some historians have dismissed them as meaningless centers of elite domination. Others assert that these bodies were more concerned with pomp and ceremony than in administering their territories. They argue that royal authorities were the ones who really governed those regions. These views also conflict with the political culture of the time, which emphasized the ideal of a *res publicae* or mixed government. The concept of *república*, however, did not signify a form of government without a king. Instead, it referred to a system of government in which civic virtue ensured liberty and stability. The true republican citizen placed the common well-being of the res publicae, or the community above his own narrow interests.[22]

There were two repúblicas in the Indies—*la república de españoles* (the republic of the Spaniards) and la *república de indios* (the republic of Indians). Both possessed forms of representation and autonomy. Although the capital cities of the república de españoles claimed to represent their entire regions, the repúblicas de indios also defended their own interests. They sent procuradores to the Peninsula from the beginning. Various studies, particularly Woodrow Borah's and Brian Owensby's analyses of the Juzgado General de los Indios (general court of the Indians), demonstrate that the natives successfully defended their interests, both in the New World and in the Old. They relied extensively on the judicial system to protect them from other groups in New Spain, which to amazing degree supported their claims.[23]

The Castilian polity also had other mechanisms that provided representation to a broad range of groups. As John Phelan has observed:

The Spanish Monarchy was absolute only in the original medieval sense. The king recognized no superior inside or outside his kingdoms. He was the ultimate source of all justice and all legislation. The late medieval phrase was, 'The king is emperor in his realm.' [It is worth noting here that the Castilian verb *imperar* meant *to govern*]. The laws that bore the royal signature, however, were not the arbitrary expression of the king's personal wishes. Legislation, and the extent to which it was enforced, reflected the complex, and diverse aspirations of all or at least several groups in that corporate, multiethnic society. The monarchy was representative and decentralized to a degree seldom suspected. Although there were no formal representative assemblies or Cortes in the Indies, each one of the major corporations, such as the [*repúbli-*

cas, or Indian governments], the cabildos, the various ecclesiastical groups, the universities, and the craft guilds, all of which enjoyed a large measure of self-government, could and did speak for their respective constituents. Their views reached the king and the council of the Indies, transmitted directly by their accredited representatives or indirectly through the viceroys and the audiencias and their aspirations profoundly shaped the character of the ultimate decisions.[24]

Margarita Garrido's book, *Reclamos y representaciones: Variaciones sobre la política en el Nuevo Reino de Granada*, the only systematic study of the question, demonstrates that all groups defended themselves against a great variety of real or perceived slights. Residents of small pueblos as well as larger cities in both repúblicas often challenged the actions of the monarch, royal officials, judges, regidores, alcaldes, and even their vecinos, the citizens of their own city or town. Sometimes they lost, but frequently they won their demands.[25] Their actions clearly demonstrate their belief in the mixed constitution and the inalienable right to influence the nature of their government.

The people of the New World also demanded the right to exercise authority in their lands. Indeed, they claimed that they should have a virtual monopoly of *cargos* (offices). Many *tratadistas* (legal scholars) in Spain and the overseas kingdoms supported this view. Perhaps the most distinguished exponent of that concept was the eminent Castilian jurist and royal official, Juan de Solórzano Pereira, who insisted that natives should have preference in appointments not only to civil but also to clerical cargos. His *Política indiana* published in 1649, after nearly two decades of experience in the Indies, held that the New World polities were kingdoms of the Spanish Monarchy that "must be ruled and governed as if the king who holds them all together were king only of each one of them."[26] It was a view that eighteenth-century Americans embraced and often repeated. As Fray Servando Teresa de Mier, one of the most distinguished defenders of the rights of Americans, declared:

It is evident that under the constitution granted by the kings of Spain to the Americas, these lands are kingdoms independent of her [Spain] without any other link but the king who according to political theorists, must govern us as though he were the king of each of them [the American realms]. When I refer to the social pact of the Americans, I do not refer to Rousseau's implicit pact. Rather, it consists of the pact between the Kingdom of New Spain and the sovereign of Castile. The rupture or suspension of that pact results, as an inevitable consequence, in the resumption of sovereignty by the Nation. When that occurs, sovereignty reverts to the original owner.[27]

The situation changed in the eighteenth century when the Bourbon monarchs sought greater control of their overseas territories.[28] The inhabitants of the New World developed a sense of their unique identity within the Spanish-speaking world. Like their counterparts in the Peninsula, Spanish Americans identified with their locality and its history. They not only wrote about the conquest and the spread of Christianity, but also embraced their Indian past. Perhaps the most distinguished exponent of this American patriotism was the *novohispano* Francisco Javier Clavijero, who published the *Historia antigua de México* in four tomes. Clavijero identified the history of his land with the ancient Mexica (popularly referred to as Aztecs) of the ancient classic world.[29] The *Historia antigua de México* not only symbolized the novohispanos' pride in their land, it also justified their desire to govern it themselves. The residents of New Spain considered it one of the kingdoms of the Spanish Monarchy and demanded the king recognize their equality.

The Bourbon reforms, which have been described as "the second conquest" by John Lynch and "a revolution in government" by David Brading, did not constitute a carefully orchestrated, determined and well-executed plan of action. Rather they consisted of a number of initiatives that responded to the particular needs of the monarchy. The *visita general* (general inspection) by José de Gálvez, the establishment of the mining tribunal, the introduction of a standing army, the creation of the system of intendancies, the formation of two new *consulados* (merchant guilds) in Veracruz and Guadalajara, and the elimination of clerical privilege unquestionably changed the relations of power in New Spain. These reforms did not, however, as many scholars erroneously assert, represent a virulent form of colonialism. Rather they were attempts by the Crown to devise efficient methods of obtaining the financial resources the Monarchy required to compete in the increasingly hostile international arena. The cities, as representatives of their regions, constituted an important obstacle to that effort because they generally opposed tax increases.[30] Therefore, the Monarchy moved to reduce their power both in the Peninsula and in America.

In the 1760s the Crown instituted municipal reforms, first in Spain and then in New Spain. Concerned that the ayuntamientos used their public funds poorly, the king ordered royal officials to examine cities' accounts. The audits demonstrated numerous irregularities. Therefore, the Monarchy established a regulatory body, the *Contaduría General de Propios y Arbitrios* (general accounting of property and arbitration), to review annually the expenditures of the cities. Subsequently, José de Gálvez carried out an audit of ayuntamiento finances in New Spain during his *visita general*. After examining the accounts of Mexico City, he accused the regidores of corruption, alleging that their transactions favored relatives and friends. Galvez and other reformers argued that the sale of offices contributed substantially to corruption and mismanagement. He recommended, and the Crown approved, the introduction of a Contaduría General de Propios y Arbitrios in New Spain.

Earlier the Crown had begun the process of reducing control of municipal government by local elites in the Peninsula and in the American realms. In 1766 Carlos III issued the "Instrucción de Diputados y Personeros" to reform municipal government in Spain. He declared: "Seeking to avoid in the pueblos all the vexations [either] of bad administration or of the system of councilmen that they may endure . . . and so that all the *vecindario* (vecinos of the town) may know how [the pueblo's funds] are handled and so that they may reflect on the most useful way [to utilize them] ... we order" that this reform be implemented.[31] The introduction of *diputados del común* (representatives of the public in the ayuntamiento) and *personeros* (officials who were concerned with the city's finances) generally has been interpreted as an effort by the Crown to establish greater control over municipal government by undermining the power of the *regidores perpetuos* (hereditary councilmen). Scholars have failed to examine the impact of the reform on political participation; it provided that vecinos vote at the parish level for *compromisarios* who in turn elected the diputados del común and the síndicos personeros. Those eligible to vote included not only nobles, professionals, and merchants, but also artisans and *campesinos* as long as they had "employment or a decent profession."

Similar elections also occurred in New Spain in the 1770s. There the officials were called *regidores honorarios* and *síndicos procuradores del común*. The number of those officials depended on the size of the city. Mexico City, for example, elected six regidores honorarios and two síndicos while Puebla chose four regidores honorarios and two síndicos. According to Reinhardt Liehr, the following cities and towns held elections: Guadalajara, Veracruz, Jalapa, Querétaro "and evidently in San Luis Potosí, Zacatecas and other cities of the viceroyalty."[32] François-Xavier Guerra states: "In New Spain many [ayuntamientos] included diputados and síndicos personeros del común, introduced by the municipal reforms of Carlos III and, therefore, elected by all the vecinos."[33] An *acta electoral* (electoral report) from the small town of Villa de Yxtlahuaca documents that suffrage might be extensive, including secular clergy, landowners, merchants, artisans, carpenters and Indians.[34] This document suggests that the municipal reforms in New Spain as in the Peninsula provided a new avenue for local representation and expanded political participation throughout the viceroyalty.

As Annick Lepérière observes: "The Spanish Crown displayed sufficient imagination to free itself from the narrow framework of urban representation that was tied to the defense of privileges and ... patrimonies .... Relying on the most accepted corporate traditions, it invented ingenious mechanisms of representation that were based on guilds and territory."[35] Simultaneously these entities provided the Monarchy new sources of revenue. The strengthening of the *Consulado* (merchants guild) de México, which had long been a rival of the capital's ayuntamiento, and the addition of two new consulados—one in Veracruz and the other in Guadalajara—are examples of the means by which the Crown sought to increase revenues. One of the most interesting, however, was the *Cuerpo y Tribunal de Minería* (corps and tribunal of mines).

The Crown approved the creation of the new institution to meet the needs of the miners and the Monarchy. Silver production was believed to have declined in the 1760s. The industry consisted of a few large mines employing large numbers of well-paid workers and many small mines worked primarily by their owners with the help of a few laborers. In 1766 workers in the Real del Monte, one of the most productive mines in New Spain, engaged in a lengthy strike. A coalition of miners had decided that decisive action was required to restore the industry. They commissioned the learned novohispano, Joaquín Velázquez de León, to write a *representación* (a request) that was submitted to the king in 1774 and proposed the establishment of a mining guild, a *banco de avíos* (bank to promote mining), and a seminar or college of mining. Two years later, the Crown approved the proposal with some modifications. The Cuerpo y Tribunal de Minería introduced a new and extensive form of representation. It ordered the *real de minas* (royal mines) to establish *diputaciónes* (committees) composed of deputies elected by the local miners. These bodies addressed local needs in a variety of ways. They also sent representatives to the Tribunal in Mexico City to address general mining interests and to oversee the management of the Banco de Avíos and the seminar. Velázquez de León became the first director of the Tribunal.[36] For the first time in its history, New Spain possessed a body that represented all regions and that met in the capital. Although the assembly neither represented all the viceroyalty's people nor concerned itself with the overall government of New Spain, it marked an important step in the development of both representative government and banking.

As the Crown expected, the new institutions contributed to economic growth. More importantly, they supported the Monarchy financially. In return for a written constitution—their *ordenanzas*—and the right of representation and self-government, the new bodies, particularly the consulados and the Cuerpo y Tribunal de Minería, raised unprecedented sums of money to support the Crown. At a time of increasing international conflict, the Spanish Monarchy desperately needed these new resources.[37]

These new institutions of *"gobierno económico"* (economic government) threatened the primacy of the cities, which lacked their resources and ability to mobilize capital. However, the municipalities did not abandon their quest to protect their rights and privileges. The persistent and increasing Crown demands for money to pay for the international wars undermined the finances of New Spain. Perhaps the greatest single disruption to the viceroyalty's economy occurred when the king extended the Royal Law of Consolidation to America in 1804. First enacted in Spain in 1798 to redeem *vales reales* (royal bonds) and other war debts, the law authorized officials to seize and auction church real estate. In return, clerical institutions would receive 3 percent on the "loans" to the government. The Crown believed that the measure would be beneficial because the action would provide small farmers and other entrepreneurs the opportunity to acquire land. However, because the church in New Spain served as the viceroyalty's principle banker, the measure could ruin the country. The principal corporations of the realm immediately challenged the law. Despite desperate and even threatening protests, the authorities enforced the consolidation decree.[38] This extraordinary act, whose negative consequences affected all social and economic groups, threatened the pact between the people and the king—the principle of mixed government that had functioned successfully for three centuries and allowed the Hispanic world to remain united for 300 years with almost no standing army in its overseas territories. It symbolized the *mal gobierno* (bad government) that traditional Hispanic political theory opposed.

It was in that context that news arrived in Mexico City in June and July 1808 of the disasters that were rapidly unfolding in Europe: the French occupation of the Peninsula, the collapse of the Spanish Monarchy, and the establishment of local juntas by Spain's provincial capitals. On July 19, the American-dominated Ayuntamiento of Mexico submitted a resolution to Viceroy José de Iturrigaray asking him to continue *provisionally* in charge of the government. The ayuntamiento utilized traditional Hispanic political theory to justify its position: "In the absence and impediment [of the king], sovereignty lies represented in the entire kingdom and the classes that form it; and more particularly in those superior tribunals that govern it and administer justice and in those corporations that represent the voice of the public."[39] Therefore the ayuntamiento proposed convening a congress of cities.

As soon as they learned of the proposal, cities such as Querétaro and Valladolid also requested the convocation of a congress of municipalities. On September 1, 1808, Viceroy Iturrigaray at the behest of the *españoles americanos* (American Spaniards) requested that the ayuntamientos of New Spain appoint representatives to a meeting in the capital. The *Real Acuerdo* (royal council), composed primarily of European Spaniards, objected to the summoning of a congress of cities. Therefore the viceroy sought to reconcile the two factions by convening four meetings of the principal corporations of Mexico City. The meetings were tempestuous. The Americans advanced a powerful argument based on juridical principles, which were consistent with Spanish political theory, and the actions of Spaniards in the Iberian Peninsula.

The European Spaniards, determined to retain power, carried out the first coup in New Spain shortly after midnight on September 16, 1808. The following morning, they informed the inhabitants of New Spain that "the people have seized the person of the . . . viceroy" for the well-being of society. As Virginia Guedea notes, the conspirators appealed to the authority of the *pueblo* in an effort to legitimate their *golpe de estado* because by that time the concept of popular sovereignty had gained considerable authority.[40] Indeed, in the Peninsula, the people had removed distrusted officials.

The crisis of the Monarchy and the events of 1808, both in Spain and in New Spain, marked the start of a significant transition in Hispanic political culture. *Los pueblos*, the cities, acted and continued to act for a time as the representatives of their regions. However, a new actor, *el pueblo*, as the representative of an inchoate and still poorly defined nation, emerged on dos de mayo—May 2—in Madrid.

The establishment in Spain of the *Junta Suprema Central y Gubernativa del Reino* (supreme central governing junta of the kingdom), which first met on September 25, 1808, appeared to be a solution to the crisis of the Monarchy. However, the body, formed by representatives of the juntas of the Peninsula, soon realized that it needed the support of the American kingdoms to conduct the war against the French. The Junta Central therefore recognized the Americans' claims that their lands were not colonies but kingdoms, that they constituted integral parts of the Spanish Monarchy, and that they possessed the right to representation in the national government. On January 22, 1809, it decreed that the four viceroyalties—New Spain, New Granada, Peru, and Río de la Plata—and five capitanías generales—Cuba, Puerto Rico, Guatemala, Venezuela, Chile, and the Philippines—each elect a deputy to represent them in the Junta Central. The election occurred in two stages. First, the ayuntamientos of the provincial capitals elected candidates. Then, the *real acuerdo* (royal council) of each viceroyalty and the advisory body in each captaincy general selected one individual to represent it in the new government of the Hispanic composite monarchy.[41] The 1809 elections constituted a profound step forward in the formation of a modern representative government for the entire Spanish nation. For the first time, residents of the New World held elections to choose representatives for a unified government for Spain, America, and the Philippines. The Americans objected, however, that they would not have equal representation. Each province of Spain possessed two deputies to the Junta Central whereas the nine New World kingdoms received one. That criticism was valid. However, as Nettie Lee Benson observes, the Junta Central was fleeing from the French, and had no idea about the size or complexity of America. There is no evidence that it planned to minimize American representation; the disparity was the result of ignorance.[42]

The authorities in New Spain granted fourteen cities the right to elect deputies. The ayuntamientos of New Spain provided their representatives to the Junta Central with detailed instructions. They interpreted the elections as an opportunity not only to obtain direct representation in the government of the Monarchy but also to seek long-desired improvements, such as universities, bishoprics, courts, and better roads. The latter goal continued the practices of the antiguo régimen; they perceived their deputies as procuradores. However, there were some indications that a new view of government was emerging. Guanajuato, for example, declared that:

> this America is not a colony but an essential part of the Spanish Monarchy, and ... that under this fundamental and invariable concept all constitutions, necessary measures, and even variations of laws and national government, New Spain will be considered the equal of the Old without any distinction.[43]

Zacatecas also presented a powerful demand for political reform. It insisted that:

> the legislative power be restored to the Nation represented in the Cortes; ... that the abuses introduced by the executive branch be reformed, and that the king's ministers be held responsible for any future wrongdoing or attempts at wrongdoing; that the most perfect, just and inviable equilibrium be established between the two branches [executive and legislative], but also in national representation in the Cortes, by means of increased representation for [New Spain] as a consequence of the sovereign declaration ... that the Americas are an essential and integral part of the Monarchy.[44]

After a lengthy election process, the *real acuerdo* selected the candidate from the city of Mexico, Miguel Lardizábal y Uribe, to represent New Spain.

Unable to stem the French invasion, the Junta Central, in an effort to strengthen its legitimacy, decreed on January 1, 1810, that the Hispanic world hold elections for a national cortes. In Spain each provincial junta and each city entitled to representation in earlier cortes could select a deputy. In addition, a deputy was to be elected for every 50,000 inhabitants. The electoral decree for the New World stated: "Deputies from [overseas territories] will have the right to participate in the national [the entire Spanish Monarchy] representation to the Extraordinary Cortes of the Realm. Those Deputies will consist of one for every *Capital cabeza de partido de estas Provincias* [the capital of each district in those provinces]."[45] After issuing the electoral decree, the Junta Central dissolved itself and appointed a Council of Regency composed of five individuals that included Lárdizabal y Uribe as the American representative.

It is clear that the Junta Central had no idea of the size of the New World and the number of partidos that existed there. According to a recent study, New Spain alone had about 250 partidos. That is more than all the deputies who attended the Cortes de Cádiz. The authorities in America were not certain what the decree meant. Some maintained that it must mean *provincial* capitals, which were fewer. However, several *partido* capitals did elect deputies to the Cortes, although not all were able to attend. The Audiencia of México, then governing the viceroyalty, determined that only provincial capitals could elect deputies. Twenty ayuntamientos, which were authorized to elect deputies, completed the process. However, only fifteen of the twenty deputies actually traveled to Spain.[46] As in 1808, the ayuntamientos provided their deputies with extensive instructions. Many still considered them, antiguo regimen-style procuradores. That changed once the Cortes Extraordinarias met in Cádiz on September 24, 1810.

As their first act, the deputies declared that they were representatives of the nation and assumed sovereignty. It was the beginning of a great political revolution. It is difficult to determine the number of deputies who attended the Cortes of Cádiz in part because they did not arrive at the same time and because many areas of America eligible to send deputies lacked the resources to do so. In South America, the autonomous juntas in New Granada, Venezuela, Río de la Plata, and Chile refused to elect deputies to the Cortes; in their view, their bond was with the monarch, not the composite monarchy. Although their juntas were autonomous, like the areas that sent representatives to the Cortes of Cádiz, they acted in the name of the king. The American deputies who participated played a central role in the parliamentary debates. The Spanish and American deputies who promulgated the constitution of the Spanish Monarchy in 1812 transformed the Hispanic world. The Constitution of Cádiz granted suffrage to adult males—with the exception of those of African ancestry, members of regular orders, domestic servants, felons and public debtors—without literacy or property qualifications. That document provided the most extensive representation in the world at that time. It constituted a great political explosion that allowed hundreds of thousands of adult men to participate in the political system.

New Spain had a long and evolving tradition of representation that reached its apogee with the Constitution of 1812. The viceroyalty implemented the new liberal Hispanic constitutional system more fully than in any other part of the Monarchy including Spain itself. It also became the basis for constitutional development after independence. In 1821 the Mexican Sovereign Provisional Governing Junta carefully followed the precedents of Cádiz. The acting legislature appointed a commission to prepare a *convocatoria* to elect the Mexican Constituent Cortes. Although the commission concluded that it lacked the authority to "convene a Congress substantially different than the Constitution of the Spanish Monarchy," the president of the regency, Agustín de Iturbide, forced the assembly to adopt a convocatoria that allocated deputies on a complex combination of corporative representatives and the number of partidos in each province. That modification changed the regional distribution of power that sparked resistance in many provinces because some areas, especially the thinly populated provinces, obtained more representatives that they would have under the Constitution of Cádiz that based elections on proportional representation.[47]

The Mexican Constitutional Cortes, elected under Iturbide's convocatoria, failed. Military and popular groups forced the body to elect Iturbide emperor. Subsequently, the new emperor disbanded the parliament so that he could govern as he wished. Provincial opposition to his usurpation of power led to Iturbide's abdication in March 1823. The provinces subsequently refused to allow the Cortes, elected under the new system, to prepare a national constitution; they considered that body illegitimate because it had not been elected according to the regulations of the Constitution of 1812. Instead, they held new elections based on the regulations of the Constitution of 1812. The new congress wrote the Constitution of 1824. The charter established a federal republic—actually a confederation—that divided sovereignty between the national government and the states. The deputies based much of the Constitution of 1824 on the charter of 1812 because distinguished novohispanos, such as Miguel Ramos Arizpe and José Guridi y Alcocer who participated in writing the Constitution of Cádiz, also drafted the Mexican charter.[48]

The Mexican document was not merely a copy of the Hispanic constitution, however. The principal innovations—republicanism, federalism and a presidency—were adopted as a result of the new Mexican reality. Because the new country was a federation, the states—not the national legislature—defined citizenship and the nature of representation. Although a few states imposed literacy and property qualifications, most followed the gaditano [Cádiz] tradition, but included individuals of African ancestry in the suffrage.

The collapse of the Hispanic world in the 1820s resulted in economic decline, political chaos, and military defeat for Mexico. Some of the nation's leaders, particularly those in the large cities, concluded that only restricting representation would restore order, prosperity, and peace. The Mexican conservative José María Luis Mora expressed their views when he declared: "All the new republics of America that . . . [have adopted] the principles of the Spanish Constitution . . . have gone without interruption from one revolution to another without being able to establish anything."[49] Despite a great struggle, the proponents of order did not triumph. The cities and pueblos controlled local politics with their ayuntamientos. In some instances, powerful interests attempted to dominate the weaker rural communities. However, the towns often imposed their interests in spite of regional, state and national opposition. In that sense, the political history of nineteenth and twentieth-century Mexico may be seen as a long and continuing process of balancing local interests with state and national concerns.

2

The Origins of the Quito
Revolution of 1809

On August 10, 1809, *quiteños*, fearing that Spain was lost to the French, took control of the government and established a *Junta Suprema de Quito* (supreme junta of Quito) to defend the Holy Faith, the king and the *patria*. Yet the other provinces of the Audiencia or Reino de Quito did not support the capital's actions. On the contrary, the cities of Guayaquil, Cuenca, and Popayán raised forces to crush the new regime in Quito. Moreover, *villas* such as Riobamba, within Quito's jurisdiction, also opposed the capital.[1] To understand why none of the other regions supported the capital, it is necessary to consider the Kingdom of Quito's experience during the eighteenth century.

THE EIGHTEENTH CENTURY

Quito was one of the oldest of the South American cities, the territory of its audiencia had once been the largest in the sub-continent, and its economy was important during the Habsburg period (1535–1700), when Quito was a major producer of textiles and artisan goods as well as a center for trade throughout the Andes. All of South America, including the Kingdom of Quito, was part of the Viceroyalty of Peru. That changed under the Bourbon King Felipe V, who established a second viceroyalty in New Granada in northern South America. The event was emblematic of the audiencia's diminishing economic and political status during the eighteenth century.

In an effort to strengthen their economic and political status, the leaders of the region repeatedly sought to gain autonomy by becoming an independent captaincy general or a viceroyalty. Instead, during the eighteenth century, the Kingdom of Quito lost control of substantial parts of its earlier territory. In 1717 the audiencia was suppressed and its territory incorporated into the Audiencia of Santa Fé de Bogotá until 1722, when it was reinstituted by the Spanish monarch. Until 1739 when the new Viceroyalty of New Granada was established, the Kingdom of Quito was subordinate to the viceroy of Peru, who resided in the capital of Lima. Contrary to what the quiteños expected, Santa Fé and not Quito became the capital of the new viceroyalty and the Audiencia of Quito remained subordinate to the new viceroy of New Granada, who resided in the capital of Santa Fé de Bogotá. During the latter part of the eighteenth and early nineteenth centuries, while former peripheral areas such as Buenos Aires and Caracas gained autonomy by becoming a viceroyalty and a captaincy general respectively, Quito lost ecclesiastic, juridical, financial and military control over some of its provinces. It ceased to be the only diocese when the bishopric of Cuenca was established in 1779 with authority over Guayaquil, Loja, Portoviejo, Zaruma and Alausí. In 1802 the eastern *gobernación* of Mainas became a bishopric administered by the viceroy of Peru, although it continued to report to Quito on juridical and other matters. Quito suffered its worst blow in 1803 when it lost military and commercial authority over Guayaquil, its most prosperous province, to Peru.[2]

During the sixteenth and seventeenth centuries the *Corregimiento* (a district or province governed by a *corregidor*) of Quito was linked to a series of prosperous, integrated regional economies extending throughout the viceroyalty of Peru, which at that time included all of Spanish South America.[3] The Corregimiento of Quito was a major producer of textiles and other manufactured products that it distributed to both the mineral-rich South and the North. In addition, quiteño merchants participated in the trade of European goods that arrived at the Portobelo fairs.[4]

The War of Spanish Succession (1700–1714) changed Quito's status. The Bourbon candidate, recognized by Castile and America as King Felipe V, decreed in January 1701 that French ships could trade with American ports. Higher quality European cloth flooded the American market, including the ports of Portobelo and Cartagena. Between 1700 and 1728, French products accounted for about 68 percent of the Viceroyalty of Peru's external trade. Because of the great volume of European goods, their price declined in the principal South American markets, such as the great mining region of Charcas (present-day Bolivia). The new Bourbon regime did little to restore the earlier system of mercantile protectionism. Feeble efforts to revive the fleet system failed and the Portobelo market ceased to exist. Predictably, Quito's textiles could not compete.[5] The eighteenth century became a period of economic decline for Quito that worsened in 1776 when the Audiencia of Charcas became part of the new Viceroyalty of the Río de la Plata. Thereafter, Buenos Aires supplied the mining center with local products and imported goods.[6]

The eighteenth-century decline of the Kingdom of Quito sparked political turmoil. A president and the *oidores* (judges) of the audiencia governed the region. Most were venal officeholders who had—or soon acquired—social, economic, and political ties with regional elites in Lima and Santa Fé as well as in Quito. Others were Americans— primarily from Lima— who frequently favored the economic and political interests of the viceregal capital rather than those of Quito. Thus, it was common for local groups to criticize these officials and their local allies, making it difficult for them to dispense justice or to fulfill the mandates of the Crown.[7] For example, two prominent Lima merchants who purchased the presidency of the Audiencia de Quito—Juan de Sosaya (1707–1716) and José de Araujo y Río (1736–1747)—generated such opposition that the authorities in the Peninsula removed them from office and punished their quiteño supporters. Subsequently, after gaining additional information, the Council of the Indies reversed the decision and punished their accusers. Juan de Sosaya's case is particularly interesting because he aroused the ire of the bishop of Quito, Diego Ladrón de Guevara, who after becoming interim viceroy of Peru continued the feud with the Sosaya from Lima.[8]

From its founding, the City of Quito had a history of social conflict. Some upheavals arose as the result of fiscal reforms or the introduction of new taxes, as in the case of the mass opposition to the *alcabala* at the end of the sixteenth century.[9] Others were ecclesiastical riots that resulted, in part, from struggles for office between peninsulares and Americans. Political changes that harmed local interests, such as the suppression of the audiencia or the arrival of a *fiscal* (crown attorney) or a *visitador* (inspector), also sparked violent upheavals. The civil and the religious disturbances often involved mass participation and frequently coincided with food shortages and epidemics. Ten such conflicts occurred between 1700 and 1780.[10]

A major upheaval, the Rebellion of the Barrios, erupted in Quito in 1765. It constituted the most extensive, the most significant, and the longest-lasting urban insurrection in Spanish America during the eighteenth century. The Jesuit historian Juan de Velasco compared it to the great 1592 Revolt of the *Alcabalas*, a violent rebellion that was etched in the shared public consciousness. The Rebellion of the Barrios, the first great reaction in America to the Bourbon reforms, would have a profound influence on later events.

Despite the area's decline, Quito continued to contribute to the *situado* (subsidy) to the fortress city of Cartagena. Nevertheless, the viceroys in Santa Fé believed that the Kingdom of Quito was capable of providing the viceroyalty more tax revenue. Because of fiscal irregularities, Quito had been the subject of investigations in the 1750s. However, the authorities took no action until Viceroy Pedro Messía de la Cerda of New Granada, who took office in 1760, concluded that the tax-farmers in Quito, who collected the alcabalas and the taxes on the *estanco de aguardiente* (monopoly of liquor), were not only poor administrators but also retained substantial sums that should have gone to the royal coffer. Therefore, he decided to impose a fiscal system capable of producing higher revenues. Under normal circumstances when instituting reforms, the viceroy sought the cooperation of both the Audiencia and the Ayuntamiento of Quito. In this case, however, Americans who had purchased their positions and were embroiled in illicit economic activities and local political disputes controlled those institutions. The culprits also included the two peninsulares on the six-member audiencia.

All social groups possessed a stake in maintaining the status quo, resisting any attempt to impose new taxes or to make the collection of existing taxes efficient. The members of the patriciate—some of whom were nobles—and the regular orders, particularly the Jesuits, possessed large sugarcane-producing estates that also distilled *aguardiente*. Some plebeians in Quito likewise manufactured aguardiente in small illegal stills; others sold this untaxed liquor in small taverns or in private houses. Like their urban competitors, the large producers—the lay owners of large heavily indebted estates and the regular orders— evaded taxes. The economic decline gave new impetus to tax evasion at all levels. The underground economy flourished in Quito's popular barrios such as San Roque, San Blas, and San Sebastian. As the city's *obrajes* (workshops) closed because their products could not compete with European textiles, many operators and other skilled workers became part of the unregulated untaxed economy that included laborers, peddlers, and artisans such as shoemakers, carpenters, and barbers. Others produced a variety of goods that they sold from their houses, or opened unofficial butcher shops, *pulperías* (a sort of grocery store), and taverns. Some, of course, worked as servants in private houses and in civil and ecclesiastic institutions. In addition, rural Indians brought a variety of foodstuffs and other items to Quito's weekly markets.[11]

Viceroy Messía de la Cerda appointed Juan Díaz de Herrera, a European Spaniard who had reformed the tax systems of Santa Fé and Popayán, to introduce a similar reorganization in Quito. The viceroy granted the official of *the Real Hacienda* (royal office of finances) independent authority. Therefore, the Audiencia of Quito could not intervene. The royal authorities in Santa Fé were well aware of the discord that reorganizing the city's taxes would provoke. Nevertheless, shortly after he arrived in Quito in October 1764, Díaz de Herrera proceeded to restructure the city's estanco de aguardiente and the alcabala taxes without consulting local authorities. The response was immediate. Regidor Francisco de Borja, a prominent member of the rich and noble families—who owned great estates, textile and hat factories and dominated Quito's economy—became the chief spokesperson for the *común* (the common people) in the ayuntamiento. The city's prelates also indicated their opposition, and on October 14, 1764, requested that the ayuntamiento hold a *cabildo abierto* (open city council) to discuss the fiscal reforms introduced by Díaz de Herrera. Not surprisingly, the ayuntamiento and the audiencia, both of which the viceroy had ignored, accepted the petition.[12]

The *oidor decano* (senior oidor), Manuel Rubio de Arévalo, presided at the cabildo abierto that met on December 7, 1764. Deputies from the ecclesiastical cabildo represented the secular clergy and several prelates spoke for the regular orders. Members of the ayuntamiento represented the city, the *protector de indios* (protector of Indians) spoke for the natives, deputies for commercial and agricultural interests represented the view of civil society, and Borja represented the *bien común*, the well-being of the community. The clergy and the protector de indios focused on moral questions, emphasizing the negative impact of the estanco de aguardiente on native society. Others emphasized the fiscal reforms' negative impact on the economic interests of all social groups. Additionally, the elite raised significant political and constitutional questions. They argued that the *pueblo* (people) had the responsibility of defending the interests of the community. The representatives of the *pueblo* argued that the king had the responsibility of governing his subjects with just laws. They maintained that reforms appropriate for one community, such as Santa Fé or Popayán, could harm others, such as Quito. The oidor Luis de Santa Cruz y Centeno insisted that the Laws of the Indies required that the authorities consult the representatives of the people before introducing far-reaching transformations. Indeed, some laws constituted *mal gobierno* (bad government). Moreover, quiteños argued that as the great political theorist Juan Solórzano Pereira demonstrated, the law had to be adapted to local conditions and needs.[13] Based on these traditional Hispanic political theories, the leaders of Quito demanded the abolition of the estanco de aguardiente and the tax reforms. Quiteños forwarded these demands to the viceroy of New Granada in the belief that the community's opposition nullified these inappropriate measures. In addition, they agreed to raise funds to send Francisco de Borja to Madrid to present their case directly to the king.[14]

Viceroy Messía de la Cerda had no intention of approving the requests of the Quito elite, whom he considered corrupt. Five months passed before he announced his decision. During that period, he contemplated sending troops to enforce his impending ruling that the fiscal reforms continue. While Quito awaited the viceroy's decision, Díaz de Herrera, who proceeded to organize the estanco de aguardiente and establish its distillery, faced only minor procedural problems. Although the viceroy rejected quiteño opposition to the fiscal reforms, he acknowledged that the city of Quito had the right to send a procurador to the court in Madrid; however, he barred Francisco de Borja, whom he considered the principal troublemaker, from that position.

On March 1, 1765, Díaz de Herrera inaugurated the distillery of the estanco de aguardiente. Sales were slow at first. Nevertheless, on May 3, he reported that prominent hacendados (large landowners) were cooperating and there was no sign of popular unrest. The situation changed dramatically after he began implementing additional elements of the fiscal reform such as assessing land values for tax purposes and collecting the new alcabala.[15] On May 20, Díaz de Herrera published a proclamation outlining the new taxes and the penalties for evasion. The following day, his assistants began registering the plots of land in the parishes of San Roque and San Sebastián. Tax officials also began collecting the alcabala on items previously exempt from taxation, including the food and provisions that the Indians brought to market, as well as gifts and alms given to clerics. Those who could not pay the alcabala had their goods confiscated. In the face of growing opposition, one tax collector threatened to erect gallows in each parish to punish violators. Unfounded rumors heightened public outrage. Agitators charged that land taxes would increase drastically, that pregnant women faced taxation for children in the womb, that women who washed clothes on stones in the river would have to pay taxes on those stones, and that the authorities planned to create estancos to control the production of tobacco, salt, potatoes, corn and sugar.[16]

The public reacted quickly. On the morning of May 22, "large cartoons, in which the thick letters appeared very legible" surfaced "on the walls of the corner of the streets of the city" announcing "as imminent an upheaval of the barrios of Quito against the aduana [customs] and the estanco de aguardiente."[17] The frightened authorities, who lacked sufficient police to quell a riot, barricaded themselves in the palace of the audiencia. The violent demonstration that followed was well organized. At about seven at night, barrio leaders fired rockets and rang the bells of the parish churches to call the people into the streets. The residents of San Roque and San Sebastián parishes met at the Plaza de Santo Domingo and from there marched to the offices of the estanco and the alcabala. They broke into the tax office, spilled aguardiente into the street and destroyed the warehouse. Curas (curates) and patrols led by oidores attempted to calm the crowd but failed. On the contrary, the patrols not only refused to fire on the rioters when ordered but many deserted. Crowds consisting of "children, men, women and persons of all classes" participated in the rioting that continued until the following day. The protestors destroyed the estanco and tax building that housed the tax assessor's property records of the barrios of San Roque and San Sebastián. The crowd finally dispersed when Oidor Hurtado de Mendoza and the Conde de Selva Florida promised a general pardon. However, the plebeians demanded that the audiencia grant formal assurances that the government would terminate the new fiscal policies and implement a general pardon to all participants. The oidores reluctantly agreed. The audiencia assembled in a formal ceremony held in the Plaza Mayor in which the Bishop Montenegro and Oidor Juan Romualdo Navarro, a native of Quito, announced the general pardon and suspended the estanco de aguardiente and the new alcabala. An uneasy calm settled on the city because the action required the viceroy's approval.[18]

The audiencia took steps to forestall future disturbances. It canceled street patrols to avoid any conflict with the vecinos of the popular barrios. Tax reformer Díaz de Herrera prudently hid in a Franciscan convent until the night of June 21, when he fled the city under an armed escort provided by the Marqués de Villa Orellana. Tensions remained high in Quito and the citizenry reacted to imagined and actual threats. A commotion in San Blas on May 26 led to a general mobilization of the barrios on the twenty-ninth to burn the houses of some royal officials, among them Oidor Hurtado de Mendoza, who was conducting an investigation into the riot. In both cases, clergymen calmed the multitudes. The European Spaniards, who were associated with the royal officials attempting to impose the fiscal reforms, believed themselves to be in danger and formed a united group that insisted on restoring order at any cost, including punishing rioters. On June 8, pasquines (posters) appeared that proclaimed *"Viva el Rey!"* (Long live the King!); *"Mueran los chapetones!"* (Death to the European Spaniards!); and *"Abajo el mal Gobierno!"* (Down with bad government!).[19] Ten days later, a crowd demonstrated in front of the bishop's palace; it demanded and received a cura of their choice for their parish of San Blas. The following day residents of the barrio attacked the jail and released a recently imprisoned member of their neighborhood. Oidor Navarro defended the jail with a well-armed unit and, after a confrontation of several hours, repulsed the rioters.[20] Corregidor Sánchez Osorio, a European Spaniard, further inflamed the barrios on June 23rd when he and a force of peninsulares arrested numerous residents of the parishes of San Roque and San Sebastian, some of whom they fined and whipped. The humiliating whipping was a provocation that aroused great anger in the barrios and contributed to the belief that the European Spaniards were planning retribution.

The lower and middle sectors of the population reacted immediately to the affront. As had transpired the previous month, anonymous *pasquines* appeared on the morning of June 24, the feast day of San Juan, urging all the barrios to unite and burn the house of Corregidor Sánchez Osorio. Rumors of another uprising rapidly spread throughout the city. The authorities divided over the appropriate response; some favored decisive action while others counseled restraint. Corregidor Sánchez Osorio and a group of peninsulares went to San Sebastián parish at 10:00 p.m. to restore order. On their way, they attempted to arrest some individuals who questioned their right to enter the barrio. When the crowd refused to disperse, they opened fire, killing two individuals. A larger group gathered, driving the patrol back to the palace of the audiencia. Along the way, the rioters attacked the house of Angel Izquierdo, a merchant from Cádiz who they believed had fired on the crowd. After a violent struggle the crowd destroyed his house, but allowed his wife and child to escape unharmed.

The struggle became one of Americans from the popular classes against Europeans. A well-armed force of about 150 men consisting of a small palace guard and peninsular volunteers protected the palace of the audiencia from the dissidents. No members of the American patriciate were present. The rebels had a few firearms, but their weaponry consisted primarily of lances, swords, sticks, and stones. According to an eyewitness, women and children collected stones to give to combatants. The latter fought from 11:00 p.m. until about 4:00 a.m. Given the disparity of weapons, the barrio residents suffered many dead and wounded while European casualties included two dead and many wounded. The following day the bishop and prominent clergymen unsuccessfully sought to calm the barrios of San Roque, San Sebastián, and San Blas. In the evening Spanish officials and their allies sought sanctuary in churches and convents. That night the people of the barrios controlled the city. Gangs took advantage of the power vacuum to attack the property of the Spaniards who were in hiding. The next day, June 26, the authorities attempted unsuccessfully to restore order. Later, Spaniards claimed that the American elite had orchestrated the revolt and that the rioters had requested the Conde de Selva Florida become king of the Reino de Quito. The assertion was false. However, it is a clear indication that the European Spaniards feared the anger of the popular classes that they had exploited.[21]

A moderate peace required that the poorer residents' anger against the peninsulars, who had exacerbated the conflict and who had killed and wounded many of their peers, be placated. The people demanded the expulsion of the Spaniards. On June 27, unable to challenge the masses, the audiencia ordered twenty-five Europeans to leave the city. However, fifty-six peninsulares, who were permanent residents of Quito and who had established economic and familial ties, retained the respect of the community and remained in the city. Interestingly, in this case, the principle of *vecindad* (residence and identity) was more important than place of birth.[22] With a few glaring exceptions, it was a pattern that was repeated throughout the Americas during the next fifty years.

To legitimize the new status quo, the authorities held a public ceremony on June 28 in front of the palace of the audiencia. The dean of the cabildo eclesiástico, some regidores of the ayuntamiento and *vecinos nobles* (respected members of the patriciate) stood on the palace balcony. Thousands of people gathered in the plaza to participate in the event.[23] The president of the audiencia began by shouting "Viva el Rey" and the crowd responded enthusiastically and repeatedly with "Viva." The most senior oidor remaining, after the peninsular oidores had gone into hiding, granted a pardon to the rebels. Then the bishop granted them absolution, which the public received on their knees. A mood of reconciliation prevailed and the crowd dispersed.

The barrios did not return to the old order, however. A new type of government emerged. The rioters consented to the appointment of barrio captains or deputies with the right to police the parishes. All the new deputies were members of the city's patriciate: the Conde de Selva Florida represented San Roque; Don Nicolas Calisto de Alarcon, San Sebastián; Don Mariano Pérez de Billups, San Blas; Don Joseph Lasso de la Vega, Santa Bárbara; and Don Manuel González and Don Francisco Borja, San Marcos. They persuaded the rioters to return the weapons they had taken from the palace of the audiencia and with the help of prominent Jesuits worked to maintain calm. On July 4, 1765, a large number of people assembled in the Plaza Mayor to return the arms, with the provision that the audiencia again pardon them. After the audiencia complied, the crowd dissolved peacefully. The restoration of order, however, did not end dissent and occasional disruptive behavior. Officials of the Real Hacienda reported that they had difficulty collecting taxes, the barrio captains reported an increase in crime, and others stated that popular disaffection remained high. In addition, barrio leaders insisted on restricting the movement of Europeans in their parishes. They also claimed the right to issue permits to peninsular merchants only for the time necessary to conduct their business.

Fearing the diminution of their status, the criollo elites acted to protect their interests. In the principal areas of the city, they organized militia companies composed of individuals whom they considered reasonable, responsible, and committed to the obligations of vecinos. These forces slowly reasserted control in the barrios. They also sought to establish urban solidarity by raising the specter of rural Indians planning to enter and plunder the city. The tactic worked because most of the residents were mestizos who felt threatened by the Indians, whom they considered their inferiors. Moreover, urban Indians did not identify with their rural brethren because they had different interests and did not want to be viewed as natives because they feared the possibility of authorities forcing them to pay tribute.

Exogenous events contributed to ending the Rebellion of the Barrios. In mid-September, the viceroy ratified the general pardon. The rebels temporarily achieved their objectives. In December American Spaniard Luis de Santa Cruz y Centeno replaced retiring President Manuel Rubio de Arévalo, a peninsular. The new president, who cooperated with the barrios, gradually restored the audiencia's authority. Finally, an epidemic ravaged the city in 1766. With many people ill, residents of the popular barrios joined other classes in combating the disease. Despite these positive developments, the royal authorities remained wary of the rebellious quiteños and the viceroy ordered troops to occupy Quito. When this news reached the city, tensions increased. The elite, the audiencia, and the Jesuits succeeded in maintaining order in the city. Fortunately, Pedro Zelaya, the governor of Guayaquil who commanded the royal forces, sought reconciliation rather than retribution upon his arrival on September 1, 1766. Thus, the city remained peaceful.

However, the Crown did not condone the actions of the people of the Andean city. Complaints by Spanish officials and others who had lost politically and economically in the upheaval resulted in a formal investigation. A royal inspector purged the audiencia pending the results of the inquiry of the events of 1765. He also ordered the implementation of the fiscal reform program. On February 14, 1767, the authorities restored the estanco de aguardiente and formulated plans to introduce new taxes in the future. Although the Rebellion of the Barrios ultimately failed to achieve its goals, it succeeded in promoting discord among elements within the quiteño elite and sharpening their awareness of the dangers of politicizing the popular urban classes.[24]

REFORM

The Rebellion of the Barrios indicated not only that royal authority had to be restored in the Reino de Quito but also demonstrated that reform was necessary. José de Gálvez, the powerful minister of the Consejo de las Indias, arranged to have one of his protégés—José García de León y Pizarro—appointed *visitador* of the Real Hacienda, governor, president of the audiencia and captain general, titles that gave him supreme military authority over the realm. These positions provided García y Pizarro independent authority within the Kingdom of Quito. No other official ever simultaneously exercised military, political, fiscal, and judicial power within the audiencia. The patriciate welcomed his arrival in 1778 since they erroneously assumed that the Crown planned to make Quito an independent captaincy general, thereby freeing it from the viceroy of Nueva Granada's authority. García y Pizarro's actions increased their expectations. He established close ties with political and economic leaders and allowed his daughter Josefa to marry Juan Josef de Villalengua y Marfil, the most influential oidor of the audiencia. He also arranged to have his brother Ramón appointed governor of the Province of Guayaquil.

President García y Pizarro believed that his writ included restoring the economic well-being of the area. After examining the socio-economic conditions of the Kingdom of Quito, which had not only suffered economic decline but also great damage from earthquakes that ravaged the sierra in mid-century, he agreed with the elite that the kingdom needed help. Writing to Gálvez on June 18, 1779, he argued that a number of problems must be resolved to restore prosperity and stability to the kingdom. Rehabilitating the textile industry would revive the economy in the sierra. However, changes in trade policy allowed lower priced European cloth to flood the market in northern South America, bankrupting many manufacturing enterprises in Quito that formerly had supplied the Andean region. These closures had far-reaching economic and political impacts. When the obrajes closed, *tejedores* (weavers)—many of whom were Indians—lost their jobs and could no longer provide for their families and pay tribute. Therefore, when officials of the Real Hacienda tried to collect that tax, they faced riots and upheavals. At the same time, the economic decline created such a shortage of specie that residents in most rural communities reverted to barter or used products like potatoes in place of money. President García y Pizarro also declared that the expanding cacao production in Guayaquil could not develop effectively because that coastal province lacked an adequate labor force. Finally, he noted that gold and silver mines in the Reino de Quito had great potential, but the high price of *azogue* (mercury) prevented their development. To change the "state of poverty in which these provinces find themselves," he proposed reducing the introduction of ordinary foreign textiles arriving via the Cabo de Hornos by 75 percent and doubling the tariffs on these imports, while exempting Spanish textiles from new taxes.[25] Once the economy improved, he believed that tax revenues from the Kingdom of Quito would increase substantially.

Minister Gálvez and the Council of the Indies asked other royal officials to comment on García y Pizarro's proposal. They consulted the visitador of the Viceroyalty of Peru, Jorge Escobedo, who in turn requested the opinion of the *consulado* (merchant guild) of Lima. That corporation, which was not an impartial body, dismissed García y Pizarro's proposal as naïve and impractical. It declared that the cloth of Quito was inferior since it was poorly woven and not as wide as foreign textiles. Moreover, the consulado claimed that *azogue* was already in short supply for the productive mines of Peru, Charcas, and New Spain; it made no sense to divert it to Quito. Finally, it insisted that slaves were too costly to work in the Province of Guayaquil.[26] As a result, the Consejo de Indias and Minister Gálvez accepted their advice and rejected García y Pizarro's proposal.

The harsh reaction convinced García y Pizarro, a consummate politician, to protect his career by changing direction. Instead of seeking concessions for the Reino de Quito from the Crown, he focused on a program of administrative, fiscal and military reforms designed to strengthen royal authority and increase government revenues. García y Pizarro created a centralized bureaucracy that collected taxes with great efficiency. He established tribunals in Quito, Guayaquil, and Cuenca. One collected the alcabala, another distilled and sold aguardiente, and a third administered the estancos of tobacco, cards and gunpowder. These bodies supervised tax offices in their jurisdictions. Ultimately, they reported to the *Dirección General de Rentas* (office of general income) in Quito. García y Pizarro filled these fiscal offices with relatives and friends to retain control and to assure loyalty.[27]

García y Pizarro dominated the Reino de Quito not only because of vast authority, but also because he and his family held the most important positions in the realm. He used this power to extract huge sums for the monarchy in the form of various taxes. As Kenneth Andrien states:

State control over local resources in the Audiencia district reached extremely high levels, particularly when compared to other European colonial systems. Although a great economic and military power, England was never able to levy taxes so effectively in its relatively prosperous North American colonies. Despite the decline of textile manufacturing in the north-central highlands, taxpayers in the Quito district paid twice as much in per capita taxes as the

English colonists in North America. The amounts paid by Guayaquil dwarfed anything collected in the thirteen English colonies. In fact, the per capita burden of Guayaquil reached nearly twice the amounts paid in England itself, which reputedly had among the highest tax levels in Western Europe. By the late colonial period, the reforms of García Pizarro created a state fiscal apparatus as powerful and exploitative as any in the world.[28]

The Captain General also substantially increased the area's armed forces. He accomplished this feat by pleasing the viceroy of New Granada, Antonio Caballero y Góngora. In four years, García y Pizarro sent more than one million pesos from impoverished Quito as the *situado* for Cartagena.[29] In comparison, his predecessor forwarded seven hundred thousand pesos in an eleven-year period. As a result, the viceroy approved requests to raise new militia forces for the Reino de Quito. In return for their support, he awarded the local elite command over those militia units by allowing titled and untitled aristocrats to purchase commissions as colonels or lieutenant colonels, the highest military ranks in the Spanish monarchy. Americans bought the majority of these posts. The prices they paid for the commissions varied on the rank and location of the posting. The Count of Selva Florida commanded the infantry regiment of Quito and Joaquín Sánchez de Orellana, son of the Marqués de Villa Orellana, served as lieutenant colonel. Manuel de Villavicencio, son of the Conde del Real Agrado, commanded the infantry unit stationed in Ibarra while Juan Pío de Montúfar, the Marqués de Selva Alegre—who had large debts—served as lieutenant colonel because he could not afford to purchase a colonelship. The wealthy and powerful merchant-entrepreneur Jacinto Rodríguez de Bejarano commanded the forces of Guayaquil with the rank of colonel. Less prominent bureaucrats, such as tax officials, bought commissions as lieutenant colonels or captains. The new commanding officers, depending on their wealth, purchased uniforms for many of their men while lower-ranking officers contributed funds to equip the rest. By 1783 the militia of the Reino de Quito consisted of: two regiments of infantry, a regiment of dragoons, and a company of artillery in Quito; a battalion of infantry in Cuenca; three companies of infantry in Guaranda; two companies of infantry in Ibarra, two companies of infantry in Loja; one company of infantry in Ambato; and in Guayaquil a battalion of white infantry, a battalion of pardo (mixed race) infantry, four companies of white dragoons, and two companies of artillery, one white and the other pardo.[30]

These forces—2,610 men in the sierra and 1,540 on the coast—contributed substantially to the maintenance of order in the Reino de Quito, which remained peaceful in the 1780's, when two great upheavals erupted in the North and in the South: the Revolt of the Comuneros in New Granada and the Túpac Amaru Rebellion in Peru. The new militias, which provided the quiteño elite with new distinctions as well as with the *fuero militar* (military privileges), reduced the resentment Americans harbored about the Council of the Indies' failure to invest in the region and provide the population more political autonomy. Since the patriciate commanded the new military units, they were also in a position to protect their economic interests from Indian revolts that had severely damaged haciendas and obrajes in earlier years. In 1803 for example, Xavier Montúfar, son of the Marqués de Selva Alegre and corregidor of Riobamba, crushed a massive Indian revolt in the partido with the militias from Quito and other units from Guayaquil.[31]

When the Crown promoted José García de León y Pizarro to the Council of the Indies in 1784, he managed to have his son-in-law, Juan José de Villanueva y Marfil, appointed to succeed him. This was a wise move because a few years later, Villanueva y Marfil was in a position to defend him against charges of corruption during his tenure in the Kingdom of Quito. The Crown initiated an investigation into García y Pizarro's activities after the death of his mentor, José de Gálvez, in 1787. The viceroy of New Granada, Francisco de Gil y Lemus, appointed Fernando de Quadrado y Valdenebro, who had a reputation of integrity, to carry out the investigation of García y Pizarro. Although Quadrado uncovered rampant corruption, Presidente Villalengua and his supporters not only impeded his investigation but also accused him of holding a vendetta against García y Pizarro. In the end, the Council of the Indies suspended the case. To resolve the problem the Council transferred Villalengua to the Audiencia of Guatemala and Ramón García y Pizarro to Salta in the Río de la Plata. The Council appointed a new president of the audiencia, Juan Antonio de Mon y Velarde, and instructed him to restore harmony in the Reino de Quito.[32]

THE BARÓN DE CARONDELET

All the presidents who succeeded José García de León y Pizarro agreed with his initial assessment of Quito's needs. His son-in-law, Juan Villalengua y Marfil (1784–1789), recommended three ways of restoring the kingdom's economy. The first was a variation of his father-in-law's recommendation. Instead of restricting European textiles as García y Pizarro proposed, Villalengua y Marfil argued for the prohibition of all cloth imports to the Andes that competed with Quito's textiles. Secondly, he proposed abolishing Venezuela's privileged access to the market in Nueva España to allow Guayaquil's cacao to enter freely the great viceroyalty to the north. The third recommendation was aid for miners in the Kingdom of Quito. Villalengua y Marfil's successor, Juan Antonio Mon y Velaverde (1789–1791), agreed with this assessment of the negative economic impact of cloth imports, and requested some relief. However, he was convinced that the extraordinary increase in taxation constituted the most significant cause of Quito's decline: "How is it possible—he asked—to continue these exactions without the total destruction of haciendas, their owners, and the Indians? And who will then pay the tribute, which is the most important tax collected in this coffer?" He maintained, "It is undeniable that they [the new taxes] have debilitated the commerce of this province, and thus harmed its inhabitants." Mon y Velaverde also insisted on the prohibition of cloth imports and on aid to miners. He concluded by assuring the Crown that, if it adopted his recommendations, royal revenues would increase by one fifth within five years "and this province will be restored to its ancient splendor and fame." His successor, Luís Guzman y Muñóz, conducted a careful evaluation of the needs of the Reino de Quito and reached the same conclusions as his predecessors.[33]

François-Louis Hector, Barón de Carondelet, president of the Audiencia of Quito from 1799 to 1807, became the kingdom's staunchest champion. The new president was a distinguished administrator with extensive experience in the Indies; he had served in Guatemala and later in Louisiana, where he not only contributed to the region's economic development but also successfully integrated the residents' French culture with that of the Spanish Monarchy. He and his family arrived in Guayaquil in December 1798 and then proceeded to Quito. During his journey, he carefully observed the prosperity of the coast and the poverty of the north central highlands, which had experienced a series of earthquakes in 1755, 1757, 1768, and 1773. The worst of these earthquakes had occurred on November 4, 1797, when the earth shook in the sierra of the Reino de Quito from Popayán in the north to Loja in the south, obliterating the relatively prosperous villa of Riobamba. The earth swallowed up entire Indian villages and landslides covered many others. Nature did not discriminate according to social rank, killing rural Indians as well as urban residents. Of the 117 members of noble families that died, 103 had perished in Riobamba.[34]

In an effort to restore the well-being of the damaged areas, Carondelet worked closely with the Audiencia and the Ayuntamiento de Quito. He requested a moratorium on the tribute for the Indians and on the debt for the hacendados. Although the crown granted a one-year suspension for the entire Reino de Quito, the new president asked for greater leniency. Given the massive destruction of their villages, the natives could not pay tribute, nor could individuals of all classes pay the alcabala or service their debts. Similarly, the elite, who had purchased Jesuit haciendas, obrajes, and other property, could not resume payment of debts. The financial crisis of the north central sierra remained a problem for years to come. In addition, Carondelet agreed with those who proposed the relocation of Riobamba to a safer location. Construction began immediately and the villa was established by January 1802.[35]

The Barón de Carondelet was an enlightened, benevolent, progressive, and pro-quiteño administrator. At the end of a long military and administrative career, Carondelet dedicated himself to the success and expansion of the Kingdom of Quito as a capstone to his public life. To achieve his goal he had to reverse the region's loss of autonomy. No president since García y Pizarro had been granted the title of "captain general." Instead, Carondelet was the subordinate of the viceroy of Nueva Granada who commanded the armed forces of the entire viceroyalty as captain general. Similarly, Quito no longer possessed an independent Dirección General de Rentas; that authority now resided in Santa Fé. In addition, Quito had lost ecclesiastical, juridical, financial and military control over several of its provinces. Despite the Kingdom of Quito's diminished status, Carondelet was determined to transform the region from a secondary and dependent audiencia to an independent realm such as a viceroyalty or at least a captaincy general with its own consulado.

To accomplish that goal, President Carondelet focused on expanding his knowledge of the region and enlisting the support of the Quito elite, particularly the nobles. Juan Pío Montúfar y Larrea, the Marqués de Selva Alegre, soon became his confidant. Montúfar y Larrea was a leading member of a group of enlightened individuals who in the 1780s and 1790s established the Sociedad Económica de Amigos del País (economic society of friends of the country) and the paper *Primicias de la Cultura de Quito*, introduced reforms in education, and fostered science, and technology. Selva Alegre was also a patron of intellectuals such as Francisco de Santa Cruz y Espejo and José Mexía Lequerica, and he hosted international scientists, including Alexander von Humboldt, in his country hacienda at los Chillos.[36] In time, Carondelet joined Selva Alegre and his friends at gatherings held at the marqués's hacienda in los Chillos, a few kilometers west of Quito. The friendship between the Barón de Carondelet and the Marqués de Selva Alegre became so strong that sometimes the president visited Selva Alegre's estate at los Chillos for days at a time and, on one occasion, spent three weeks there.

Although no records exist of the conversations between Carondelet and Selva Alegre and his friends, it is evident from Carondelet's actions that they must have discussed how to improve the sad economic and political state of the Reino de Quito. The Barón de Carondelet concluded that the *obrajero* economy would never recover and that Quito should produce other commodities to sell in various markets. He believed that it could grow tobacco, sugar, cotton, grains, fruits and vegetables for the mining regions of Chocó in the northwest. In his view, the entire northern coast would be more accessible from Quito if a road were built via Malbucho to Esmeraldas on the coast and from there to Panama, rather than Santa Fé or Popayán, which were separated by high mountains. He also believed that improving the road from Quito to the southern coastal city of Guayaquil would stimulate industrial production and economic diversification in both the highlands and the littoral. He initiated work on those roads in 1801 and 1802, but lack of funds from the viceroy of Nueva Granada and from Madrid stalled the project.[37]

President Carondelet submitted a series of proposals for improving the Reino de Quito over the years. The most important of these was a lengthy and well-documented *memoria* (petition) in which he presented his program of regeneration for the Audiencia of Quito, a proposal that was very similar to the desires the Quito elite expressed. He argued that Quito was poor because its interests had been blocked by New Granada and Peru. However, it was not a poor country; it was the "Sicilia Americana" whose inhabitants "are endowed with all talents." Quito was in an excellent position to supply the *"tierra riquísima* [wealthy land] of Chocó," which was rich in mines but lacked basic resources including foodstuffs. Moreover "Panama, which lacks the principle resources," could be supplied by the bountiful resources of Quito. The Kingdom of Quito could accomplish much if it were relieved of the burden of the situado, which consumed hundreds of thousands of pesos in currency and left the country strapped for money. He therefore insisted that former territories be returned to the Reino de Quito, that it become an independent captaincy general, that its armed forces be increased to address internal and external threats, that a consulado be established, that Guayaquil be subordinated to Quito's full authority, and that funds be allocated to carry out these projects.[38]

When towards the end of his life the Crown rejected his grandiose plans for the Kingdom of Quito, Carondelet sought solace in his close friendships with the capital's nobles. At this point, the gatherings at los Chillos likely centered on the irresponsible nature of the current government in Spain. Early in 1807 an ailing Carondelet retired to los Chillos to convalesce. His health continued to deteriorate, however, and he died at the marqués's hacienda.

Carondelet's death contributed to the reemergence of a climate of apprehension and distrust in the Kingdom of Quito, particularly because his successor, Count Ruiz de Castilla, was a weak eighty-four-year old man who was incapable of forcefully representing the interests of region's residents. At the same time, the audiencia was reduced to three quarrelsome oidores who were incapable of fulfilling their responsibilities to adjudicate civil and criminal cases and to act as an advisory council to the president. Thus the quiteño elite, who no longer had privileged access to the highest authority in the land, felt exploited by peninsular officials and merchants. The economic depression, as well as the loss of authority and status, engendered significant discontent among the kingdom's elite. In this atmosphere of heightened political and social tensions, the competition between Americans and peninsulares for business opportunities, government jobs, and honors was intense.

THE QUITO REVOLUTION OF 1809

Despite the crisis of confidence that gripped the region in the late eighteenth and early nineteenth centuries, the people of the Kingdom of Quito responded to the 1808 crisis of the monarchy with great patriotism and determination. They recognized Fernando VII as their legitimate and beloved king, rejected Napoleon, contributed funds to support the war in the Peninsula, and prepared to defend the nation from French oppressors. The city of Quito, for example, received the news October 6, 1808, that:

Napoleon Bonaparte, Emperor of the French has imprisoned Our King and Natural Lord, the Señor Don Fernando Septimo, with his Royal Family . . . [The] Ayuntamiento [of Quito] . . . endowed with the most just sentiments of its love, and loyalty for its Religion, the Sovereignty of its King, and the Patria, gives its most vehement demonstrations of loyalty, including its willingness to sacrifice its lives and properties . . . . It does not delay in informing the World that this faithful City does not recognize any other Sovereign, nor will it recognize any other Sovereign than Señor Don Fernando Septimo, even if it costs the last drop of blood in its veins, which it would shed with the most great Glory.[39]

The capitals of the kingdom's other provinces reacted with similar patriotism.

The Marqués de Selva Alegre invited a group of his *allegados* (close colleagues) and relatives, to join him at los Chillos on December 25, 1808. The group included Dr. José Luis Riofrío, the local cura; Capitán Juan Salinas; the lawyers Dr. Juan de Dios Morales, Dr. Manuel Rodríguez de Quiroga, Dr. Antonio Ante, and Dr. Juan Pablo Arenas; as well as don Nicolás de la Peña, don Francisco Javier Ascásubi and Pedro Montúfar, the marqués's brother. Although patriotic historians assert that these men conspired to declare independence from the Hispanic composite monarchy, there is no evidence to support the allegation.[40] It is quite probable that they discussed the defeats that Spanish forces had suffered in the Peninsula and the fact that provinces in Spain were establishing governing juntas.[41] According to the later testimony of Rodríguez de Quiroga, the group discussed the need to establish a local junta to retain Quito safe for King Fernando VII in the event that the French conquered Spain. While other Spanish Americans discussed these questions, the desire to remove Ruíz de Castilla from office and replace him with someone who would act on Quito's behalf was a contributing factor. But it is highly unlikely that the members of the group went beyond words to form a plan for taking over the government as some Ecuadorian historians maintain.[42]

The participants of that Christmas Day gathering at los Chillos appear to have shared their views about the need to establish a junta similar to those in Spain with a number of people, one of who denounced them to the authorities. As a result, royal authorities arrested Selva Alegre, Rodríguez de Quiroga, Morales, Salinas, Riofrío, and Peña in March 9, 1809. Rodríguez de Quiroga presented an excellent defense demonstrating that the transfer of the crown to Napoleon was illegal, that in the absence of the king sovereignty reverted to the people, and that Quito, like towns in Spain, had the right and responsibility to form a junta to defend the Holy Faith, the king, and the patria from the French. In addition to expounding these views on traditional Hispanic political theory, he argued that Fernando VII had sent a letter from Bayona asking "all my pueblos to defend their rights to independence and religion from the enemy." Since Quito was one of the king's realms, it possessed as much right as Asturias to establish a governing junta.[43] Despite Rodríguez de Quiroga's excellent *alegato* (allegation), he could not secure his release or that of his colleagues. Instead, the Marqués de Selva Alegre used his influence to convince President Ruiz de Castilla to ensure their acquittal.[44]

News that arrived in March, April, and May 1809 of Spanish victories temporarily elated the people of the kingdom. Guayaquil, Quito, Cuenca, and other cities made "public displays *en acción de gracias [thanksgiving]* for the victories of the Spanish *armas [arms]* that the patria madre, *obtained* against the Emperor of the *French*."[45] At the same time, the reports that arrived of the formation of the Supreme Central and Governing Junta of the Kingdom fostered the belief that the situation in the Peninsula was improving. During March, April, and May the cities and towns of the Reino de Quito held public ceremonies to recognize the authority of the Junta Central and to pledge support to the new government of the Spanish Monarchy. Early in March, "after a solemn Mass in the hands of the illustrious Señor Obispo," Quito celebrated the swearing of recognition of the Junta Central at the cathedral in ceremonies that included the president of the audiencia, the oidores, the ayuntamiento, the clergy, the nobility and other groups. At the end of that month, Cuenca held similar ceremonies. In early May, the Ayuntamiento de Guayaquil swore to obey the Junta Central Gubernativa del Reino and to defend "our sacred Catholic, Apostolic, Roman religion . . . our august Sovereign . . . our rights, *fueros*, laws and customs."[46]

The establishment of the Junta Central appears to have offered a solution to the crisis of the monarchy. That organism not only recognized the rights of the Spanish provinces, but it also agreed that the American kingdoms constituted integral and equal parts of the monarchy. The Junta Central decreed on January 22, 1809, that the kingdoms of America could elect a representative to that body.

The cities of the Kingdom of Quito—Popayán, Pasto, Ibarra, Quito, Riobamba, Cuenca and Loja—participated in the elections of New Granada. Guayaquil, which the viceroy of Peru took under his control, participated in the elections of that kingdom. When the Ayuntamiento of Quito met on June 9, 1809, to elect its representative to the Junta Central, Pedro de Montúfar, captain of the militias and alcalde of the first vote, declared: "Although there are many subjects in the City who are capable and worthy of the task," there are three "local subjects" already in the Peninsula—the conde de Puñonrostro, a *grande* (great noble who could wear his hat in the presence of the king) of Spain, and two young military officers, sons of quiteño nobles, Carlos Montúfar y Larrea and José Larrea y Jijón. Therefore, Pedro de Montúfar voted for them. Virtually all the members of the ayuntamiento agreed. Their names were placed "in a Chinese jar" and a seven-year-old child, Antonio Albufa, selected the name of José Larrea y Jijón.[47] Although pleased that they had participated in the election of a deputy for a government of the entire Spanish Monarchy—the Junta Central—the leaders of Quito were distressed because they were ineligible to elect their own deputy. They complained bitterly that "isolated in a corner of the earth, they had no one to sustain its hopes, dissipate its fears, or to take any measure in its defense."[48]

As news arrived of French victories in Spain, tensions between peninsulares and Americans escalated. Many on both sides were convinced that Napoleon's forces would defeat Spain. Quiteños believed that Ruíz de Castilla would accept French rule in order to retain power in America while the peninsulares were convinced that the Americans favored independence. In these circumstances, rumors spread that some *chapetones* (a negative name for Spaniards), including some royal officials, planned to assassinate the quiteño nobility on August 19, 1809. These rumors accentuated the tensions that had arisen in January during the ayuntamiento elections of 1809, when the Spaniard Pedro Muñóz had protested "in the name of his nation" because no peninsulares had been elected, and later when Selva Alegre, Rodríguez de Quiroga and the others had been arrested and released.[49]

The "middle class" professionals who had attended the Christmas gathering and who feared incarceration again decided to act. The lawyers Morales and Rodríguez de Quiroga convened meetings on August 7 and 8, 1809, to organize the ouster of Ruíz de Castilla and the establishment of a junta de gobierno. Key to the success of the movement was Captain Salinas, a highly experienced officer and the commander of an infantry company in Quito, whose task was to take control of the garrison of Quito and remove the president and other authorities.[50] Although we lack details of their debates, it is evident from their actions that they did not wish to involve the plebes from the popular barrios in the movement. No doubt they feared a repetition of the 1765 rebellion. The brief acta (official document) prepared on August 7 and possibly revised on August 8, indicated that

the barrios of the Center of the City or Cathedral, San Sebastián, San Roque, San Blas, Santa Bárbara . . . [named] as their representatives the marqueses de Selva Alegre, de Solanda, de Villaorellana and de Miraflores and the señores Manuel Zambrano, Manuel de Larrea y Manuel Matheu so that in the Junta of representatives named by the Cabildos of the provinces that form the Presidency of Quito, will form a Supreme Junta Suprema that will govern the Presidency in the name and as a representative of Fernando VII. We also appoint as Ministers Secretaries of States, Don Juan de Dios Morales, Don Manuel [Rodríguez de] Quiroga, and Don Juan de Larrea, the first, for the office of Political Affairs and War, the second for Grace and Justice and the third for Finance; the

Jefe de la Falange (chief of the army) Colonel Juan Salinas and Auditor of War Don Pablo Arenas. We also agree to form a Senate, composed of two chambers for the administration of civil and criminal affairs.[51]

The proclamation clearly attempts to appear as if it resulted from consultations with the barrios. Had that been done, there would have been widespread reaction, particularly in the popular barrios of San Roque, San Sebastián, and San Blas, and the plotters might have lost control of events. Instead, the plotters contacted a small group of vecinos who agreed with them and signed authorizations to appoint the representatives to the Junta Suprema Gubernativa of Quito.[52] Although the plan appointed nobles to the *Junta de Representantes* (committee of representatives), Morales, Rodríguez de Quiroga, and Larrea awarded themselves key posts in the new government while Salinas was promoted to colonel and put in command of the army.

The plotters met again on the evening of August 9 to carry out their plan. Salinas, who had already won support among a few officers and troops, went to the general quarters to take control of the local garrison. After winning over many officers and men, he arrested the *jefes* (high-ranking officers) Joaquín Villaespesa and Bruno Rezua and assumed command of the military as the new colonel. After midnight, Salinas informed the other plotters. Later on the morning of August 10, they informed Ruíz de Castilla that he was no longer president. Messengers also notified the nobles elected to the junta. At the same time, Colonel Salinas dispatched armed units to arrest senior officials who were peninsulares. The *golpe* had been conducted efficiently and without bloodshed.[53]

The new government consisted of the Marqués de Selva Alegre, president; Bishop José Cuero y Caicedo, vice president; and a junta of the leading members of the Quito elite, including many nobles. The new body, composed entirely of Americans, declared in a manifesto to the public that the Junta Central had been "truly extinguished" and that therefore it was necessary to establish a government to defend the Holy

Faith, the king, and the patria.[54] Subsequently, it reaffirmed its right to act as a representative of the pueblo of Quito declaring that, "the imperious circumstances had forced them to secure the sacred interests of their Religion, their Prince and their Patria." It then proceeded to enumerate the grievances of the people of Quito: The Spaniards controlled "all the public offices in their hands;" the criollos "had been viewed with contempt and treated with ignominy . . . The Spanish Nation, devastated, oppressed, humiliated, and betrayed by an unworthy favorite, had seen a young monarch wrenched from its arms."[55]

During the nearly three months that it governed, the Junta Suprema de Quito sought to establish legitimacy through public celebrations and economic reforms. It reduced some property taxes and the cost of sealed paper that was required to abolish all debts, eliminated the estancos de tobacco and aguardiente, and abolished the situado for Cartagena. Although the changes appealed to the plebe, the actions benefitted the elites. The properties of the nobles and other members of the upper class had large debts and were subject to onerous taxes. The monopolies were widely considered an unreasonable burden on producers and consumers. Moreover the situado extracted specie from Quito.[56]

These were not the only the only ways in which the elite advanced their interests. President Selva Alegre received a salary of six thousand pesos; the income of other officials, most of whom were members of the elite, ranged from two thousand to one thousand pesos. Many new positions became available when the Junta Suprema removed the governors of Popayán, Cuenca and Guayaquil and replaced them with relatives, such as Javier Montúfar, the son of the president, or with influential members of the elite. In addition the government created new ayuntamientos in towns like Guaranda and Otavalo where individuals including José de Larrea, the president's cousin, and José Sánchez, son of the Marqués de Villaorellana, received appointments.[57] Naturally, all these individuals obtained remuneration appropriate to their rank.

The imposition of these new officials by the Junta Suprema de Quito alienated the other provinces of the realm. In addition, the junta's proposal to implement the Carondelet plan to incorporate the coast north from Esmeraldas to Panama into the Reino de Quito undermined the authority of Popayán, stripping it of its prosperous coastal regions, and threatened Guayaquil's dominance of the coast. The governors of Popayán, Guayaquil, and Cuenca—whom the Junta Suprema ordered removed—organized forces to subdue the insurgents in the capital. At the same time, the viceroys of New Granada and Peru prepared to mount major assaults. Even the towns of Latacunga, Ambato, Riobamba y Guaranda rebelled against the Junta Suprema, despite the fact that they received higher status. The lower classes in Quito, who had not been included in the movement, also demonstrated little interest in defending the new regime. Isolated and blockaded by hostile forces, the junta split into factions. Selva Alegre resigned and the others decided to reinstate Ruíz de Castilla. On October 24, 1809, the junta reached an agreement with the deposed president that restored him to office while absolving its members of all charges stemming from their actions. On November 2, Ruíz de Castilla cancelled the junta's economic reforms.[58]

The following month, after the Junta Suprema had dissolved its forces, troops from Lima occupied the city and units from other provinces stationed themselves nearby. On December 4, 1809, the forces of the viceroy of Peru arrested the leaders of the junta, as well as the soldiers who had backed them. The fiscal Tomás Aréchaga, who had earlier been a supporter of Selva Alegre, sought the death penalty for forty-six of the accused and perpetual exile for the others. President Ruíz de Castilla, however, decided to transfer the proceedings to Santa Fé, allowing the viceroy to adjudicate the case.[59]

It is clear that the Quito Revolution of 1809 was not a movement for independence. By ignoring the interests of the rest of the audiencia, and of the viceroyalties of New Granada and Peru, it doomed the movement for autonomy and set the stage for civil war.

3

Clerical Culture in the
Kingdom of Quito

The Catholic faith played a fundamental role in uniting the Spanish Monarchy. Although the people of its various realms retained their languages, laws, and customs, they all had to be Catholics. The "one true faith" defined Hispanic society. After the defeat of the last Muslim kingdom of Granada and the expulsion of Jews in 1492, non-Catholics could not reside in the lands governed by the Spanish rulers who, starting with Isabel and Fernando, called themselves "Catholic Kings."[1] The great political theorist Juan de Mariana recognized that reality when he declared, "religion is the bond of human society and by it [religion] alliances, contracts and even society itself is sanctioned and sanctified."[2] Moreover, as Tamar Herzog indicates, the fact that the Hispanic community "was by definition a Catholic community was rarely discussed. It was so obvious to contemporaries and so consensual in nature that there was no need to spell it out."[3] However, it is important to remember that in the Hispanic world the Catholic Church was not autonomous. It was subordinate to the Spanish monarchs who had obtained administrative control over the church through the *patronato real* (royal patronage), because of the papal donation of 1493 and the papal bulls of 1501 and 1508.

As was true in other Catholic, Protestant, and Muslim lands, religion permeated all aspects of life. Although religious ceremonies and the ringing of church bells punctuated the daily life of Hispanics, few lived in a world dominated by prayer. Individuals within the church, like their secular counterparts, had multiple social, economic, and political roles and interests. Therefore, it is not surprising that members of the clergy frequently participated in secular activities, including politics,

and at times held views that were in conflict with official church policy. Moreover, the Catholic Church in the Spanish Monarchy was not
a monolithic institution controlled by the pope. Rather, it was highly
fragmented and decentralized. At the broadest level, the church consisted of secular clergy and the regular orders. The secular clergy, as
the name suggests, served the needs of the laity. They were organized
geographically into areas administered by archbishops and bishops
selected by the king and approved by the pope. *Curas* administered
the parishes, the subdivisions of the dioceses (districts). They were
the "magistrates of the sacred" who ministered to their parishioners
and had the most contact with society. In contrast, the regular orders
were organized vertically and responded, not to the archbishop or to
the bishop, but to their own authorities and ultimately to the pope.
Nevertheless, within the Spanish Monarchy, the king also controlled
the regular orders. Orders such as the Franciscans, Dominicans, and
Jesuits played a major role in the acculturation and conversion of non-
Catholic peoples in Iberia and later in the Indies. However, to undermine the regular clergy's authority, it was the policy of the monarchy
to transfer jurisdiction over the new regions to the secular clergy as
quickly as possible.

In essence, the Hispanic church responded to the king and was a
pillar of the monarchy. Churchmen held numerous government posts,
including the position of viceroy. The practice of appointing clergymen
to government office was so common that in 1665, quiteño Fray Gaspar
de Villarroel, referred to the Hispanic church as one of the king's two
swords.[4] When acting as government officials, churchmen represented
the king, not the pope. The clergy, particularly the members of the regular orders, also dominated higher education and provided most social
services. Moreover, many clerics were lawyers who practiced in civil
as well as clerical courts. Ecclesiastics in their non-clerical capacities
are generally indistinguishable from their secular counterparts since
both often studied the same subjects at the same institutions. They
were not "ignorant, fanatical priests" as John Adams and other prominent Protestants believed.[5] On the contrary, many were distinguished

scholars and scientists who addressed non-religious topics. The great constitutional scholar Francisco Martínez Marina, for example, was a priest. Moreover, the Jesuit Juan de Mariana developed radical political ideas including the principle of tyrannicide.[6]

THE KINGDOM OF QUITO

Quito was one of the oldest of the South American capital cities, the territory of its audiencia was once the largest in the sub-continent, and its bishopric supervised not only parishes of the sierra and the coast, but also the missions in the Amazon jungle. It ceased to be the only diocese in the audiencia when the Crown created the Bishopric of Cuenca in 1779 with authority over Guayaquil, Loja Portoviejo, Zaruma and Alausí. In 1802 the eastern Gobernación of Mainas became a bishopric that reported to the Viceroyalty of Peru; however, it continued to report to Quito on juridical and other matters.[7]

During the sixteenth and seventeenth centuries, the Corregimiento of Quito linked a series of prosperous, integrated regional economies extending throughout the Viceroyalty of Peru, which at that time included all of Spanish South America.[8] The city's prosperity contributed to the growth of clerical institutions. The principal orders— Franciscan, Dominican, Augustinian, Mercedarian, and Jesuit—built important monasteries in the capital that became centers of healing, art and education. In the seventeenth century, the orders established three universities in the city of Quito: the Universidad de San Fulgencio (Augustinian), the Universidad de San Gregorio (Jesuit), and the Universidad de Santo Tomás (Dominican). Quito became a city of learning that attracted students from many parts of South America.[9] To pay for these institutions the orders invested in a variety of enterprises. Haciendas that produced sugar for aguardiente and textile obrajes were the most important sources of revenue for these institutions.[10] Churchmen were economically as well as religiously important in the region.

The situation changed during the eighteenth century, when economic and political reforms introduced by the Bourbon kings diminished Quito's role within Spanish America.[11] Despite economic and political decline, the second half of the eighteenth century was a period of cultural and intellectual progress in Quito. The clergy played a central role in this flowering. The convent libraries of the city of Quito contained not only religious and traditional books but also the works of the leading contemporary European scientists and scholars. All of them included the publications of Fray Benito Jerónimo Feijóo, who introduced and popularized the scientific and technical achievements of the age. His approach was critical, exposing the fallibility of physicians as well as false saints and miracles, and consistently advancing the cause of modern analytical thought. The colleges and universities of Quito incorporated some of these works into their curriculum. As a result, the French geodetic mission (1736–1743) that arrived in Quito to measure the equator discovered that the city was home to many intellectuals. They found that in some families, women as well as men read French works. They also met village curas interested in science. More importantly, they worked with several local scientists. Although the leader of the geodetic mission, Charles Marie de la Condamine, mentions various local scientists in his diary, two were outstanding: Father Juan Mangín and Pedro Vicente Maldonado. A professor at the Universidad de San Gregorio, Mangín wrote extensively about mathematics, astronomy, and Descartes. He also mapped or charted the Jesuit missions in the Amazon. Maldonado, a member of a noble family, collaborated with the geodetic mission. He also wrote about mathematics and prepared detailed maps of the Kingdom of Quito. At the recommendation of La Condamine, the Academy of Science in Paris elected Mangín and Maldonado members of the prestigious society.[12] The geodetic mission furthered quiteños' interest in contemporary science. After the mission departed, some intellectuals in Quito established an informal group to study modern physics and astronomy. In 1766 members of the group and others, including students, formed the Academia Pichinchense, a cultural center devoted to the discussion of scientific and social questions. Among the young men who joined the Academia were scholars such as Eugenio Santa Cruz y Espejo and the clergyman Miguel Antonio Rodríguez, who would distinguish themselves in later years.[13] There remained, of course, traditionalists who questioned experimental science and who opposed its teaching in the universities. Nevertheless, a cadre of experimental scientists existed. Many of them were members of the clergy who remained professors and trained future generations of progressive thinkers.

The expulsion of the Jesuits in 1767 had a significant impact on the universities of Quito. Initially, the authorities attempted to continue operating the former Jesuit Universidad de San Gregorio by appointing Franciscans with academic experience to some of the principal *cátedras* (chairs) and secular scholars to teach courses in cannon and civil law. The Jesuits were difficult to replace, however, in part because they had led the introduction of scientific advances, such as the Copernican system and Newtonian physics, and they had invested a significant portion of their wealth in the Universidad.[14] The other orders were unable to provide sufficient resources and the authorities closed the institution in 1769. The other universities and colleges continued to function, but they could not fully address the education needs of the Kingdom of Quito. The crisis in higher education that lasted nearly two decades eventually resulted in a complete restructuring of the academic institutions into one large "public" university, the Real Universidad de Santo Tomás. The newly expanded institution, which included the faculty of medicine, consisted of both ecclesiastic and secular professors. In addition, the rectorship was to alternate between an ecclesiastic and a layman.[15] In 1791 the recently arrived Bishop José Pérez Calama, after consulting with the leading intellectuals of Quito, introduced a new plan of studies for the university. Pérez Calama, who as bishop of Valladolid, Michoacán in New Spain had contributed to the spread of the Enlightenment in that city, not only emphasized modern empirical science in the plan of studies but also included cátedras in economics and politics. A new generation of educators who were conversant with modern empirical science and with a critical approach to government, law, and society taught students who would become political leaders when the crisis of the Spanish Monarchy erupted in 1808.

The exiled American Jesuits became the most vehement advocates of the New World. Far from home, in a hostile Europe, they wrote histories of their patrias. In his three-volume *Historia del Reino de Quito*, Juan de Velasco endowed his native land with a prehistory as brilliant as that of Peru and New Spain. He defended the moral, civic, spiritual, and intellectual abilities of the Indians. He also demonstrated the glories of Quito by extolling its geography, climate, mineral resources, flora and fauna. The third volume traced the history of the Reino de Quito until the expulsion of the Jesuits. Velasco, like the other exiles, contributed significantly to the creation of a sense of local identity.[16]

The arrival of Bishop Pérez Calama contributed to the consolidation of a group of intellectuals who continued and expanded the efforts of the Jesuits to promote experimental science and the new modern critical thought. Nobles, particularly Juan Pío Montúfar y Larrea, the Marqués de Selva Alegre, served as patrons of the intellectuals. Prominent among them was Eugenio Santa Cruz y Espejo—a disciple of the distinguished Jesuit scholars Juan Bautista Aguire and Juan Hospital—known for his enlightened thought and his critical writings. Most historians, both Ecuadorian and foreign, consider Espejo the precursor of independence. Martin Minchom, however, has described him as "a hired pen" in the service of "enlightened patrons, ecclesiastics or local factions."[17] Starting in 1780 Espejo wrote a series of polemics against conservative clerics, educators, royal authorities and individuals. In his *Cartas riobambeñas*, for example, he accused María Chiriboga, a member of one of Riobamba's most prominent families, of adultery. The targets of his vitriol complained to the authorities, who on occasion exiled him from Quito. Finally, in January 1795, after important segments of the elite withdrew their support, the authorities in Quito arrested Espejo for *infidencia* (conspiracy). Espejo appealed his case to the viceroy in Santa Fé. On October 20, after reviewing the charges, Viceroy José de Ezpeleta dismissed the accusations and ordered Espejo released. He died on December 27, 1795, shortly after obtaining his freedom.

Bishop Pérez Calama relied on elite intellectuals to advance his program of reform. With their backing he introduced a *Sociedad Económica de Amigos del País* (economic society of friends of the country), an organization similar to others founded in Spain and America to promote useful knowledge.[18] At the inaugural session held on November 30, 1791, Bishop Pérez Calama paid tribute to the distinguished women who participated in the event. The Sociedad appointed Espejo editor of its journal *Primicias de la cultura de Quito*. Bishop Pérez Calama also arranged to have him appointed director of Quito's first public library, which held the collections of the former Jesuit library. The bishop supported Espejo because of his abilities, as did younger intellectuals, such as Miguel Antonio Rodríguez and José Mejía Lequerica.

Bishop Pérez Calama's failure to take into account the negative impact of Espejo's earlier polemics, however, led to the destruction of the careers and premature deaths of the two men. The Dominicans, who believed themselves marginalized, opposed the new plan of studies for the Real Universidad. They and other ecclesiastics lobbied the *cabildo eclesiástico* (clerical council) to support their position. They felt vindicated when the radicalism of the French Revolution provoked the king's chief minister, the Conde de Floridablanca, to impose press censorship in 1791 in an attempt to inoculate the Hispanic world from the French revolutionary virus. After Spaniards criticized this outrageous act, however, the King ousted him within a few months, naming as new chief minister the Conde de Aranda, who ended censorship. However, when news of the 1791 decree reached Quito, President Luís Guzman y Muñóz resigned from the Sociedad Económica de Amigos del País and suspended publication of the *Primicias*. The Sociedad held its last meeting on March 10, 1792. These events encouraged the clergy who opposed Bishop Pérez Calama. Later that year the cabildo eclesiástico removed the bishop from office and declared the episcopal chair vacant. Although President Guzmán y Muñoz rescinded the action, the clergy insisted on maintaining the vacancy. Angered by the *golpe* (overthrow) Bishop Pérez Calama left Quito for Spain on November 29, 1792. He drowned when the ship taking him to Acapulco sank.[19]

To put the events in Quito in perspective, it is useful to compare them to those that occurred in England, the land of representative government. "Quito and England followed exactly the same cycle: enlightened debate followed by reaction, (including in England, too, the dissolution of voluntary associations) which finally culminated in a climate of repression, denunciation, and real or imagined conspiracies."[20]

THE QUITO REVOLUTION OF 1809

The people of the city of Quito responded to the 1808 crisis of the monarchy with great patriotism and determination. Religion played a prominent role during the crisis. Quiteños held public prayers, formal masses, and *Te deums* (song of the church giving thanks to God) on behalf of the king and the nation.[21] However, French armies defeated Spanish forces throughout Spain. News of these calamities alarmed Americans, many of whom believed that the Spanish Monarchy would not survive as an independent entity. They also worried that the authorities in Spain might surrender America to the French. The climate of fear profoundly influenced New World actions.

Although the clergy played an important role in the Quito Revolution of 1809, their intentions remain unclear. Although the conspirators elected Bishop José Cuero y Caicedo, a native of Cali, vice-president, he cautiously opposed the movement. When the revolution began, the bishop convened the cabildo eclesiástico to discuss how they should respond to the political transformation. The members of the cabildo agreed with Cuero y Caicedo that to maintain order and peace they should cede "for now to the force and violence of the *mandones* [those giving orders] who are backed by troops and weapons; that, in consequence, his Illustrious Lordship believed that the members of the cabildo should attend the Cathedral Church where the factious will hold mass and swear allegiance under the most solemn protest that they did not adhere to the principles advanced by those seditious [men]." The bishop and the other members of the cabildo, among them Dr. Calixto Miranda, signed the document and then entrusted it to the Mother Prioress of the Carmen de la Nueva Fundación to be kept confidential until the bishop— or in the case of his death, the cabildo eclesiastico—requested it.[22]

Although Bishop Cuero y Caicedo was elected vice president, he refused to attend any meetings of the new government.[23] When he learned that other provinces of the Kingdom of Quito—Guayaquil, Cuenca, and Popayán—were organizing forces to subdue the insurgents in the capital and that the viceroys of New Granada and Peru were preparing to mount major assaults, the bishop instructed the clergy of Quito not to support the movement. Instead, he instructed them to pray for peace. As a result, they refused to allow "revolutionaries" to use the churches either to elicit supporters or to publicly endorse their "radical" decrees. The bishop and the clergy's overwhelming opposition to the junta convinced some members of that body that attempts to mobilize the masses were dangerous.[24] Isolated, blockaded by hostile forces, and threatened by popular groups, the junta split into factions. The Marqués de Selva Alegre resigned and the others decided to return Ruiz de Castilla to office. Through the good offices of Bishop Cuero y Caicedo, the junta reached an agreement with the deposed president on October 24 that restored him to office while absolving its members of all charges stemming from their actions.[25] However, the month after the junta had dissolved its forces, troops from Lima occupied the city, and units from the other provinces of the Kingdom of Quito stationed themselves nearby. On December 4, 1809, the forces of the viceroy of Peru arrested the leaders of the junta, as well as the soldiers who had backed them.

The Quito revolution of 1809 aroused debate among the church hierarchy. Dr. Andrés Quintian Ponce de Andrade, bishop of Cuenca, published a letter to the Marqués de Selva Alegre criticizing him for actions that, in his view, undermined the nation's government as it fought a war against the atheist French who sought to conquer the entire Spanish Monarchy. Dr. José de Silva y Olave, a guayaquileño who was chantre (presenter) of the cathedral of Lima as well as a newly elected deputy to the Junta Suprema Central in Spain, replied: "Quito was moved by an excess of loyalty and because great passions and great virtues are difficult to control." A spokesperson for the city agreed with Silva y Olave, arguing that Quito's actions were in keeping with traditional

Hispanic rights and obligations to protect and defend the realm. The Junta de Quito had acted exactly as the Junta Central had acted in the Peninsula. No wrong had been committed, except perhaps excessive loyalty, as Silva y Olave noted. Bishop Cuero y Caicedo did not contribute publicly to the debate because he was under investigation for *infidencia* (conspiracy) at the time. However, his testimony repudiated the actions of the Junta de Quito.[26]

Fiscal Tomás Aréchaga, who had collaborated with the "revolutionaries," prosecuted the cases. Just as he had earlier turned against the royal authorities, he denounced his former colleagues and friends. Aréchaga and the commander of the Peruvian troops, Colonel Manuel Arredondo, insisted on severe punishment for the "rebels." Aréchaga sought the death penalty for 40 of the leading participants and 40 of the 160 soldiers who served in the garrison the night of August 10—the latter chosen by lot—and perpetual exile for the remaining garrison forces. The proposed sentences were so draconian that President Ruiz de Castilla decided to transfer the proceedings to Santa Fé, where the viceroy would adjudicate the case. Tensions increased between the occupying forces and the residents of Quito in the months that followed. The Peruvian troops, the pardo fusiliers of the Real de Lima, behaved as though they were conquerors, not defenders of the Spanish nation to which they and the quiteños belonged.[27]

While the viceregal authorities investigated the matter, groups in Quito attempted to free the prisoners. On August 2, 1810, a well-organized movement attacked the prison holding the "revolutionaries" and freed them. Another group attacked the barracks of the Peruvian soldiers, killing its captain and wounding others. At the same time, members of the plebe killed some soldiers in the street. The Peruvian troops reacted violently to the attack. In revenge, they killed the captives, among them the leaders of the revolt, Juan de Dios Morales, Manuel Rodríguez de Quiroga and Captain Juan Salinas.

Terror and consternation for a moment were visible in the countenance of the president [Ruiz de Castilla] and officers, when, on a sudden, the . . . soldiers rushed from the barracks into the streets, shouting revenge! revenge! Our captain is murdered. Scarcely was the alarm given, when the infuriated soldiers abandoned their posts, and running up and down the streets, murdered every individual they met with, without distinction either of age or sex: the drums in different parts of the city beat an advance, and murder and pillage raged in this horrid manner till three o'clock, all the officers standing on the esplanade of the palace, without making any effort to check the massacre: at length, the soldiers having expended their stock of cartridges began to return to the barracks, some of them so laden with plunder, that they had left their arms they knew not where.

The number of prisoners confined in the cells, many of whom were secured with irons, and fell as a sacrifice to the insubordination of the soldiery, and the imbecility of the officers, was seventy-two. . . . In the streets of Quito about three hundred individuals perished, including seven . . . soldiers, killed by some Indian butchers, whom they had repeatedly insulted. Such was the fury displayed by the pacifying troops, that a party of them having met a captain in his uniform, who belonged to the Guayaquil cavalry, a soldier seized his sword of his captain, and ran him though the body, laying him weltering in his gore not fifty yards from the door of the barracks.[28]

No powers of language can describe the anxiety that this dreadful affair excited in the minds of the inhabitants, who ignorant of the origin, considered it as an unprovoked slaughter of their countrymen, and consequently dreaded that it might be again repeated in the same manner. Only five of the soldiers who left the presidio entered the barracks—had twenty entered, they doubtlessly would have succeeded in liberating the prisoners; but these were murdered while those were engaged with the guard at the door.

The streets of the city were entirely deserted; groups of people were scattered about on the neighboring hills, looking wistfully at their apparently deserted town; dead bodies lay in the streets and squares and all was horror and dismay. During the night the bodies of the prisoners were conveyed to the church of San Agustin, and those that were murdered in the streets, to the nearest churches. The two succeeding days, the third and the fourth of August, the inhabitants kept within their houses, and, except for the soldiers not an individual ventured into the streets.[29]

On the third day after the bloodbath, Bishop Cuero y Caicedo, with a crucifix in hand, and his vicar general Dr. Manuel José Caycedo by his side, ventured into the streets of the city calming the public and promising to expel the Peruvian troops from the city. Responding to the bishop's demands, Ruiz de Castilla convened an assembly of notables at the viceregal palace on August 4 to formulate a plan to pacify the people. Bishop Cuero y Caicedo insisted that the "foreign troops" leave the city and the Kingdom of Quito and that the events since August 10, 1809, be disregarded. Dr. Miguel Antonio Rodríguez, a secular priest and an eminent scholar, agreed with the bishop, concluding, "The people of Quito could no longer consider their property and lives secure, unless those individuals who had . . . forfeited their title of pacificators were removed from the country."[30] All the representatives of the city approved the recommendations. Colonel Manuel Arredondo, commander of the Peruvian troops, accepted the verdict and withdrew his forces the next day.

Carlos Montúfar, son of the Marqués de Selva Alegre, arrived from Spain on September 12, 1810, as royal commissioner with full powers to remedy the situation in Quito. Montúfar, who had fought the French in the Peninsula, insisted on sharing command of the armed forces with President Ruiz de Castilla. They convened a junta of notables on September 19, which resolved that "this city and its province recognize the supreme authority of the Council of Regency as representative of our well beloved King Fernando VII . . . while it controls any part of the Peninsula which is free from French domination . . . . [It also agreed to establish a] Superior Junta of Government, dependent only to the Council of Regency." In this manner, Quito once again declared its autonomy from both Santa Fé and Lima. The junta would consist of Ruiz de Castilla, president, and the royal commissioner, the bishop, and eleven representatives of the corporations, classes, and parishes of the city as members, elected "in the accustomed form."[31]

Three days later, the representatives of the cabildo eclesiástico, the ayuntamiento, the nobility, and the five urban parishes met with the authorities. They reviewed and approved the previous actions, elected members to the Junta Superior, and unanimously named Juan Pío Montúfar, the Marqués de Selva Alegre, vice president. Seven of the eleven individuals elected to the Junta Superior had served in the Junta of 1809. Finally, they declared "the purpose of this Superior Junta is the defense of our Catholic, Apostolic, and Roman religion which we profess; the preservation of these dominions for our legitimate sovereign Sr. D. Fernando VII; and to seek all the well-being possible for the nation and the patria."[32]

As had occurred in 1809, the other provinces of the Kingdom of Quito refused to accept the capital's authority. Popayán and Pasto to the north, Cuenca and Loja to the south, and Guayaquil to the west organized forces to oppose Quito. Encircled by hostile provinces and cut off from the autonomists in Santa Fé de Bogotá, Quito took the offensive. It formed armies to subdue the recalcitrant regions. Carlos Montúfar assumed command of the force, which marched south to oppose Guayaquil and Cuenca, while his uncle Colonel Pedro Montúfar led another to the north. In the months that followed, the armies of Quito established control over most of the sierra. Cuenca, however, remained under royalist control and became the headquarters of the royalist government and military forces.

This time, unlike 1809, Bishop Cuero y Caicedo and the clergy of Quito supported the new junta. The massacres and the sack of the city had affected them profoundly. Nine clergymen, including the bishop, participated actively in the junta; many, known as *predicadores revolucionarios* (revolutionary preachers), supported the movement publicly, and more than half the curas of the Corregimiento de Quito took up arms in its defense. In addition, numerous members of both the regular and the secular clergy assumed command of forces and led them into battle. Finally, when Bishop Cuero y Caicedo subsequently became president of the junta he assumed the title of "Commanding General of the Army." Loyalist clergymen also existed in the areas under royal authority. However, they appear to have had less involvement in the armed forces because their side had more trained officers and men. Nevertheless, Bishop Quintian Ponce de Andrade of Cuenca publicly brandished a sword while proclaiming his loyalty to the king.[33]

Familial and political rivalries divided the quiteños. The Montúfar family appeared wedded to the regency whereas others, led by Jacinto Sánchez de Orellana, the Marqués de Villa Orellana, favored an autonomous junta. The sanchistas—those supporting the junta—sought to dilute the power of the montúfares in the Junta Superior and were especially critical of Carlos Montúfar both for his military failures and for maintaining his role as royal commissioner. In May 1811 the sanchistas forced Carlos Montúfar to abandon his command of the armed forces. After months of intrigue, on October 11, the partisans of autonomy fomented a riot in Quito that forced Ruiz de Castilla to resign as president of the junta. As vice president, Juan Pío Montúfar, the Marqués de Selva Alegre, should have succeeded Ruiz de Castilla to that office. However, the sanchistas blocked him and instead elevated Bishop Cuero y Caicedo to the presidency.

The new regime convened a congress to determine the appropriate course of action. The ayuntamiento, the ecclesiastic cabildo, the secular clergy, and the regular orders each elected one deputy; the nobility two; and Quito's five parishes, one each. In addition, the administration allocated one representative to each of the provincial capitals of Ibarra, Otavalo, Latacunga, Ambato, Riobamba, Guaranda, and Alausí, the sierra regions that the junta controlled. Half of those elected were clergymen.

The eighteen-member congress met in Quito in December 1811. Dominated by the montúfaristas, whose partisans had won many of the elections, the assembly elected Bishop Cuero y Caicedo president and the Marqués de Selva Alegre vice president. The growing threat of the royalist provinces that encircled Quito convinced many representatives, including some montúfaristas, that the time had come to end relations with the Council of Regency and the Cortes of Cádiz. On December 11, the congress voted to establish an autonomous government, "subject only to the supreme and legitimate authority of Señor Don Fernando VII."[34] Three distinguished clergymen and intellectuals, the Canon Manuel Guizado, Dr. Miguel Antonio Rodríguez and Dr. Calixto Miranda, prepared constitutions. On February 15, 1812, the congress promulgated the Solemn Pact of Association and Union Among the Provinces the State of Quito, written by Rodríguez, which "recognizes and will recognize as its monarch Señor Don Fernando VII, provided that free of French domination, . . . he is able to govern [the kingdom] without prejudice to this Constitution."[35] The new charter established a representative government with a plural executive, a legislature and a judiciary.[36]

Personal rivalries quickly resurfaced. Only the montúfarista majority ratified the new constitution. The sanchistas withdrew to Latacunga, where they formed another government. They rallied the army of the South and marched on Quito. To avoid civil war, the newly elected authorities resigned. Since the sanchistas accused the Marqués de Selva Alegre of conspiracy to crown himself king, the Montúfar family fled to avoid prosecution. President Cuero y Caicedo attempted to maintain a united government to no avail. Political divisions in Quito permitted the royalists, led by a new and more effective president, General Toribio Montes, to triumph by the end of 1812. The royal authorities arrested and imprisoned many of the leaders of the autonomist regime, among them Cuero y Caicedo. A few managed to flee.[37]

Some scholars consider the Quito revolution, particularly the second phase, a religious movement because of the clergy's role. Bishop Cuero y Caicedo served first as vice president of the Junta of 1809 and later of the Junta of 1810; the congress subsequently elected him president of the second junta. Moreover, many priests participated in both events. The French historians Yves Saint-Geours and Marie-Danielle Demélas and the Spanish historian Leoncio López-Ocón Cabrera maintain that the Quito movement was a "religious war" rather than a political movement. Most of their evidence centers on the second Junta de Quito that functioned from 1810 to 1812. However, these historians fail to account for the fact that churchmen played very different roles in the two periods. Saint-Geours and Demélas argue that it was a religious war because Bishop Cuero y Caicedo played a leading role and because he and other clergymen utilized religious language such as "We the Dr. Don José Cuero y Caicedo *by the grace of God and the will of the people president.*"[38] They also maintain that clergymen were "the ideologues of the Junta" because three ecclesiastics—Manuel Guizado, Calixto Miranda and Miguel Antonio Rodríguez—authored draft constitutions in 1812. López-Ocón Cabrera also asserts that it was a religious war because Bishop Cuero y Caicedo was its leader, about half the clergymen of the Audiencia of Quito were insurgents, and Cuero y Caicedo ended "three centuries of the patronato, which the clergy poorly tolerate."[39]

Research demonstrates that it was a political rather than a religious movement. It is evident that subsequently Bishop Cuero y Caicedo and Miranda changed their opinions about the movement and its leaders, whom they had called "factious" and "seditious" in the first period. This transformation, however, does not mean that they later waged a religious as opposed to a political struggle. The massacre and sack of Quito fundamentally changed their political outlook. Moreover, Bishop Cuero y Caicedo's acknowledgement that he received the office of president of the junta "*by the grace of God and the will of the people*" is in accord with the oath Fernando VII took when the Constitution of Cádiz was restored in 1820. Similarly, there is nothing new about clergymen functioning as intellectual leaders in the New World and in Europe. They had done so for centuries. Moreover, as stated earlier, ecclesiastics within the Hispanic Monarchy often played political roles. About one-third of the members of the Cortes of Cádiz were clergymen. The novohispano ecclesiastics José Miguel Ramos Arizpe and Miguel Guridi y Alcocer, for example, contributed to the writing of the Constitution of Cádiz and later to the Mexican Constitution of 1824. Research on elections in Quito and in New Spain/Mexico (1812–

1824) demonstrates that clergymen were the most important political group at all levels of government. When they functioned as politicians, they did not represent either the church or religion. As was true of their secular colleagues, ecclesiastics held a wide variety of opinions. Moreover, some of the most virulent anti-clericals were men of the church.[40] Finally, the constitutions written by Miranda and Rodríguez are neither religious nor different from charters authored by laymen. All the constitutions of the Hispanic world at the time recognized the Catholic faith as the only one permitted in their lands.

THE CONSTITUTIONAL REGIME

After restoring order, President Montes issued pardons to those who swore allegiance to the Constitution of Cádiz. He also instructed local officials to publish the Constitution of Cádiz, that is, to have it read in formal ceremonies in all the cities, villas, and towns of the kingdom. Then he ordered curas and local officials to conduct parish censuses to determine the size of the population eligible to participate in elections. After months of effort, the electoral census of the Kingdom of Quito, which did not include the Province of Guayaquil now under the authority of Lima, was completed in June 1813. It determined that the realm possessed a politically eligible population of four hundred thousand and that therefore Quito had the right to elect six deputies to the Cortes.

The crisis of 1808 and the Constitution of 1812 provided an opportunity for laymen and ecclesiastics to enter politics in new arenas. The new political system required elections to three representative institutions—the towns, the province, and the Cortes. The complex electoral process, which started at the parish level, began with prayer. The election officials, the parish priest, and the public attended a solemn Mass of the Holy Spirit, at which the cura emphasized the election's importance. As directed by the Cortes, the junta's instructions for holding elections allocated significant authority to the curas. They were charged with establishing the number of citizens in their parish, determining the individuals eligible to vote, and "explaining to their faithful the object of these juntas and the dignity in which they elevate the vecinos of each pueblo because in their vote and willingness [to participate in the election] they assume the high character of representatives of the Sovereign Nation."[41]

After Mass at their respective parish churches, the officials and the people returned to their polling places. The elections resembled a cabildo abierto since the proceedings were public. The eligible voters elected a secretary and two *escrutadores* (scrutinizers). Then the president read the relevant articles of the constitution. Afterwards, he asked if any citizen wished to express a complaint regarding bribery or conspiracy to elect specific individuals. If the public replied "no," the voting began. After the citizens cast their votes, the officials went to the municipal building where they counted the votes and announced the names of the winners to the waiting public. The parish electors met the following day to select the city's officials.

The elections for the constitutional ayuntamientos during the months of September 1813 and January 1814 proved to be both exciting and confusing. Officials and the public asked if women, bastards, illiterates and clerics had the right to vote. Although *vecinas* (women heads of families) *had* previously possessed the right to vote, the higher authorities replied that under the Constitution of Cádiz, men voted as individuals and not as heads of household. Women family heads, therefore, were not entitled to vote. Since the constitution did not differentiate between legitimate and illegitimate men, bastards possessed political rights. Similarly, illiterate men who were otherwise qualified could vote since the charter did not impose literacy requirements until 1830. Finally, according to the constitution, only secular clergy had the right to vote. The regular clergy were disenfranchised because they did not have the right to make decisions as individual citizens. Despite some people's consternation at the new voting regulations, most segments of the population who were allowed to, participated enthusiastically in the electoral process.

The elections of deputies to the Cortes and to the Provincial Deputation of Quito proved to be lengthier and more complicated, since many regions were in the midst of factional struggles. After months of effort, the eighteen partido electors met in the city of Quito on August 24–26, 1814, to elect six deputies to the Cortes as well as two suplentes, and the seven deputies and three substitutes to the provincial deputation. The electors met at the palace of the president of the audiencia and, with "an open door" so that the public could hear, selected a secretary and two scrutinizers who examined the electors' credentials. The following day, after attending a solemn Mass of the Holy Spirit, they assembled in the palace. Again, the proceeding took place with an open door. President Montes inquired if any citizen wished to make a complaint of bribery or conspiracy. When no one challenged the electoral process, the electors voted. Two of the six deputies to the Cortes were clergymen. After the election, the newly chosen deputies, the other participants, and the public attended a *Te Deum* at the cathedral. The next day, following the same procedures, the partido electors chose seven deputies to represent Quito, Cuenca, Latacunga, Ambato, Riobamba, Loja and Otavalo, and three suplentes for the Diputación Provincial de Quito. This time, three provincial deputies were ecclesiastics, among them Dr. Calixto Miranda author of one of Quito's Constitution of 1812. The substitute deputies represented Riobamba, Pasto, and Ambato; one of them was a clergyman.[42] The elections for representatives to the Cortes and to the Provincial Deputation of Quito concluded in August 1814. Shortly thereafter news arrived that King Fernando had suspended the constitution. As a result, its six deputies were not able to attend the Cortes and the Provincial Deputation of Quito does not seem to have met. However, the restored Hispanic Monarchy was incapable of completely reestablishing the traditional system. The political awareness of many lower class and rural people had expanded and they continued to be active within the new political spaces.

Discontented liberals in Spain eventually forced the king to restore the Constitution of Cádiz in March 1820. News of its restitution arrived in the Kingdom of Quito in July and August. On August 27, 1820, General Melchor Aymerich, president of the audiencia, publicly announced this news and immediately ordered the members of the constitutional ayuntamientos of 1814 be restored to office while an electoral census was prepared and new elections were scheduled.

The elections proved to be lengthy and complicated because republican forces from the north and the south threatened the former Kingdom of Quito. In the sierra, elections for constitutional ayuntamientos took place in 1821. The people of the highlands, particularly the Indians, participated extensively in the elections. By the end of the year, countless reports of constitutional electoral returns arrived in the capital not only from the cities and towns of the former Kingdom of Quito, but also from areas of New Granada that were still in royalist hands, such as Panama. As in the previous elections, citizens selected many clergy as their representatives. The more complex elections to the Cortes and the provincial deputation occurred in the early months of 1822. When the republican forces subsequently took control of the sierra, they compelled the royalists to terminate the elections.[43]

THE REPUBLIC OF ECUADOR

The final battle for Quito occurred on May 24, 1822, when the royalist forces were defeated. Although the leaders of Quito, like those of Guayaquil and Cuenca, preferred to establish an independent nation, the Bolivarian commanders forced them to accept the sovereignty of Colombia (Gran Colombia). President Simón Bolívar arrived in Quito from the north with a large army on June 16. Since he possessed extraordinary war powers, Bolívar governed as an absolute ruler who could act without consulting congress or local authorities. He declared the Kingdom of Quito a department of Colombia, the Department of the South, naming General Sucre its first intendant.

The former Kingdom of Quito had achieved independence from the Spanish Monarchy but not liberty. General Bolívar placed the Department of Quito or of the South, as it was sometimes called, under martial law. Officials from other parts of Colombia, as well as from other countries, replaced local authorities. To pay for the liberation of Peru, Bolívar restored Indian tribute, as well as the salt and tobacco monopolies that the Spanish Cortes had abolished. These actions and other coercive tactics to supply the army with men and material eroded popular support among all segments of the population. This disaffection laid the foundation for the breakup of the Republic of Colombia in 1830 into three nations: Venezuela, Nueva Granada, and Ecuador.[44]

Although the clergy remained prominent in the areas of education, health, and welfare, their political role diminished in the Republic of Ecuador. Lay politicians and military men dominated local, provincial, and national politics. The nineteen constitutions of Ecuador, however, all recognized the Catholic religion as the only one permitted in the nation. The new nation not only remained Catholic, it also became more conservative. Indeed, President Gabriel García Moreno dedicated the nation to the Sacred Heart of Jesus in the 1860s. The situation changed, however, with the Liberal Revolution of 1895, which introduced a secular society in which the clergy no longer dominated education, health and welfare.[45]

4

Citizens of the Spanish Nation

INDIANS AND THE CONSTITUTIONAL ELECTIONS
IN THE KINGDOM OF QUITO

The Constitution of 1812 triggered a great political revolution throughout the Hispanic world. Beginning with the pioneering article published by Nettie Lee Benson in 1946, scholars studied the nature of the new constitutional elections, primarily in Mexico City.[1] As a result, some academics have interpreted the constitutional revolution as a phenomenon limited strictly to the principal cities and to the elites. According to these studies, the rural population—the vast majority of the Indians—did not enjoy the rights and privileges of citizenship. Historians such as Eric Van Young have held, for example, that the Indians neither knew nor understood the nature of the new elite politics. Moreover, they maintain that the natives' vision of the world was limited to the confines of their village and that they were not interested in events beyond the sound of their church bell.[2] A few, like Jean Piel, argue that during the independence period Indians "killed each other without a thought. To the majority the idea of an independent . . . [nation] meant nothing."[3] A number, including Marie-Danielle Demélas-Bohy, assume that local elites easily manipulated the natives, excluding or including them as they wished.[4]

While these arguments may reflect aspects of political reality in some places at specific times, they do not explain the broad, multifaceted processes that engaged the citizenry in the new constitutional system. As is true today of individuals and groups living in lands with representative governments, some citizens of the new constitutional monarchy of the Spanish nation were uninformed, apathetic, or easily swayed by elites who were protecting their social, economic, and political interests. However, such individuals and groups lived among others—from all sectors of society—who were well informed, politically active, and used the new constitutional order to advance their interests and those of their families, groups, and communities.

The elections in the Kingdom of Quito, which had become a provincial deputation, provide an interesting example of how the new constitutional system affected an area with a large native population and refute many widely accepted ideas about that important transitional period.

In the immediate aftermath of the forced abdication of Fernando VII, American elites in the city of Quito formed an autonomous junta to govern the region in the name of the king. The southern region of the Kingdom of Quito remained in the hands of the royalists; Cuenca became the capital of the audiencia. Indians from the southern highlands, the provinces of Cuenca and Loja, joined urban groups in fighting for their "beloved king." In March 1812 quiteño units retreated north under constant attack by royalist Indians. At the end of the year, royalist forces commanded by General Toribio Montes crushed the Junta of Quito.[5]

After restoring order, General Montes introduced the new constitutional system. First, he instructed local officials to publish the Constitution of 1812, that is, to have it read in formal ceremonies to the civil, ecclesiastic, and military authorities and to the public in all the cities, towns, and villages of the kingdom. Those present swore to obey the Constitution of Cádiz, and the occasion was celebrated with the ringing of bells, *Te Deum*, Mass in the cathedral and other solemnities, as well as popular events, such as bullfights.[6] Montes, *jefe político superior* (superior political chief) under the constitution, began the process of overseeing popular elections by ordering curas and local officials to conduct parish censuses to determine the number of eligible voters.[7]

A local official provides a sense of the scope of the instruction when he wrote that he had received

Your Excellency's Superior instruction . . . [which] indicates that in order to fulfill the important objectives established by the wise

Political Constitution of the Spanish Monarchy in forming new cabildos, electing representatives [to the Cortes] and provincial deputies, it is necessary that I carry out without delay a census of all the inhabitants of the towns in my local jurisdiction, including both sexes, all ages, classes, and castes, with the exception of those who appear to be slaves.[8]

Montes's actions startled most people in the realm. Countless local officials requested copies of the constitution, as well as further instructions in order that they might better understand the new political system. Some officials asked for clarification whether Indians really were Spanish citizens. One official in the Marañon, the eastern jungle region, argued that he could not conduct an electoral census of the towns in his jurisdiction because most were twelve to fifteen days' walk in the jungle and, in any case, their residents were Indians. From Quito, Superior Political Chief Montes replied that those individuals were citizens of the Spanish nation and therefore possessed the same rights as any other citizen. The chastened official replied that he would soon complete the census of those "*individuos selváticos*" (jungle individuals).[9]

Montes faced a complex task in implementing the new constitutional electoral system. Since the system provided for proportional representation, the *jefe político superior* ordered local authorities to complete a census of eligible voters in each district. For the purpose of the election, he needed to divide the provinces of the former Kingdom of Quito into districts called *partidos*, which subsequently subdivided into parishes. Then, based on the size of the eligible population, he established the number of *compromisarios* in each partido and the number of parish electors in each district. The constitution specified that there would be one elector for every two hundred politically eligible persons. If the parish had the right to select one elector, the parish junta could elect eleven compromisarios by a plurality of votes; if it could name two electors, it had the right to elect twenty-one compromisarios, and if it had the right to choose three electors it could select thirty-one compromisarios. Small towns that contained twenty politically eligible inhabitants could elect one compromisario; those with thirty to forty could elect two; those with fifty to sixty, three; progressively, until they reached the maximum of thirty-one compromisarios. Towns with less than twenty politically eligible inhabitants "will unite with the most immediate [towns] in order to elect a compromisario." The indirect electoral process required that the parish electoral juntas elect the compromisarios who in turn selected the parish electors. These individuals traveled to the capital de partido—Cuenca or Loja, for example—where they met to elect the partido electors who, in turn, traveled to the capital of the province—Quito—to select the deputies to the Cortes from the province and the deputies to the provincial deputation.[10]

After months of effort, the royal authorities completed the electoral census of the Provincial Deputation of Quito in June 1813. The authorities determined that the region numbered 465,900 inhabitants. The figure included a conservative estimate of the population of those areas that remained in "enemy hands." It also inflated the number of Indians eligible to vote.

Article 25 of the constitution indicated that a man lost his political rights if he were a domestic servant. Since many Indians in the Kingdom of Quito lived on haciendas in *concertaje*—a form of servitude—the crown attorney determined that they were in effect rural domestic servants and therefore not eligible to vote.[11] According to Udo Oberem, in 1805, 46 percent of the Indians were *indios sujetos* (subject Indians) in the haciendas of the highlands.[12] Since the Indians constituted the majority of the kingdom's population, the number of eligible voters was less than half of those reported in the census. However, the authorities deducted only 65,900 individuals, who were either not citizens or precluded from exercising political rights. As a result, the Provincial Deputation of Quito's politically eligible population of 400,000 had the right to six proprietary deputies to the Cortes and two suplentes as well as eighteen partido electors.[13] But if Oberem's calculations are correct, the number of persons eligible for representation in the Provincial Deputation of Quito would have been around 250,000, and the province would only have had the right to elect three deputies to the Cortes.

Since the census also determined the number of compromisarios for each parish and the number of parish electors for each partido, it is evident that local officials inflated the number of independent Indians who were citizens to increase the representation of the Provincial Deputation of Quito in the Hispanic Cortes.[14] Although many scholars have argued that the Spaniards reduced American representation in the Cortes by excluding persons of African ancestry, the cases studied, including Oaxaca, Guadalajara, Guayaquil and Quito, demonstrate that the Americans were able to defend their right to full representation and to compensate for any inequality resulting from the efforts of *peninsulares* to restrict American representation in the Cortes.[15] Moreover, in the New World, the royal authorities conspired with local groups to increase representation.[16]

While local officials were eager to expand the representation of the Provincial Deputation of Quito in the Cortes, they were also determined to restrict the number of individuals from the indigenous community and urban lower classes who voted at the parish level in order to protect the power of provincial authorities and the upper classes. To that end, they strictly interpreted Article 25 in determining the number of parish electors charged with selecting the partido electors who, in turn, elected deputies to the Cortes and to the provincial deputation. For example, when the citizens of the Parish of Chambo in the Partido of Riobamba y Macas insisted that—based on the size of their population of 2,385 inhabitants—they were entitled to more than one parish elector, the fiscal replied that half of the individuals in the parish counted in the census were conciertos and therefore were ineligible to vote.[17]

The Cortes also gave the *curas* great authority in the new electoral process. They were responsible for determining the number of citizens in their parish, ascertaining who could vote, and "explaining to the faithful the object of these electoral processes, the dignity to which the vecinos of each town are elevated in the process as well as the fact that the high character of representatives of the Sovereign Nation had its origin in their vote and will."[18] The curas and the representatives of the ayuntamientos presided over the parish elections. Although the electorate for this first popular election had expanded to include illiterates and men without property as well as Indians and mestizos—and probably blacks and mulattos as well—the voters picked prominent members of society as their parish electors.[19]

In the Provincial Deputation de Quito, as in many other parts of Spanish America, Indians constituted the majority of the population. Given their numbers, they had the potential to dominate most governments in the province. To achieve that goal, however, they would have required a shared ethnic identity that transcended extended family, community, linguistic, occupational, and other affiliations. There is little evidence of such Indian unity in the Reino de Quito.[20] Instead, the documents record conflicts between former *pueblos sujetos* (subject towns) and *cabeceras* (head towns), interethnic alliances, and intraethnic struggles for political power.

Despite a lack of cohesion among and within the indigenous populations, most Indians identified as active citizens, that is, citizens eligible to vote, and cast ballots and were elected to various offices. In small towns, illiteracy was not an impediment for participating in local politics at the parish level and in some cases, at the level of the ayuntamiento. Many individuals and groups took advantage of the new constitutional system to further their interests and those of their relatives and friends. In some cases, they formed coalitions that ousted entrenched groups who formerly had monopolized local political power.

Extensive documentation on the southern provinces, under the Constitution of 1812 called the *partidos* of Cuenca and Loja, provides a nuanced picture of the varied roles of Indians in the new political system. After the publication of this charter, Indian communities in the region formed constitutional ayuntamientos. They based their actions on Article 310, which stated, "ayuntamientos should be established in towns that lack them." The article's most significant clause declared that ayuntamientos "could not be prevented from being formed in those [places] which, in them, or in their *comarca* (surrounding area) reach [the number of] a thousand souls."[21] According to local officials, once the Indians learned that they were Spanish citizens with full political rights, they proceeded to form an "infinity of [constitutional] cabildos . . . in the most wretched towns and haciendas [of the region]."[22]

Despite repeated explanations by government representatives that they could not establish constitutional ayuntamientos inside private property, Indians throughout the region continued "to form ayuntamientos in . . . haciendas, estancias, and *hatos* [land for animals] in violation of the Constitution and applicable regulations, causing grave damages."[23] Their actions concerned the landowners and "all right-thinking citizens who insisted that the Constitution be obeyed." In defense of their activities, and to prove that the charter of Cádiz granted them the right to establish those governments, the Indians exhibited copies of Article 310 of the constitution, underlining the clause that ayuntamientos should not be prevented from being formed in those places with a population of a thousand souls. Diego Fernández de Córdova, the constitutional *alcalde* (magistrate) of the city of Cuenca, worried that unknown people were seducing "ill advised Indians."[24]

Political tensions increased when Lic. Juan López Tornaleo—*teniente letrado* (legal advisor to the governor) and, in his absence, the acting governor—proposed the establishment of 242 ayuntamientos constitucionales in the Partido de Cuenca, which possessed only 23 pueblos principales (head towns). The carefully crafted proposal submitted to the royal authorities on April 29, 1813, listed the number of vecinos and other individuals in each town. It also indicated the number of alcaldes, *regidores* and *procuradores* that each should have under the Constitution of 1812. Cuenca, the capital and the largest city in the partido, for example, would have two alcaldes, sixteen regidores, and two procuradores. Smaller towns such as Paute would be allocated one alcalde, two regidores, and one procurador.[25] Many Indians supported the proposal because it granted their settlements the status of towns with ayuntamientos constitucionales. As might be expected, the region's elites bitterly opposed López Tornaleo's plan. Alcalde Fernández de Córdova argued that "he [López Tornaleo] has distributed towns in all the haciendas and hatos in the district . . . . Some places only have livestock, others are peopled by blacks, and most of them only have Indian domestic servants."[26] Jefe Político Superior Montes ordered the teniente letrado to "appear before next Monday's [real] acuerdo to explain his proposal in detail." He also ordered that he "explain to that Alcalde [Fernández de Córdova] . . . that he has exceeded his authority."[27] López Tornaleo argued that his plan was preliminary and that he would submit a fuller report later to the diputación provincial. However, he insisted that the small settlements deserved to have their own ayuntamientos constitucionales and that the establishment of those governing bodies in formerly dependent villages would allow the "rustics" to learn how to function within the new political system. They would, he said, become "civilized." Montes accepted the teniente letrado's explanation and instructed him to await the election of the Provincial Deputation which, under the constitution, was responsible for "overseeing the establishment of ayuntamientos."[28] Despite the concerns local authorities expressed, officials in Quito refused to take action to prevent "Spanish citizens" from establishing ayuntamientos where the requisite population existed.

In an effort to reduce confusion and tensions, the authorities in Cuenca and in Loja appointed commissioners and curas to assist in establishing ayuntamientos and in holding elections. These actions did not have the desired results. In late 1813 and early 1814 the authorities in both partido capitals received numerous reports of discord in towns throughout the region. On July 14, 1813, the military commander of Cuenca, Colonel Antonio García, notified Jefe Político Montes that the "unhappiness and commotion of the Indians" of the region began "the day the Constitution was published."[29]

When the charter of Cádiz granted Indians equality, it also abolished their special privileges under the república de indios. All citizens, Indian and non-Indian, were now eligible to serve in the former Indian governments. Conversely, Indians could aspire to office in the former Spanish ayuntamientos.[30] In addition, since the constitution allowed towns with 1,000 souls or more to form constitutional ayuntamientos, small towns were no longer subject to larger cities and, in the former repúblicas, the *pueblos sujetos* were no longer subject to the *cabeceras*. The changes naturally disturbed individuals and groups who had benefited under the antiguo régimen.

The electoral process exposed conflicts within indigenous society and provided opportunities for formerly excluded Indians to aspire to offices and perquisites formerly held by native elites. In some instances, the old Indian "*Governadores, Casiques y Mandones* [governors, chiefs, and authorities] . . . of those pueblos" were ousted in the elections. Having lost their jobs, they also lost their salaries and other remunerations. Several former officials alleged that the curas and commissioners appointed to oversee the elections were responsible for their ouster. Some former Indian officials refused to support the new constitutional system and threatened revolt to restore the old order. García reported that the discontented former Indian leaders did not oppose the constitution; however, they blamed curas and the commissioners for encouraging and supporting the election of new Indian groups as well as some non-Indians. Exaggerating, the former Indian officials charged that "the curas and commissioners only elected whites; it is very strange that in one pueblo an individual, who was not a *vecino* and had come from this city [of Cuenca], govern a pueblo of only Indians. The latter are just as good as the former. And the pueblo would be better governed by its own compatriots who know their own customs." García believed that the residents ousted the Indian officials from their positions because "no one has explained the Constitution in its true sense to these unfortunates . . . . [Moreover, he complained,] no educated person has been commissioned" to explain the new system to them.[31]

Actually, the power struggle pitted the old Indian officials who sought to retain their prerogatives against younger natives who understood the new constitutional order and used it to influence their communities. In addition, the *forasteros* (migrants of all ethnicities who lived in the community) who in the antiguo régimen were ineligible to participate in the governance of the pueblos, were now citizens under the Constitution of Cádiz and, therefore, participated in local elections. They represented a new political force, which opposed the old caciques who formerly had ignored them.

Commander García tried to mollify the former native officials by telling them that Jefe Político Montes would resolve the issue, but he believed that quick action was necessary to avoid violence. In his communication to the authorities in Quito, he declared: "This city needs at least two hundred fusiliers so that the king's forces will have the respect they deserve and no one dares to disturb the peace."[32] The official concluded: "I beg your excellency to provide a solution for these unfortunates by retaining them in the *casicasgos* [authority of the cacique] and other posts they had before . . . . Moreover," he declared, "those positions and jobs are necessary to assist in the collection of tribute, mail, and other services in the República [de indios]."[33] Nevertheless, in Quito, the crown attorney recommended that the authorities refrain from acting unless proof of fraud or collusion justified overturning the elections.

Although some former Indian officials complained that they had lost elections because of fraud or collusion, none was able to present credible evidence during the first constitutional period, from 1813 to 1814. After the constitution's restoration in 1820, however, former "Regidores del Ylustre Ayuntamiento del Pueblo de San Juan del Valle," near the city of Cuenca alleged that prior to the election "the parish cura of said pueblo . . . sent many *papeluchos* [slips of paper] with the names of those to be elected; all the slips of paper had the same names and were written by the same hand."[34] The papeluchos were distributed not only to a few individuals, but "the entire pueblo . . . received those seductive papers." They had tolerated such actions in the elections of 1814 "because then we did not entirely understand the Constitution." Now that they understood the new political system, the former regidores realized that the charter prohibited such action. Instead, they asserted, it required "that each individual name the persons he wished to support. Since we witnessed the infraction that distorted the sovereign authority [of the Constitution], they declared, we opposed such a criminal act." In their lengthy allegation, they argued, "no elector even though he is the parish cura or any other high dignitary should intervene [arbitrarily in the electoral process]." The people had the right to act of their own volition. The former regidores also emphasized the significance of the clergy's moral authority. The "faithful who respect the parish cura," they noted, "could not but agree to vote as those papeluchos [indicated]." That was the only reason, they alleged, that the people accepted "those seductive papers." Moreover, they asserted that "the sovereign Constitution" determined that such an election "is null and without merit." They insisted that the authorities hold a new and free election in San Juan del Valle.[35]

The authorities in Cuenca, who were already involved in another investigation of fraud concerning elections in the city itself, did not immediately respond to the charges. Therefore, the former regidores of San Juan del Valle brought their charges to the interim *Juez de Letras*. The judge appointed the alcalde of the city of Cuenca, Dr. Diego Fernández de Córdova, to investigate the matter. The alcalde determined that indeed, there had been collusion, and ordered new elections. Those who had won the original elections appealed to the higher authorities in Quito. The crown attorney agreed that the election of the ayuntamiento of San Juan del Valle had been irregular and approved Fernández de Córdova's recommendations. The conflict, however, was between members of the old Indian elite and younger men who used the constitutional system to seek office much earlier than would have been possible in the antiguo régimen. The new elections produced mixed results. Voters chose one alcalde and four regidores from among the old Indian elite but their younger opponents retained four seats. The town of San Juan del Valle remained bitterly divided for years.[36]

Local pressures rather than the requirements of the constitution or of electoral decrees of the Cortes prompted the crown attorney to annul the first election in San Juan del Valle. In a similar situation in Mexico City, after an extensive investigation, the authorities determined that distributing prepared slips with the names of electors was not illegal. Such activity was not prohibited either by the constitution or by any of the electoral decrees of the Cortes. In the Mexico City instance, the authorities agreed that it was difficult to remember the names of all the electors to be chosen and therefore it was reasonable for people to carry lists to the election. They also agreed that pre-electoral campaigning had taken place on all sides and that it was not illegal for individuals to propose electoral lists to the voters.[37]

The struggle for the control of the ayuntamiento constitucional of the city of Cuenca highlights the significance of the Indian vote. Cuenca, like other large cities, contained urban as well as rural parishes. The city's nine rural parishes—Sidcai, Déleg, Baños, Nabón, Paute, Taday, Nirón, Pagcha y Gualaceo—were populated primarily by Indians as well as some mestizos and a few mulattos and blacks. Although not repúblicas, the rural parishes traditionally had been administered by Indian officials. Interethnic coalitions began to form shortly after the constitution was published. Local notables, who maintained strong ties with Indian elites, appear to have assumed that they would easily win the elections.

To their surprise, Lic. López Tornaleo formed an interethnic coalition of Indians and mestizos that won the elections in the rural parishes. Although the two urban parishes were the most populous, the rural parishes were more numerous. As a result, the urban parishes only possessed twenty parish electors while the nine rural parishes had a total of thirty-five. Since López Tornaleo and his allies won virtually all the rural elections as well as a few electors in the city, they gained complete control of the Ayuntamiento of Cuenca. Naturally, the defeated criollo and Indian elite vehemently protested the results. They alleged fraud and collusion; the two most important charges were: (1) that the curas and the electoral commissioners appointed by López Tornaleo had "seduced innocent" illiterate natives who did not realize who they were voting for, and (2) that the interim governor had disenfranchised numerous Indians by falsely claiming that they were conciertos.

After a lengthy investigation, the authorities in Quito determined that the election indeed had been fraudulent. They ruled that Indians who did not live in haciendas had been deprived their rights as Spanish citizens.[38] The ministers of the Real Acuerdo declared that a new election had to be held because "all the members of the people [that is, the Indians,] had not participated" in the first.[39] Jefe Político Montes removed interim governor López Tornaleo and ordered new elections. This time, Indians allied with the criollo elite won the elections in the rural parishes and together with their white confederates gained control of the Ayuntamiento of Cuenca. The triumphant alcalde, Diego Fernández de Córdova, expressed great pleasure that "the Spanish Monarchy is one of laws" and that his "fellow citizens," the Indians, had voted.[40] In this instance, the older pre-constitution, interethnic coalition defeated López Tornaleo's new coalition of Indians and mestizos. In both elections, the Indian vote determined the outcome.

Indians also played a significant political role in Loja, the Province of Quito's southernmost highland city because the area's elites were divided into two opposing coalitions. The region had been a corregimiento whose economy relied on raising livestock and on the production of *cascarrilla* (plant species of the genus Croton) in the large Jesuit estates in the area. After the expulsion of the Jesuits, local notables gained control of those estates.[41] The Corregimiento de Loja, although isolated in the southern sierra region of the Reino de Quito, had a mixed population at the end of the eighteenth century. In 1778 the corregimiento had a population of 23,810; 23.6 percent were white, 53.9 percent Indian, and 22.6 percent people of color, most of whom were free. Loja experienced considerable racial mixture and social mobility. By the beginning of the nineteenth century, mestizos were included in the category "white" and blacks were not recognized as a separate group. They had either become mestizos through miscegenation or migrated to the prosperous coastal region. Subsequently, Loja came to be considered a "white province." That is, the elite claimed white status even though the demographic evidence suggests otherwise.[42] The 1813 electoral census does not indicate if the Partido de Loja had a substantial African-origin population. No mention is made of their having been eliminated from the electoral rolls. The conflict that arose there, as we shall see, only involved Indios conciertos.

José Manuel Xaramillo y Celi, a wealthy patriarch who lived in his haciendas near the city of Loja, led one group of notables. In 1813 Xaramillo y Celi, who was sixty-nine years of age and served as alcalde primero of the Ayuntamiento of Loja, was supported by the other alcalde and the regidores, as well as other local notables and the Dominicans.[43] Another group led by the corregidor Tomás Ruiz de Quevedo, who had governed the area for twenty-two years, opposed them. The corregidor's principal supporters were various officials, among them the secretary of the ayuntamiento, José Agustín de Celis, the sacristan of the cathedral and other secular clergymen, and the captain of the militia, Tomás Ramirez.

The struggle for control of the region began as soon as the constitution was published in May 1813. Corregidor Ruiz de Quevedo decided that under the new system, he was now jefe político of the region. Xaramillo and his allies objected and were supported in the matter by the higher authorities in the capital who determined that there could only be one jefe político in the Province of Quito.[44] Ruiz de Quevedo traveled to the city of Quito to appeal the decision that had diminished his authority. During his absence, on June 16, Alcalde Xaramillo convened a *cabildo abierto* in which he announced that he had prepared a list of those eligible to vote in the constitutional election. The roster excluded a large percentage of the city's population, including Indians in the rural parishes of San Sebastian and San Juan del Valle. Facing strong public opposition, particularly from rural groups, Alcalde Xaramillo postponed a final decision on the voting list until clarification arrived from Quito.[45]

Former Corregidor Ruiz de Quevedo returned to Loja on June 18, 1813, with instructions to conduct the elections. He immediately rejected Xaramillo's voting list and restored to the voter roll all Indians who were not serving as conciertos in haciendas. The officials of the ayuntamiento protested and organized demonstrations in the urban areas of the city of Loja. Ruiz de Quevedo responded by jailing Alcalde Xaramillo and ordering Captain Ramirez to maintain order in the city. Fearing reprisals, Xaramillo's allies fled to Cuenca and filed grievances against the former corregidor. They insisted that the Indians lacked the knowledge (*luces*) to vote freely.[46]

After months of investigation, the authorities in Quito determined that both sides were at fault, declaring, "both parties have exceeded [their authority], both have strayed from the path of reason."[47] Nevertheless, they upheld Ruiz de Quevedo's decision to restore the Indians to the voting roll. In the subsequent election, both groups sought and won support from Indian voters. Ruiz de Quevedo and his allies won the majority of seats in the elections for the constitutional ayuntamiento of Loja. Xaramillo and his supporters, however, won the elections for deputy to the provincial deputation. Political power in the region remained divided for years, but, as in the case of Cuenca, the Indian vote, which was not monolithic, became central in the struggle to control the ayuntamiento of Loja.[48]

Concerned about the rapid proliferation of constitutional ayuntamientos in the Partido of Loja, on July 25, 1814, the leading citizens of the city sent a detailed plan to control the formation of such governments in their region to Jefe Político Montes. They maintained that it was crucial "to determine which towns should have ayuntamientos and which should remain united with their neighbors." The plan stressed the need for a citizenry with *hidoneydad* (suitability) and an appropriate number of whites in order to establish a constitutional ayuntamiento. It began by arguing, "This city [Loja] should remain with its two [neighboring] parishes of San Sebastian and San Juan del Valle, both because the latter are made up of Indians and because they together with the city constitute one town."[49] The rest of the plan identified the towns and their annexes that should have constitutional ayuntamientos and carefully identified the number of *blancos hidoneos* (suitable whites) they contained. Catacocha and annexes, for example, had "3,308 souls, among them 716 suitable whites"; Celica and annexes had "2,232 souls, among them 1,189 suitable whites"; and so forth. In Quito, Montes postponed action by determining that the provincial deputation, which had not yet been elected, should resolve such matters.[50] In practice, this meant that any town with a population of a thousand inhabitants could establish an ayuntamiento regardless of its ethnic composition. It also meant that Indian support had become crucial for winning any election. The new order, therefore, strengthened the political power of the natives.

The Indians were not simply concerned with elections and government; they were also determined to protect their rights. Many Indian communities in the region of Cuenca and Loja were exempted from tribute because of their Cañar ancestors' contributions to the Crown. According to tradition, the Inca Tupac Yupanqui had conquered the natives of the region, the Cañaris, after years of warfare. The triumphant Inca was then said to have slaughtered thousands of Cañaris. The Cañaris subsequently avenged themselves by siding with the Spaniards against the Incas. As a result, they enjoyed special status and were exempted from various obligations. The native communities of the area had the reputation of being loyal to the Crown and fought in the name of the king against the Quito insurgents during the years from 1809 to 1812.[51]

Although the Cortes' abolition of tribute in 1811, and the constitution, made Indians full citizens of the Spanish nation, thereby ending special obligations based on ethnic origin, General Joaquín Molina, then fighting the autonomist Junta de Quito, did not publish the decree abolishing tribute on the principle of *se obedece pero no se cumple* [obey but do not imply]. After crushing the Junta of Quito in December 1812, his successor, General Montes, ordered that Indians throughout the new Province of Quito, including Cuenca and Loja, pay tribute to defray the costs of subduing the insurgents.[52]

The reaction among the Cañaris was immediate. On January 18, 1813, in the city of Quito, "Agustín Padilla, Indian of the town of Cañar and soldier of cavalry of the City of Cuenca," submitted a formal petition to General Montes requesting the right to resign from the army and return home. He declared:

Although I have the obligation to support my poor wife and children and elderly parents with the sweat of my labor, I gladly abandoned those tasks voluntarily in order to serve the just cause that has brought me [to this city of Quito]. I would gladly continue to serve, but as I have now become an Indian who pays Royal Tribute, it is necessary for me to return to my land and work in order to fulfill that obligation. Since I cannot at the same time fulfill both obligations, I beg Your Excellence to have pity . . . and grant the request.

Captain of Dragones Juan Benites supported Padilla's request, stating that he was a brave and loyal soldier and that the burden of having to pay tribute was very real, not only for Padilla but also for all the tributary Indians in his company. Other petitions soon followed. Within a month several hundred Cañar soldiers, men who had constituted the backbone of the royalist forces, returned home.[53]

The former soldiers played a central role in mobilizing their communities' opposition to the tribute. In the months that followed, Indians throughout Cuenca and Loja refused to pay tribute on the ground that the constitution had made them Spanish citizens and therefore, they were not required to bear such burdens. When local authorities disagreed, the Indians justified their refusal to pay tribute by producing hand-written copies of the articles of the constitution that sustained their position.

Fearing that curas were inciting their parishioners, the governor of Loja asked the bishop to instruct priests not to undermine the government. The bishop complied, urging the parish curas "to abstain from influencing directly or indirectly matters that may affect public tranquility or may result in insubordination against the legitimately constituted authorities."[54] In an effort to "quiet the Indians," Jefe Político Superior Montes reduced the rate of the tribute. For a time, it appeared as if the agitation against tribute had ended. However, it reappeared in early 1814, when Jose Ygnacio Checa, a local official in the pueblo de Tablabamba in the Partido de Loja, was stoned when he tried to "inform them about the reduction of the rates." As Checa noted, "seducers have made that contribution repugnant."[55]

This time, to justify their actions, Indian leaders exhibited printed copies of the constitution. After an extensive investigation, the authorities determined that the documents were entering Loja from the neighboring Peruvian partido of Trujillo. Since the southern region of Loja lay within the jurisdiction of the bishop of Trujillo, the civil authorities requested his assistance in preventing the circulation of inappropriate materials. Although the bishop ordered an investigation, he was unable to confirm that a cura within his jurisdiction was encouraging Indians not to pay tribute. Instead, the investigation revealed that Indians from Loja were spreading word that the Indian communities in Trujillo, which in the past had been subject to tribute, no longer had to pay because the constitution forbade it. Some distributed *esquelas* (small notices) stating that "what the King grants, he does not take away." Others argued that "if the entire kingdom pays that tax" they too would pay tribute because that was the meaning of citizenship: they were all equal under the law.[56]

The indigenous population's actions demonstrate that they did not live in isolation. They communicated extensively, not only with their counterparts in other jurisdictions, but also with other groups in society. They did not depend entirely on curas for their information, particularly about politics. They knew and understood the issues that affected them and ably defended their interests.[57] Unable to enforce the collection of tribute in large areas of the Province of Quito, Jefe Político Superior Montes ordered its abolition in May 1814.

The successful efforts of Indians to defend their rights with regard to tribute were not the only unforeseen consequences of the new constitutional order. The leaders of the indigenous population continued to demonstrate their sophisticated understanding of the new political order. Many Indians, former members of repúblicas de indios, invoked their status as Spanish citizens to refuse to perform personal service or forced labor, including building or repairing public projects such as roads and government buildings. They also steadfastly refused to pay either the tribute or the tithe on the grounds that the constitution had ended those obligations. Many no longer contributed to the support of their parish curas.[58] Some refused to attend mass or to send their children to school. In a few instances, Indians became drunk and disorderly because, they said, as free men they could do what they wanted.[59] Others used the constitution as a justification for refusing to pay their debts. The dismayed local authorities could only complain about the Indians' "incredible effrontery" to higher officials in the hope that they would restore order.[60]

The introduction of the Constitution of 1812 triggered a profound socio-political revolution that scholars are only beginning to study. The new system transformed power relations. The Indians of the Kingdom of Quito quickly learned to defend their interests within the evolving political system. Although some authorities and many members of the elite resisted recognizing the Indians' new political status, records in the Archivo Nacional de Historia in Quito indicate that most royal officials attempted to implement the new revolutionary system. That is not to say that they did not seek to influence events. They clearly inflated the number of souls with a right to representation in order to increase the number of deputies the Province of Quito could elect to the Cortes. Similarly, they reduced the number of residents when establishing the number of parish electors, to control elections to the Cortes and the provincial deputation. Despite these manipulations, the officials staunchly defended Indians' participation in the new political system at the local level in the constitutional ayuntamientos. They had no choice. The Indians—particularly those from Cuenca and Loja, who had supported the Crown against the quiteño insurgents—proved equally energetic in pursuing their own interests under the new system. Although most Indians living in private estates were conciertos, they nonetheless established numerous constitutional ayuntamientos, defending their actions with strong constitutional arguments that the officials in Quito did not challenge.

The Indians did not constitute a monolithic block. As was true of other groups of society, individual, family, and local interests divided them. The majority of Indians participated in interethnic coalitions. Like their fellow citizens, Indians supported a variety of political positions. Their participation in local contests for political control endowed Indians with power and influence.

The Indians' political activism continued after independence. On September 28, 1822, the natives of the pueblo de San Felipe refused to work in the powder factory of Latacunga. They argued "that the Constitution of Colombia, the Code which governs us, declares that no republican man may be subject to any other or forced to render any service against his will. [The Constitution] conceives men as free and in full use of the sacred rights they possesses. Therefore, no one can subject another through violence or force to serve in any task, unless it is undertaken of his own free will." Moreover, they asserted, "Indians enjoy the same privileges as any other citizen. No one may intercede to represent them. We Indians enjoy the freedom to speak for ourselves."[61]

Only four months after the defeat of the royalists in the battle of Pichincha, the natives of the former Kingdom of Quito were using the Constitution of Colombia to defend their interests in the same way that they had relied on the Constitution of Cádiz.[62] It is clear that the Indians were not the passive victims often described by some historians. They, like many of their fellow citizens, were active participants in the formation of the new nation of Ecuador.

Table 1: Partido of Cuenca (Head of Cuenca) and its region

	COMPROMISARIOS	PARROQUIAL ELECTORES
Cuenca	31	20
Sigcai	31	5
Déleg	31	3
Baños	31	4
Nabón	31	3
Paute	31	4
Taday	11	1
Niron	31	3
Pagcha	21	2
San Juan del Valle	31	3
Gualaceo	31	7
Azogues	31	6
Biblián	31	4
Oña	21	2
Cumbe	21	2
San Bartolomé	31	6
Sigsig	21	2
Taday	21	2
Cañaribamba	11	1
Cañar	31	7
Chuquipata	31	4
Guachapala	21	2
Pucará	11	1

Source: Archivo Nacional de Historia, Quito, Gobierno, Caja 63, 26-viii-1813, 19–22, 31.

Table 2: Partido of Loxa (Head of Loxa)

	COMPROMISARIOS	PARROQUIAL ELECTORES
Loxa	31	5
San Sebastián	5	—
San Juan del Valle	16	2
Zaruma	21	2
Yulu	11	1
Saraguro	11	1
Santiago	—	3
Chuquiribamba	8	1
Catacacha	21	2
Guachanamá	4	—
Valladolid	4	1
Chito	—	3
Celica	21	2
Sosoranga	11	1
Cariamanga	11	1
Gonzanamá	11	1
Malacatos	11	1
Pagcha	11	1
Amalusa	11	1

Source: Archivo Nacional de Historia, Quito, Gobierno, Caja 63, 26-viii-1813, 19–22, 31. The five compromisarios from San Sebastián should reunite with the sixteen of San Juan del Valle, and elect in that town parish electors. The three electors from Santiago should reunite with the eight from Chuquiribamba and name a parish elector there.The four from Guachanamá, the four from Valladolid, and the three from Chito should reunite in one of the three Pueblos, which one that it is most convenient, and name a parish elector.

5

The Emancipation of America

The emancipation of most of America—that is, the Western Hemisphere—is a complex process that began as a series of reactions by the settlers to the events that occurred in their *madres patrias* (motherlands). Although Spanish-American, British-American, and French-American societies were profoundly different, each began the process of independence in response to metropolitan threats to their self-interests and to their sense of being an integral and important component of their respective monarchies.[1] The leaders of the independence movements considered themselves Spaniards, Britons, and Frenchmen defending their rights. The social and political structure, resource base, and, most of all, the timing and context of each region's emancipation affected the process and determined the future of the newly independent nations.

THE NEW SOCIETIES

The monarchies that conquered and settled the New World during the sixteenth and seventeenth centuries were not modern nation-states.[2] Although the Spanish, English, and French crowns first gained ascendancy over neighboring territories in the Old World, the nature of those conquests forged different kinds of relationships between the newly included peoples and the dominant society.

The Spanish rulers, for instance, initially incorporated into their Iberian kingdoms peoples—Jews and Muslims—who, although Caucasian, essentially belonged to different cultures. Further expansion into North Africa and the Canary Islands brought other groups into the confederation that became the Spanish Monarchy. At its height, the Spanish Crown claimed the entire Iberian Peninsula, Sicily, parts of

Italy, France, the Germanies, Flanders, the Netherlands, parts of North Africa, the west coast of Africa, islands in the Mediterranean, as well as America, islands in the Pacific, the Philippines, and parts of India.[3] Although the Spanish monarchs imposed religious unity by force in 1492, they sought neither linguistic nor cultural uniformity.[4] Heirs to centuries of Muslim domination of the Iberian Peninsula, the Spanish rulers conceived of their universal monarchy as being composed of many lands, peoples, and cultures, who, although not of equal status, enjoyed particular prerogatives and privileges. Thus, the Indians of the New World constituted one more special group.

The Spanish New World had two legal systems: the *república de indios*—Republic of Indians—and, for everyone else, the *república de españoles*—Republic of Spaniards. The Indians became subjects of the Spanish Crown, although in a subordinate status much as the Jews and Christians had been under Muslim rule.[5] The monarchy also established the office of *Protector de Indios* (protector of Indians), responsible for guarding the well-being of the native populations.[6]

The distinction between the Indians and Spaniards, however, proved impossible to maintain. The Spanish Monarchy was too vast and the lands it occupied too populous for Europeans to become the largest group in America. Within a few years of the conquest, miscegenation and economic development had transformed the kingdoms of Spanish America into multiracial societies in which the Indians, although legally protected, entered the larger society as cultural and often as biological *mestizos* (Euro-Indians). The Africans and Asians brought to the New World underwent a similar process of cultural and biological integration. Although a racial hierarchy of castes emerged, economic development and population growth permitted considerable racial and social mobility, particularly during the second half of the eighteenth century.[7]

The English experience differed significantly from that of the Spanish. Although the conquest of Ireland and the incorporation of Wales and Scotland were at times violent, they did not constitute the inclusion of fundamentally different cultures. The English, however, viewed the Catholic Irish as barbarous savages "only nominally Christian, and generally intractable."[8] Later, they perceived the North American Indians in the same way: wild, savage peoples who were incapable of being incorporated into "civilized society."[9] Thus the Indians in the regions conquered and settled by the English Crown lost their land and frequently their lives. The *Mayflower* settlers advanced the theory of *vacuum domicilium* (empty domicile), a view that was widely held and eventually approved by the philosopher John Locke, who was also the secretary of the Carolina Colony in England. Moreover, as early as 1622, Robert Cushman described the natives as no better than "foxes and wild beasts." That same year, the settlers responded to the natives' attack declaring that they would conduct a harsh assault "even to . . . the rooting them out for being no longer a people upon the face of the Earth."[10] The policy of Indian extermination continued not only during the colonial period, but also until the late nineteenth century. Thus, from a pre-conquest population of about five million, the natives declined to approximately two hundred forty thousand at the end of the nineteenth century. Even distinguished intellectuals and political leaders such as Thomas Jefferson supported the principle of extermination.[11]

As Patricia Seed notes: "While the Spanish Crown officially declared all Indians its subjects and vassals in 1542, Indians collectively never became subjects of the English Crown (save in isolated instances), and did not become citizens of the United States until 1924."[12] Likewise, both the free people of color and the large African-origin slave population, who lived principally in the South, remained at the margins of society. By the second half of the eighteenth century, the British-American colonies had become lands dominated by a people who excluded non-whites—and even some whites—from full participation and who abhorred racial mixture.[13]

French explorers, missionaries, traders, and settlers established themselves in North America—Canada and Louisiana—during the sixteenth and seventeenth centuries, and later in the Caribbean islands. France lost its thinly populated possessions in North America in 1763, in the treaty ending the Seven Years' War. Britain obtained Canada and Spain received Louisiana.[14] The extremely valuable islands in the Caribbean, however, remained French. Initially, during the late seventeenth century, French plantation owners recruited *engagés*—indentured servants who signed three-year labor contracts—in the West Indies. As the plantation economy expanded, large numbers of African slaves—a permanent, reliable labor force—replaced the *engagés*. By the end of the eighteenth century, the planters of Saint Domingue imported thirty thousand African slaves a year to meet their labor needs.

The exploited slave majority constituted the base of the social pyramid. Above them were a group of free people of color, *gens de couleur*, composed primarily of racially-mixed persons and a few blacks. Some of them were a wealthy, sophisticated, and cultured elite with ties to France. The Europeans of Saint Domingue did not constitute a socially homogeneous group. The *grands blancs*, planters, high officials, and large merchants constituted the political, social, and economic elite of the island. In contrast, the *petits blancs*, many of them descendants of the seventeenth-century *engagés*, were in an ambiguous position. They considered themselves racially superior to the *gens de couleur* elite but lacked their wealth and education.

As Franklin Knight indicates, the social structure of the French colony reflected "the structural distortion" of a "slave plantation exploitation society."[15] Race as well as socioeconomic status divided the population: the *grands blancs* held the *petits blancs* in contempt; the latter feared and despised the free people of color who were often their economic and cultural superiors; and the *gens de couleur*, while disdainful of the *petits blancs*, feared and loathed the exploited slaves.[16]

THE SOCIAL COMPACT

The three monarchies governed their American possessions by consent, not by force. All three were obliged to grant their settlers greater autonomy than their European subjects, both because the crowns lacked the resources to develop the regions themselves and because the New World provided more economic opportunities to its residents than the Old. As a result, in differing degrees, the three crowns exercised a form of rule that has been characterized as "benign neglect." During the seventeenth century and the first part of the eighteenth century, royal power was scarcely felt by the inhabitants of America; they essentially governed themselves. Despite this similarity, the three monarchies maintained their authority in the New World in very different ways.

At first glance, the structure of the Spanish Monarchy appears to have been highly centralized. The king administered his American possessions through the Council of the Indies, which oversaw viceroyalties, captaincies general, and other administrative subdivisions governed by viceroys and other royal officials. In reality, however, the Crown lacked the fiscal and coercive resources to enforce its will. Although New World kingdoms did not exercise their right to establish *cortes* (representative assemblies), numerous other bodies represented their residents' interests.

Native societies, which enjoyed rights to lands, language, culture, laws, and traditions, under the Republic of Indians also possessed their own governments, popularly known as *repúblicas*. Located in the settled pre-Hispanic areas, these regional governments consisted of the *cabecera* (head town), the principal town and seat of administration, and *pueblos sujetos* (subordinate villages). The *repúblicas* did not exist in isolation. Even in areas of dense Indian population, those polities coexisted with Spanish cities, mestizo and *mulatto* (Afro-Indian) towns, and rural estates of various kinds. Indeed, San Juan Tenochtitlan and Santiago Tlatelolco, the successors of the two island cities that made up pre-Hispanic Mexico City, coexisted during the entire *antiguo régimen* with the Spanish capital city of Mexico, the greatest metropolis in the Western Hemisphere.[17]

The Republic of Spaniards, which expanded over time not only because of population growth but also because of miscegenation and acculturation, possessed countless representative corporate bodies including *ayuntamientos* (municipal councils that governed districts), universities, cathedral chapters, convents, mining and merchant organizations, and numerous craft guilds. These organizations elected officials who represented their constituents. The corporate entities as well as the *repúblicas* enjoyed a large measure of self-government and transmitted their views to the higher authorities such as the *audiencias* and viceroys or directly to the Council of the Indies and the king.[18]

Spanish Americans believed that an unwritten constitution required consultation between the royal authorities and the king's New World subjects. As John Phelan observes, "Usually there emerged a workable compromise between what the central authorities ideally wanted and what local conditions and pressures would realistically tolerate."[19]

British America, like its Spanish counterpart, was, in Jack Greene's words "a consensual empire."[20] The great difference was that it possessed a substantially larger white settler population. They—not the Indians, the free people of color, or the slaves—are the ones whom U.S. historians have in mind when they write about the rights and opportunities available in the thirteen colonies.[21] Only if one limits consideration to that important group, and ignores all the others, is it true that British Americans possessed greater rights and liberties than the other Americans. They alone enjoyed the right to convene local assemblies.

The French West Indies developed a form of self-government by the early eighteenth century. Limited to the white minority, and dominated by the *grands blancs*, a system of superior councils emerged that proved able to overturn royal ordinances not to their liking. Indeed, some councils aspired to play the role of the *Parlement* (regional high court) of Paris, claiming the right to register the king's laws. Although the nature of representation and negotiation was much weaker in French America than in Spanish or British America, the region nonetheless offered its minority white population more autonomy than the people of France possessed.[22] Thus, in varying degrees, Greene's observation that "What was legal, what was constitutional, was determined not by fiat but by negotiation," is true of the three Americas.[23]

THE MATERIAL CONDITIONS

The natural endowments of each region determined the life in the New World. The thirteen colonies of British America possessed widespread, fertile agricultural lands. Additionally, easy coastal communications and extensive, navigable river systems enhanced the natural endowments of each colony. The Louisiana Purchase of 1803, which included the mouth of the Mississippi River, would further facilitate transportation and contribute to the dramatic expansion of the young United States. Because of the greater availability of agricultural land and of efficient low-cost water transportation, most white British Americans acquired property and many exported a variety of agricultural products to Europe and the West Indies. These conditions helped create the dynamic propertied classes who constituted the "egalitarian social orders of the free segments of these settler societies [who] would provide a sturdy foundation for the limited egalitarian impulses of Revolutionary and early republican [British] America" described by Greene.[24] By the end of the eighteenth century, about 5.5 million people, excluding Indians, lived in the former British American colony, the United States.

Spanish America, although claiming the vast majority of the continent, possessed very limited fertile agricultural land. The best soil was located in the thinly populated periphery in the extreme South and in the North. Only about 15 percent of present-day Mexico is arable without irrigation. The vast fertile Pampas of present-day Argentina, like the Great Plains of North America, had limited economic utility in the eighteenth century because contemporary technology did not allow cultivation.

Massive mountain ranges, jagged canyons, great deserts, and extensive rain forests characterized the settled areas of eighteenth-century Spanish America, the region's heartland, posing formidable barriers to communication. Despite extensive shorelines on both sides of the continent, coastal shipping was restricted by the lack of good harbors and by the location of the major population and production centers in the highlands, away from the coast. Moreover, as none of the settled areas possessed navigable rivers, the cost and difficulty of land transportation, universally more expensive than water, limited external trade to a few tropical agricultural products and valuable exports such as silver. As a result, the Spanish American kingdoms, although part of the same monarchy, had little contact with one another unless they were neighbors.

The physical environment not only determined the nature of the economy but also of society. New Spain, which had vast deposits of silver, developed a complex and wealthy economy. Its large and advanced Indian population rapidly adapted to the new political and social system, learning to protect its interests within both the Republic of Indians and the Republic of Spaniards. The viceroyalty gradually became a multiracial society whose members to varying degrees shared a hybrid mestizo society that was neither Indian nor Spanish.[25] At the end of the eighteenth century, New Spain, with a population of about six million, was the richest, most populous, most developed portion of the Spanish Monarchy in America. In contrast, the Viceroyalty of the Río de la Plata, a thinly populated peripheral region far from Europe, remained isolated and economically marginal during most of the period. It was elevated to the status of a viceroyalty only in 1776. Previously, the interior sold its agricultural and livestock production to the silver mines in Upper Peru (present-day Bolivia), while Buenos Aires and the Pampas raised livestock. The area did not expand rapidly until 1776, when Buenos Aires became the outlet for trade from the interior, particularly the silver mines in Charcas, present-day Bolivia. By 1800 the region, excluding Upper Peru, possessed a population of about five hundred thousand, composed of a tiny white elite, a small mestizo middle group, and a large Indian population.

Saint Domingue, although occupying only the western third of the island of Hispaniola, became during the second half of the eighteenth century the most productive colony in the West Indies. David Geggus observes that in 1780 through the 1790s, Saint Domingue accounted for "some 40 percent of France's foreign trade. On the coastal plains of this little colony little larger than Wales was grown about two-fifths of the world's sugar, while from its mountainous interior came over half the world's coffee."[26] Its productivity doomed most of Saint Domingue's inhabitants to exploitation within a tropical plantation society. As Knight indicates, "A white population of approximately 25,000 psychological transients dominated the social pyramid that included an intermediate subordinate stratum of approximately the same number of free, miscegenated persons . . . and a depressed, denigrated, servile and exploited majority group of some 500,000 workers of Africa or African descent."[27]

Two contradictory tendencies emerged in the Atlantic world during the second half of the eighteenth century: the assertion by Americans—both Spanish and British—of a *conciencia de sí* (sense of unique identity), and the attempt of the Bourbon and Hanoverian monarchies to gain control of their Americas and transform them into profitable colonies. From the Río de la Plata in the south to New England in the north, the peoples of the settler societies identified with their *patrias* or localities, which they thought of as "America." Though educated members of both communities emphasized the unique characteristics of their lands and peoples, the Spanish Americans incorporated their Indian heritage into their identity while the British Americans did not. This distinction is evident in two great works of the time: Francisco Javier Clavijero's *Historia antigua de México* and Thomas Jefferson's *Notes on the State of Virginia*.[28] The latter exalted white British Americans while the former glorified the ancient Mexicans.

As noted previously, Americans considered themselves true Spaniards or Britons, the possessors of all the rights and privileges of those peoples. Spanish Americans developed a compact theory of government in which they derived their rights from two sources: their Indian progenitors, who originally possessed the land, and their Spanish ancestors, who in conquering the New World obtained privileges from the Crown, including the right to convene their own *cortes*. The compact was not between America and Spain, but between each New World kingdom and the monarch.[29] Similarly, British Americans based their claims to self-government on their rights as Englishmen. In particular, "they insisted that each of their own local legislatures enjoyed full legislative authority and exclusive power to tax within its respective jurisdiction."[30]

Although both the Spanish and British crowns had considered asserting more control over their American possessions in the 1740s and 1750s, they accomplished little until the advent of the Seven Years' War. That conflict, a world war fought in Europe, America—both North and South—and Asia, changed the balance of power in the New World. France withdrew from the continent in 1763, leaving Spain and Britain as the principal contenders for control of the region. Both monarchies established standing armies for the first time and introduced new regulations and structures designed to enable them to exercise greater control over their vast and distant possessions. Impressed by the great wealth that France extracted from its Caribbean islands, particularly Saint Domingue, Spain and Britain not only attempted to exercise greater control of their Americas, but they also sought increasingly to profit from them. Since these changes in the Spanish world are called the "Bourbon reforms," the comparable transformations in the British are best conceived of as the "Hanoverian reforms."

THE BRITISH-AMERICAN REVOLUTION

As was to be expected, Americans, both British and Spanish, objected to the new imperialism. Why British Americans objected so strongly to the new measures—such as the introduction of a standing army, the Stamp Act, the Navigation Acts, and the Tea Act—and why the British government insisted on imposing its authority, remain open to debate.[31] The British monarchy clearly feared that the colonials would demand independence if their demands were met. At the same time, the British Americans were convinced that the Hanoverian reforms sought to deprive them of their rights and liberties as Englishmen. Clearly, the revolution resulted from "the inability of the disputants to agree upon the nature of the British Empire."[32] In addition, the British, like the Spanish subsequently, proved unwilling to accept a settlement comparable to the later British Commonwealth.

The nature and process of the struggles for emancipation were as different as the three Americas. The war for U.S. independence became an international conflict in which France and Spain fought Britain on both land and sea. At the height of the struggle, France fielded a force of more than ten thousand men in North America—an army larger than the royal army in New Spain—while Spain's troops harassed the British along its vast border with New Spain, and the combined French and Spanish navies neutralized the British fleet at sea. As a result of foreign involvement, the United States obtained its independence through an international settlement, the Treaty of Paris of 1783.[33]

Many of the founders of the new nation were members of the oligarchy. During the struggle for independence, the British-American upper and upper-middle classes shared moderate goals. Although other social groups participated in the conflict, they did not challenge the elites. No social revolution threatened their interests.[34] Traditional military engagements characterized the U.S. War of Independence. Local insurgents with goals fundamentally different from those of the elite are notable for their absence. No rural insurrection occurred. The black slaves did not revolt against their masters. Moreover, the Indians did not take the opportunity to recover the lands that the settlers had taken[35]

Although regional tensions existed, and although the first U.S. constitution, the Articles of Confederation, was rapidly discarded in favor of the stronger Constitution of 1787, the British-American elite managed to control the new nation without serious challenges from other social groups.[36] As Greene notes:

Despite the universalistic pronouncements of the Declaration of Independence and the apparent inclusiveness of the phrase "We the People" in the Constitution, the [British] American Revolution was a limited revolution that really fully applied, immediately, only to adult white independent men. Because such a large proportion of the American population fell into that category, the [British] American Revolution seemed to contemporaries to be far more egalitarian and inclusive than it actually was. But whole groups of people—slaves, servants, propertyless workers, women, minors, free people of African and Amerindian descent, and even, in some places, non-Christians—were systematically excluded from the suffrage and the public space that the suffrage guaranteed.[37]

The United States, therefore, emerged as an oligarchic republic, which slowly incorporated other groups into full political participation, a process that continues today.

The origins of the revolution in Saint Domingue, as Knight observes, "lie in the broader changes of the Atlantic World during the eighteenth century."[38] The British-American Revolution, for example, directly affected France. The cost of aiding the British-American rebels contributed to the fiscal and constitutional crisis of the French monarchy. When the nobility refused to accept increased taxes, the monarchy was forced to convene the Estates General, and when that parliament met in 1789, a coalition of the third estate (urban middle and upper class groups) and a significant minority of liberal nobles, transformed the body into a national assembly, thereby initiating the French Revolution.

The French Revolution influenced the nature and evolution of the Haitian Revolution. As Knight indicates:

The *grands blancs* saw the Rights of Man as the rights and privileges of bourgeois man, much as the framers of North American independence in Philadelphia in 1776. Moreover, *grands blancs* saw liberty not as a private affair but rather as greater colonial autonomy, especially in political matters. [In this, they were following the earlier political tradition of their superior councils]. They also hoped that the metropolis would authorize more free trade thereby weakening the restrictive effects of the mercantilist *commerce exclusif* with the mother country. *Petits blancs* wanted equality, that is, active citizenship for all white persons, not just property owners, and less bureaucratic control over the colonies. But they stressed a fraternity based on whiteness of skin color that they equated with being genuinely French. *Gens de couleur* also wanted equality and fraternity, but they based their claim on an equality of the free regardless of skin color, since they fulfilled all other qualifications for active citizenship. Slaves were not part of the initial discussion and sloganeering, but from their subsequent actions they clearly supported liberty. It was not the liberty of the whites, however. Theirs was a personal freedom that undermined their relationship to their masters and the plantation, and jeopardized the wealth of a considerable number of those who were already free.[39]

The white population of Saint Domingue initiated a struggle for autonomy in 1790. As the *grands blancs* and the *petits blancs* fought for control of the colony, they not only armed themselves but also their slaves. When the French National Assembly granted political rights to the free *gens de couleur*, the whites temporarily united to limit political power to their race. Naturally, the free people of color also armed their slaves to defend their interests. The slaves, after two years of fighting for the liberty and equality of the free people of Haiti—white and non-white—rebelled to secure their own freedom. Commanded by former slave Pierre-Dominique Toussaint L'Ouverture, the rebels won a temporary victory for the slaves in 1793, which the National Assembly in France ratified by abolishing slavery. However, the ouster of the Jacobin government resulted in the reestablishment of slavery. The struggle for manumission continued for another decade. The British and the Spanish as well as the French intervened in the conflict, but Toussaint L'Ouverture's forces drove them from the island, controlled internal dissent, and even captured Spanish Santo Domingo.

When Toussaint L'Ouverture named himself governor-general for life in July 1801, however, he did not declare independence. French attempts to reassert control of Saint Domingue caused the final rupture. The new emperor of the French, Napoleon Bonaparte, who wished to restore French power in America, seized Louisiana from the Spanish, and in 1802 dispatched a massive French army to restore order in Saint Domingue. The French army captured Toussaint L'Ouverture and sent him to prison in France, where he died. However, his cause survived. His successor, Jean-Jacques Dessalines, defeated the French and declared Haitian independence on January 1, 1804.[40] As Knight observes:

Haiti was a unique case in the history of the Americas: a thorough revolution that resulted in a complete metamorphosis in the social, political, intellectual, and economic life of the colony. Socially, the lowest order of the society—the slaves—became equal, free and independent citizens. Politically, the new citizens created the second independent state in the Americas, and the first independent non-European state to be carved out of the universal European empires anywhere. Their model of state formation drove fear into the hearts of all whites from Boston to Buenos Aires.[41]

THE INDEPENDENCE OF SPANISH AMERICA

The upheavals in the Spanish world differed significantly from those in British and French America. The independence of Spanish America did not constitute an anti-colonial movement, as many assert, but formed part of not only the *revolution* within the Spanish world, but also the *dissolution* of the Spanish Monarchy. Indeed, Spain was one of the new nations that emerged from the breakup of that worldwide polity.[42]

Spain, like Great Britain, attempted to reorganize Spanish America during the last years of the eighteenth century. It established a small standing army and a large force of provincial militias, reorganized administrative boundaries, introduced a new system of administration— the intendancies—restricted the privileges of the clergy, restructured trade, and limited the appointment of Americans to government in their *patrias*.

Although Spanish Americans objected—sometimes violently— to the Bourbon reforms, they did not imitate their northern brethren by seeking independence. The Spanish Monarchy was sufficiently certain of its American subjects' loyalty that it fought Great Britain during the British-American struggle and signed the 1783 Treaty of Paris, which granted independence to the United States.

The Bourbon reforms, however, generated massive opposition in Spanish America, as those harmed by the changes used every legal remedy to stymie or modify the new system and, on occasion, turned to armed resistance to redress their grievances. Tax increases, the expulsion of the Jesuits, and other changes led to protests and to violent riots in Quito in 1765, in central New Spain the following year, and in Upper Peru during the years 1777 to 1780. The Spanish Crown eventually subdued the most serious upheavals—the Túpac Amaru Rebellion, which threatened to engulf the entire Viceroyalty of Peru during 1780 to 1783, and the Revolt of the Comuneros in New Granada in 1781—with a combination of compromise and the use of force.[43]

Spanish Americans opposed the innovations that injured them and managed to modify many to suit their interests. Although the Bourbon reforms initially harmed some areas and groups, even as they benefited others, the existing political and administrative structures appeared capable of negotiating acceptable accommodations and establishing a new equilibrium as they had after periods of rapid change for three centuries. The monarchy believed that the political system was flexible enough to reconcile these competing interests. Events in Europe, however, prevented an orderly readjustment. The French Revolution, which unleashed twenty years of war in which Spain became an unwilling participant, further eroded stability. Thus, at the end of the eighteenth century, the Spanish Monarchy faced the greatest crisis of its history.[44]

The political revolution of the Spanish world began, as Virginia Guedea observes, "with the great imperial crisis of 1808."[45] The collapse of the Spanish Monarchy, because of the French invasion of the Peninsula and the abdication of its rulers, triggered a series of events that culminated in the establishment of representative government throughout the Spanish world. The first step in that process was the formation of local governing *juntas* in Spain and America, which invoked the Spanish legal principle that in the absence of the king, sovereignty reverted to the people. While the peninsular provinces made that transition easily, the American kingdoms faced the opposition of royal officials, resident Europeans, and their New World allies.

Events in Spain had profound effects in the New World. Unwilling to accept French domination, the people of Spain opposed the invader.[46] Although initially divided, the provinces of the Peninsula ultimately joined forces on September 25, 1808, to form a government of national defense, the *Junta Suprema Central Gubernativa del Reino* (supreme central governing junta of the realm), and to wage a war of liberation. The Spanish national government, however, could not defeat the French without the aid of its overseas territories. Therefore, the new regime had to recognize the equality of the American kingdoms and in 1809 invited them to elect representatives to the Junta Central.

Although restricted to small elite, the elections enhanced the political role of the municipalities, the *ayuntamientos*, and were the first of a series of elections that provided Spanish Americans with the opportunity to participate in government at various levels. When the Junta Central convened a national assembly, the *Cortes*, in 1810, it invited the American kingdoms to send delegates.[47] The elections to the *Cortes* extended political participation more broadly than those for the Junta Central, including "Spaniards born in America and Asia . . . those domiciled and resident in those lands as well as Indians and the sons of Spaniards and Indians."[48] Before the Cortes met, the Junta Central dissolved itself, appointing a Council of Regency to act as the executive.

The deputies of Spain and America who enacted the political constitution of the Spanish Monarchy in March 1812, transformed the Hispanic world. The Constitution of Cádiz was not a Spanish document; it was as much an American charter as a Spanish one because the American deputies to the *Cortes* played a central role in its drafting. The charter of Cádiz abolished seigniorial institutions, Indian tribute, forced labor—both in America and in the Peninsula—and asserted the state's control over the Catholic Church.[49]

The constitution not only expanded the electorate, it also dramatically increased the scope of political activity. The new charter established representative government at three levels: the municipality (the constitutional ayuntamiento), the province (the diputación provincial), and the monarchy (the Cortes). By permitting cities and towns with a thousand or more inhabitants to form *ayuntamientos*, it transferred political power to the localities by incorporating vast numbers of people into the political process. Studies of the popular elections in Spanish America demonstrate that although the elite dominated politics, hundreds of thousands of middle- and lower-class men, including Indians, mestizos, and colored castes, participated in politics.[50]

Despite the unparalleled democratization of the political system, civil war erupted in Spanish America because some groups that refused to accept the government in Spain formed local *juntas,* while others, who recognized the new authorities in the Peninsula, opposed these juntas. Supporters of autonomy grounded their arguments on the *unwritten* American constitution, the compact between the individual kingdoms and the monarch. According to their interpretation, if that relationship terminated, nothing bound an American realm to Spain or to any other New World realm. However, Spaniards and Spanish Americans in the New World who opposed the formation of local juntas, believed that the Council of Regency and the Cortes constituted the only legitimate government. Conflicts also erupted in some American kingdoms when provincial cities concluded that they too possessed the right to form their own local governments, a view that the capital cities rejected with force.

Civil wars erupted in the New World, pitting supporters of the Spanish government formed to defend the monarchy against the American juntas, the viceregal capitals against the provinces, the elites against one another, and the towns against the countryside. Local conditions determined the nature and manner in which the conflict developed. Because of the European coup of 1808, the autonomist movement in New Spain began with urban conspiracies that subsequently erupted into widespread rural insurgencies. With the exception of Peru, the kingdoms of South America established governing juntas in 1809 and 1810 that assumed authority in the name of the imprisoned king and sought to dominate their regions.

Because all areas of the Spanish Monarchy possessed the same political culture, these movements, including the insurgencies in New Spain, justified their actions on the same grounds and in virtually identical terms. They argued that because of the imprisonment of the king, sovereignty reverted to the people. Most South American juntas initially consisted of both peninsulars and Americans. Once it appeared that Spain might fall completely under French domination, however, radical Spanish Americans took control, ousting the Europeans from government. Although most governing juntas acted as though they were independent and a few eventually formally declared independence from the Spanish Monarchy, the vast majority of the politically active population of Spanish America desired to retain ties with the Spanish Monarchy as autonomous realms.

The Spanish American movements of 1810, like those in Spain in 1808, arose from a desire to remain independent of French domination. The great difference between the Peninsula and America was that the regions of Spain fought an external enemy, while the New World kingdoms grappled with internal and external divisions and the fear of falling under the control of the French atheists. The conflict in Spanish America waxed and waned during the first constitutional period from 1810 to 1814, and, at times, when the authorities acted with restraint, accommodation seemed possible.

King Fernando VII's return provided an opportunity to restore the unity of the Spanish world. Virtually every act since 1808—the struggle against the French, the political revolution enacted by the *Cortes*, and the movements for autonomy in America—had been taken in his name. Although he abolished the constitution, at first it appeared that the king would implement moderate reforms; however, he instead opted to rely on force to restore royal authority in the New World. Free from constitutional restraints, the royalists in the New World crushed most autonomy movements, such as those in New Spain, Venezuela, Nueva Granada, Quito, and Chile. Only the isolated Río de la Plata remained beyond the reach of a weakened Spanish Monarchy.

The Crown's repression prompted the minority of Spanish America's active population, which favored independence, to act decisively. In South America, self-proclaimed generals like Simón Bolívar, and former professional soldiers such as José de San Martín, gained immense power and prestige as the leaders of the bloody struggles to in independence.

It was clear by 1819 that King Fernando VII needed more troops to retain control of America. But raising yet another expeditionary force to reconquer the New World only increased discontent in the Peninsula.

The liberals, exploiting the army's disenchantment with war in America, eventually forced the king in March 1820 to reinstate the constitution. The return of constitutional order transformed the Hispanic political system for the third time in a decade.

The restoration of constitutional government elicited disparate responses in Spanish America. When the news arrived in May, the people of New Spain and Guatemala (Central America) enthusiastically reestablished the constitutional system. In the months that followed, they conducted elections for countless constitutional *ayuntamientos,* provincial deputations, and the *Cortes.*

New Spain's deputies to the *Cortes* proposed a project for New World autonomy that would create three American kingdoms governed by Spanish princes and allied with the Peninsula. The proposal to form a Spanish commonwealth preceded the formation of the British Commonwealth. Indeed, the proponents argued that they did not wish to follow the example of the United States. Instead, like Canada, they sought to retain ties with the monarchy. The Spanish majority in the Cortes, however, rejected the proposal that would have granted Spanish Americans the home rule they had been seeking since 1808.[51]

At the same time, New Spain's autonomists convinced the prominent royalist Colonel Agustín de Iturbide to accept their plan for autonomy, which resembled the one presented to the Cortes. New Spain achieved independence in 1821, when Iturbide and his supporters won the backing of the majority of the royal army. Mexico achieved its independence not because the royal authorities had lost on the battlefield but because New Spaniards no longer supported the Crown politically.[52] Central America also declared independence and joined the new Mexican Empire. Mexico abolished the empire in 1823; Guatemala seceded peacefully, forming a separate nation.

The newly independent Mexicans carefully followed the precedents of the Spanish constitutional system. Although they initially established an empire, they replaced it in 1824 with a federal republic, modeling their new constitution on the Spanish charter because it had been part of their recent political experience. Distinguished New Spanish statesmen such as José Guridi y Alcocer and Miguel Ramos Arizpe, who had participated in writing the Constitution of 1812, also served in the Mexican Constituent Congress. To many Mexicans, the Constitution of Cádiz was as much their charter as Spain's. In keeping with Hispanic constitutional practices, they formed a government with a powerful legislature and a weak executive branch. Federalism in Mexico arose naturally from the earlier political experience; the provincial deputations simply converted themselves into states.[53] Like Mexico, the new Central American republic established a federation based on Hispanic constitutional practices.

In South America, the restoration of the Spanish constitution provided advocates of independence with the opportunity to press their campaign to liberate the continent. In contrast with New Spain, the South American insurgents defeated the royal authorities in battle. Two pincer movements, one from the north and the other from the south, eventually converged on Peru, ending Spanish rule.

THE RESULTS OF INDEPENDENCE

The economic and political success of the new nations depended largely on timing. The British-American struggle for independence constituted part of a larger international conflict. The new nation gained both its independence and diplomatic recognition as part of an international agreement, the Treaty of Paris of 1783. Consequently, the United States had neither to spend large sums of money for its defense, nor, like the Spanish-American countries, to devote years of political and diplomatic effort to obtain recognition from an aggrieved motherland. Fortuitously, the United States enjoyed a post-independence prosperity engendered by twenty years of war in Europe. The French Revolution of 1789 and the subsequent wars generated an insatiable demand for products from the United States. Moreover, Spain's involvement in those wars created a great commercial opportunity for the young republic because that monarchy had to rely upon neutral shipping to conduct its trade with Spanish America. Thus, prosperity alleviated political and social tensions within the United States.

The independence of the United States, moreover, did not result in the political and economic destruction of the British world. Despite brief and relatively minor conflicts, cultural, economic, and diplomatic relations continued between the former metropolis and the former colony. More significantly, during the nineteenth century Great Britain became the preeminent industrial, commercial, financial, technological, and naval power in the world. The history of the United States would have been considerably different had Spain achieved that preeminence while Britain collapsed. In a world dominated by a country with a different language, religion, and culture, the United States would have been less privileged politically and less able to exploit its rich endowment of easily available resources. Furthermore, it would have had to contend with powerful neighbors. That situation, of course, did not occur. Instead, the United States grew territorially through conquest, expanded economically, and maintained a stable political system that became increasingly democratic.

Although Haiti began its process of independence like the rest of America, by continuing patterns and processes that had been evolving for years, it experienced a dramatic social as well as political revolution. At first, Saint Domingue participated in the transformations of the French Revolution, but the slaves, who were not initially included in those changes, insisted upon freedom and equality. The bloody and destructive wars that were necessary to achieve those goals jeopardized the country's future. As Knight observes, "The Haitians dramatically transformed their conventional tropical plantation agriculture from a latifundia-dominated structure into a society of *minifundist*, or small-scale, marginal self-sufficient producers who re-oriented their production away from export-dependency to an internal marketing system supplemented by a minor export market sector."[54] In addition, a revolution of former slaves—people of African ancestry—terrified the white societies of both America and of Europe. When their armies failed to subdue the Haitians, the Europeans isolated the new country. Although some Haitians sought to continue sugar exports, most countries refused to trade with them. Instead, European nations introduced profitable tropical agriculture to other Caribbean islands. Thus, the citizens of Haiti, an impoverished, politically and economically isolated land, proved unable to form an economically prosperous and politically stable nation.

The emancipation of Spanish America did not merely consist of separation from the mother country, as in the case of the United States; independence also destroyed a vast and responsive social, political, and economic system that had functioned relatively well, despite its many imperfections. For nearly three hundred years the worldwide Spanish Monarchy was a flexible system capable of accommodating social tensions and conflicting political and economic interests. After independence, the former Spanish Monarchy's separate parts functioned at a competitive disadvantage. In that regard, nineteenth-century Spain, like the American kingdoms, was just one more newly independent nation groping for a place in an uncertain and difficult world.

By 1826 the overseas possessions of the Spanish Monarchy, one of the world's most imposing political structures at the end of the eighteenth century, consisted only of Cuba, Puerto Rico, the Philippines, and a few other Pacific islands. In contrast to the United States, which had obtained its independence in 1783, just in time to benefit from the insatiable demand for its products generated by the twenty years of war in Europe that followed the French Revolution of 1789, the Spanish world achieved emancipation after the end of the European conflicts. Not only did the new nations have to rebuild their shattered economies, but they also faced a lack of demand for their products. Instead, Europe and the United States were eager to flood Spanish America with their goods. The new countries thus did not enjoy prosperity during their formative years as the United States had. Rather, the Spanish American states had to face grave internal and external problems with diminished resources.

Spain's and Spanish America's nineteenth-century experiences provide stark proof of the costs of independence. The two regions suffered political chaos, economic decline, economic imperialism, and foreign intervention. Both the Peninsula and the nations of the New World endured civil wars. In their efforts to resolve their political and economic crises, Spain and Spanish America experimented with monarchism and republicanism, centralism and federalism, and representative government and dictatorship. Unfortunately, there was no simple solution for nations whose economies had been destroyed by war and whose political systems had been shattered by revolution.

Only in the last third of the nineteenth century did the nations of Spanish America and Spain begin to consolidate their states. By then, Spain and most Spanish-American countries had established stable governments and undertaken the difficult process of economic rehabilitation. However, the former Spanish Monarchy languished during fifty crucial years in which Britain, France, Germany, and the United States advanced to a different stage of economic development. In the period since the great political revolution had dissolved the Spanish Monarchy, the North Atlantic world changed dramatically. During those decades, Western European and U.S. industrial corporations and financial institutions achieved such size and strength that the emerging economies of Spanish America and Spain simply could not compete. Consequently, the members of the former Spanish Monarchy had to accept a secondary role in the new world order.

6

U.S. Independence and Spanish American Independence

After independence, the United States of America became one of the most successful nations in the world. It has enjoyed a stable representative government and economic prosperity for more than two centuries. Observers argue it is natural, therefore, to believe that it owes its success to its form of government. A prominent historian, for example, recently asserted, "the American Revolution was an event of truly global importance. . . . . Thus, it would be no exaggeration to say that the origins of our modern world of states can be traced back to the . . . American Revolution."[1] Scholars base such interpretations on the belief that the U.S. independence movement was not only the first to create a successful nation-state, but also the first to advance the principles of liberty, self-determination, and representative government. Those assumptions are incorrect.

The independence of the United States provided an example of political change, but it did not represent a radical departure from the shared Western European culture that based its political concepts on ancient classical thought and on late medieval Catholic theories. The Hispanic world, a major segment of Occidental civilization, played a central role in developing and transmitting those ideas in the Americas.

Political theorists and other intellectuals in the universities and colleges of Spain and Hispanic America reinterpreted the basis of modern Hispanic political thought during the late eighteenth and early nineteenth centuries. Among the concepts advanced by sixteenth- and seventeenth-century legal commentators such as Fernando Vázquez de Menchaca and Francisco Suárez, two would become significant in the early nineteenth century: the principle of popular sovereignty (*potestas populi*) and the notion of a compact (*pactum translationis*) between the people and the king.[2] Natural law theories of government also were widely accepted in the Hispanic world. Joaquín Marín y Mendoza, appointed by King Carlos III to the *catedra* (chair) of law at San Isidro, for example, published *Historia del derecho natural y de gentes* (History of natural law and people) in 1776. He and other professors of law introduced their students to a number of European authors who developed natural law and contract theories of government, among them Gaetano Filangieri, Christian Wolf, Emmerich de Vattel, and Samuel Pufendorf. These lesser-known authors, rather than the more famous Jean Jacques Rousseau, prepared several generations of Hispanic students to reinterpret the relationship between the people and the government.[3]

The redefinition of the relationship between rulers and their subjects encompassed the economic as well as the political sphere. As was the case of Hispanic political thought, economic theories evolved in a parallel fashion with ideas in Protestant countries and in France. During the reign of Carlos III (1759–1788), a number of distinguished reformers in the Spanish Monarchy discarded mercantilism in favor of free trade as a means of promoting economic growth. Their work culminated in the activities of the great Spanish economist and statesman, Gaspar Melchor Jovellanos. In 1774 before Adam Smith published the The *Wealth of Nations*, Jovellanos issued a legal opinion that supported the free market: "We would like to restore liberty completely, which is the soul of commerce, the one which grants merchandise its value, based on its abundance or scarcity, and the one that establishes prices with natural justice." Both in his political actions and in his subsequent published work, the Spaniard sought to eliminate privilege and to advocate commercial and political liberty. He declared, "The first political principle . . . is to provide men the greatest freedom possible. Protected by liberty, industry, commerce, population, and wealth will increase."[4] During his long and distinguished career, Jovellanos advocated free trade and attacked privilege. He opposed government interference in the economy and defended individual property rights and self-interest.

In his view, the role of government was to foster economic liberty by protecting private property and interests and to promote economic development by providing social and economic infrastructure, such as education, roads, canals, irrigation, ports and other facilities.[5]

The eighteenth century was a period of warfare in Europe. A prominent feature of that struggle pitted the British and Spanish monarchies against each other on four occasions: the War of Spanish Succession (1700–1714), the War of Jenkins's Ear (1739–1740), the War of Austrian Succession (1740–1748), and the Seven Years' War (1756–1763), which proved disastrous for the Spanish Monarchy.[6] In those conflicts, the British sought new territories in the New World and control of maritime trade in the Atlantic and the Pacific.

The American continent underwent significant transformation in the wake of the Seven Years' War, when both the Spanish and British Crowns restructured their possessions in America, a process known in the Spanish world as the Bourbon reforms. Although both Spanish and British Americans objected to many of these changes, the Spanish kingdoms in the New World did not imitate their northern brethren by rebelling against the Crown. On the contrary, the Spanish Monarchy was sufficiently certain of its American subjects that it fought Great Britain during the British-American struggles and signed the Treaty of Paris of 1783, which recognized U.S. independence. Although the Spanish Americans opposed certain aspects of the Bourbon reforms— sometimes violently—they did not seek separation from the Spanish Crown. Only when the Spanish Monarchy collapsed in 1808 because of the French invasion of the Iberian Peninsula—thirty-two years after the British Americans had rebelled—did Spanish Americans insist on home rule.[7]

The independence of the United States did not influence the Spanish Americans to separate from the Spanish Monarchy. Their failure to act did not stem from ignorance. On the contrary, numerous printed works provided them with detailed information about events in North America.[8] From 1763 forward, the *Gaceta de Madrid* and the *Mercurio histórico y político*, which circulated widely in the Hispanic world, reported the results of the Seven Years' War and provided details about the treaty that ended that conflict. In subsequent years, they offered extensive accounts of the discontent in the British colonies of North America, such as the revolt of Chief Pontiac and the public reaction to British reforms such as the Sugar Act and the Stamp Act. The two papers devoted considerable space to the Townsend Acts, which restricted the authority of local assemblies and increased taxes on a variety of goods. Readers of the *Gaceta de Madrid* and the *Mercurio histórico y político* learned of the Boston Tea Party, in which citizens of that port refused to pay the increased taxes on tea and, dressed as Indians, boarded ships in the harbor and threw their contents in the water. The newspapers also provided detailed information about the emergence of groups in those colonies who opposed British royal authority. Both papers, but especially the *Gaceta de Madrid*, recounted the establishment of the Continental Congress and the Declaration of Independence of July 4, 1776. They indicated that the Congress had vacillated when considering separation from the British Crown, but a pamphlet entitled *Common Sense* had ended those doubts. Portions of that publication appeared in the *Gaceta de Madrid*, which erroneously attributed authorship to "Mr. Adams one of the deputies to the Congress."[9]

After Spain entered the war against Great Britain in 1778, Madrid newspapers carried detailed reports of the U.S. struggle for independence. That same year Francisco Alvarez published an account of the history, government, and customs of the British Americans.[10] Subsequently, a Spanish translation of the U.S. Constitution of 1787 appeared in the Madrid press. In 1783 José de Covarrubias published *Memorias históricas de la última guerra con la Gran Bretaña, desde el año de 1774: Estados Unidos de América* (Historic memoirs of the last war with Great Britain since the year 1774: United States of America), which provided much information about those newly formed states.[11] Interest in the conflict and in the formation of the United States remained high. During the years 1786 and 1789, Antonio de Alcedo y Bejarano, a native of Quito, published a *Diccionario geográfico de las Indias Occidentales o América* (Geographic dictionary of the Occidental Indies or America) in five volumes. The *Diccionario*, which circulated widely in Spain and in America, was essentially an encyclopedia of the American continent. Besides geographic information about the states and the principal cities of the United States, it gave a long account of the causes and the process of independence. Alcedo included his own translation of a 1774 proclamation exhorting the inhabitants of Boston to take arms against the brutal British government. The proclamation ended with the exhortation: "Awaken Americans, the regions in which you habituate have never seen such dark clouds. You are called rebels because you refuse to pay tribute; well, justify your pretentions with your valor or seal the loss with your blood."[12] Such inflammatory words, however, did not cause Spanish Americans to revolt.

In 1806 at a time when the Spanish Monarchy had become a satellite of the French Empire and therefore an enemy of Great Britain, the Royal Press in Madrid published *Historia de la administración del Lord North, Primer Ministro de Inglaterra, y de la Guerra de la América Septentrional hasta la paz* (History of the Administration of Lord North, First Minister of England and the War of North America until Peace). The English-language edition, which had been published in Dublin, was critical of the British government and favorable to the British Americans. A later French edition glorified the British American Revolution. The Spanish-language edition translated from the French also assumed an extremely positive interpretation of the independence of the United States. The government of the Spanish Monarchy, however, does not seem to have been concerned with the impact that such a publication might have on its New World realms.[13]

The works listed above are but a sample of the many published materials about the independence of the United States available to the inhabitants of Spanish America. With few exceptions, such as the conspiracies of the Venezuelans Manuel Gual and José María España, and the activities of the Jesuit exile Juan Pablo Viscardo y Guzmán, there is little evidence of serious efforts to separate from the Spanish Monarchy. The activities of intellectuals such as Antonio Nariño of New Granada or Eugenio Espejo of Quito do not appear to have been revolutionary.

Much of the evidence against them expresses the paranoia of royal officials who created or imagined conspiracies where none existed.[14]

In 1807 Napoleon Bonaparte obtained permission to cross Spain and occupy Portugal to enforce his continental system. Once his troops entered the country, the emperor of the French decided to replace the Spanish Bourbons. Using a dispute over the Spanish Crown as an excuse, Bonaparte lured the royal family into France, where he compelled them to abdicate in his favor. Then he granted the Spanish Monarchy to his brother Joseph.

Although the governing elites in Spain capitulated, the people of the Peninsula and the New World were virtually unanimous in their fidelity to Fernando VII, opposition to the French, and determination to defend their faith. Inspired by the legal foundations of the monarchy, most agreed that in the absence of the king, sovereignty reverted to the people who possessed the authority and the responsibility to defend the nation.[15] The years 1808 to 1810 were fraught with apprehension, particularly in the Americas, where a French victory would result in the loss of autonomy and incorporation into Napoleon's empire. This possibility led some groups to rebel against royal authority, unleashing civil wars in the New World. However the overwhelming majority preferred a political resolution to domestic problems. They were active participants in the political process from 1808 through 1812 in which the composite monarchy became the *Nación Española*, a representative government with the most radical constitution of the nineteenth century.[16]

The establishment of autonomous governments generated widespread debate. Public discourse had intensified after 1808. The printing press, which became the indispensable instrument of politics, fueled an explosion of political activity in the entire Hispanic world. In the months and years that followed, important notices—particularly the debates in the Cortes—, decrees, laws, minutes of special meetings, reports of elections, statements from prominent persons, and other matters of interest were published rapidly. News publications from Europe, the United States and other regions of the New World circulated widely in the capital cities and in the provincial towns. As they formed their new governments, the leaders of the various regions of Spanish America discussed the utility of U.S., British, and French models as well as those from earlier centuries, including the Dutch Republic, the Italian city-states, and ancient Rome and Greece. However, they overwhelmingly preferred Hispanic traditions and practices.[17]

Although the translations of writings by prominent figures in the U.S. independence movement appeared in Spanish publications before 1810, the principal works identified by scholars who believe that the influence of the United States was important in shaping movements for autonomy in Hispanic America, appeared *after* those movements began.[18] In many cases, students of this topic rely on similarities in wording as evidence of influence. Such assertions ignore the different domestic conditions that gave rise to the independence movement in the United States and the early autonomous movements in Spanish America. More importantly, they also disregard the fact that a content analysis of the large number of pamphlets published in Spanish America during the period does not corroborate the assertions that U.S. publications significantly influenced the wide-ranging debate. Similarly, an analysis of the debates within juntas and later constituent assemblies uncovers only fleeting references to the United States; the majority of these references relate to reasons the northern republic's government was *not* an appropriate model for Spanish America.

A review of the works selected by those who insist on U.S. influence demonstrates their limitations. For example, in 1810 the Venezuelan José Manuel Villavicencio translated and published in Philadelphia a copy of the second U.S. charter, the Constitution of 1787. Although scholars have not found copies of his pamphlet in Spanish America, five pages of that work appeared in the *Gazeta de Caracas* and subsequently in the *Aviso al público*. Nothing else appeared in those periodicals. In January 11, 1811, the *Diario político de Santafé de Bogotá* announced that Villavicencio's translation was on sale for three *reales (silver coins)*.[19] Copies probably circulated in other parts of Spanish America, as was the case with a handwritten copy of the 1787 Constitution found in the Río de la Plata, purportedly translated by an English merchant in Buenos Aires by the name of McKinnon.[20] These cases are interesting, but prove nothing about the influence that that document may have had in those two countries.

The Venezuelan Constitution of 1811 and the U.S. Constitution established federal systems. However, the two documents were rooted in particular domestic situations resulting in vastly different governments. The federalist U.S. Constitution of 1787 established a stronger government than the Articles of Confederation adopted by the Continental Congress in 1777 and ratified by all thirteen states in 1781. In contrast, the provinces of Venezuela, following established Hispanic tradition, insisted on the right to local government. Moreover, leading Venezuelans, such as the prominent jurist Fernando Peñalver, were highly critical of the U.S. Constitution because it granted too much power to the slave-owning southern states.[21] There were other significant differences between the two charters. The U.S. document does not impose a religion while the one from Venezuela recognized "the Catholic, Apostolic, Roman religion as the exclusive one of the State and the exclusive one for the inhabitants of Venezuela." The U.S. charter granted considerable power to the executive, since it established a presidential system. In contrast, the Venezuelan Constitution created a powerful legislature and a weak executive branch, consisting of a triumvirate. The U.S. Constitution equalized representation by allocating two senators to each state regardless of its size and population. In contrast, Article 45 of the Venezuelan charter maintained proportional representation by assigning "a number of individuals whose proportion will not exceed a third, nor will it be less than a fifth part of the representative of the assembly." The Venezuelan Constitution was much more detailed and extensive than the U.S. charter.[22] The similarities in the two constitutions derive from the fact that both nations based their charters on the ancient Roman Republic. However, the system that Venezuelans constructed reflected their country's realities rather than some abstract model.

Although the Mexican Constitution of 1824 is widely believed to be based on the U.S. charter, there is no evidence of such influence.

True, both are federal constitutions. However, Mexico became a federal republic because its leaders in the Cortes of Cádiz such as Miguel Ramos Arizpe, had introduced provincial governments into the Constitution of 1812. Later, those governments, called *Diputaciones Provinciales* (provincial deputations), became the basis for the states of the independent First Federal Republic of Mexico. An analysis of the debates of Mexico's Constitutional Congress of 1823 indicates that the U.S. Constitution of 1787 had virtually no influence on the Mexican charter.[23]

Another Venezuelan, Manuel García de Sena, also published translations of works in Philadelphia that scholars wishing to demonstrate U.S. influence cite. These publications include *La independencia de la Costa Firme justificada por Thomas Paine treinta años ha* (The Independence of Costa Firme [Venezuela] justified by Thomas Paine thirty years ago), which appeared in 1811. A second publication deemed important, *Historia concisa de los Estados Unidos desde el descubrimiento de América hasta en año de 1807* (Concise history of the United States since the discovery of America until the year 1807), appeared the following year.[24] These works seem to have circulated in the port cities of South America. However, their influence is not evident. Venezuela, for example, declared independence in July 1811, before the first volume justifying U.S. independence arrived. Moreover, Paine's arguments had little to do with Venezuelan reality. The South American territory was more concerned with France's domination of the Spanish Monarchy than grievances against its rulers.[25]

Some scholars also cite the U.S. Declaration of Independence written by Thomas Jefferson as proof that the northern nation influenced authors of Spanish American declarations of independence. They fail to note that the Dutch drafted the first formal declaration of independence in 1581. Indeed, upon reading the U.S. document, Prince of Orange William V, considered it "a parody of the proclamation issued by our forefathers against King Felipe II."[26] Although the U.S. declaration was not the first, it certainly was a brilliant document, whose phrases were adapted for use in other contexts.

Two examples from the extremes of the continent will serve our purpose. In August 1810, Mariano Moreno, the secretary of the Junta Provisional of the Capital of the Río de la Plata, issued the following declaration:

> When, in the course of human events, it becomes necessary for one people to dissolve the political bonds, which have connected them with another, a decent respect to the opinions of mankind requires that they should declare the causes, which impel them to the separation. The Capital of Buenos Ayres, inseparable from the means of moderation that it has proposed, attempted to unite closely to Montevideo.[27]

The words address two radically different situations. In this case, Buenos Aires was trying to dominate the entire former Viceroyalty of the Río de la Plata, and Montevideo, like other provinces, was not willing to cede power to the *porteños* (people of Buenos Aires). Moreno plagiarized Jefferson because of his brilliant writing, not because the original document encouraged him to seek independence from the Spanish Monarchy.

The second example comes from Béjar, Texas, which declared its independence on April 6, 1813. In this case, the unknown authors of the document paraphrased the last part of the U.S. Declaration of Independence as follows:

> We the people of the Province of Texas, swearing before the Supreme Judge of the universe the rectitude of our intentions, declare that the bonds that kept us under the domination of European Spain are forever dissolved, that we are free and independent, that we have the right to establish our own government and that henceforth all legitimate authority emanates from the people, who alone possess that right, that from now on and forever we are absolved of any duty and obligation to any foreign power.[28]

In this case, the rebels—including British Americans—used the terminology to justify separating Texas from the Viceroyalty of New Spain and making the region part of the United States. Their plans did not work at that time; however, they would succeed twenty-three years later.

The residents of the Hispanic world knew about the U.S. Declaration of Independence and other documents relative to its struggle against the British. However, these texts were neither unique nor a factor in the Spanish American independence movements. The leaders of the United States had themselves followed earlier traditions. When they called their provinces "estates," for example, they were following the Dutch tradition. Moreover, their first constitution, the Articles of Confederation, also drew on the Dutch experience. The second U.S. charter, the Constitution of 1787, drew from the ancient Roman tradition of a bicameral legislature with its Senate and House of Representatives. This is not to say that the Founding Fathers of the United States merely copied earlier practices. They did not! They adapted previous documents to their circumstances. That is what the people of the Spanish world did as well. Like their British-American brethren who relied on Roman and English sources, the leaders of Spanish America relied heavily on their Roman and Hispanic traditions.

Here it is useful to recall the words of the great Mexican political theorist, Servando Teresa de Mier, who declared in the Mexican Constituent Congress of 1823:

The United States was not constituted until after the war with Great Britain ended. . . . And how did they govern themselves in the meantime? With the rules they inherited from their fathers. Even the Constitution which they later promulgated was no more than a collection of those [laws]. . . . And in the meantime with what do we govern ourselves? With the same laws that we have had until now. With the Spanish Constitution, the laws in our code books that have not been derogated, with the decrees of the Spanish Cortes until the year 1820 and those which the [Mexican]

Congress has introduced and will continue to enact in accordance to our present system [of government] and our circumstances.

Although the independence of the United States had little influence on the independence of Spanish America, the northern federation held a great attraction for the new nations of Spanish America. That appeal was not based on its form of government, which some Spanish Americans—Vicente Rocafuerte chief among them—praised.[29] This interest reflected the belief that as within the United States, independence and representative government would foster economic prosperity and political order in Spanish America. Since that did not occur, many contemporary and numerous current scholars concluded that the failures of the new nations of Spanish America were attributable to their lack of preparation for self-government and the adoption of inappropriate foreign political models. That is incorrect; new research demonstrates that the inhabitants of the Spanish Monarchy possessed a long history of representation and a significant degree of autonomy within the Hispanic composite monarchy that had prepared them to govern themselves in fact. Furthermore, the great political revolution started by the Constitution of Cádiz provided the people of Spanish America with widespread experience in electing their representatives to the Cortes, the provincial deputations, and the constitutional ayuntamientos. Moreover, the Hispanic Constitution of 1812 provided more extensive suffrage than those of Britain, the United States, and France.

Given their history, why did Spain and Spanish America experience political instability and economic decline during the nineteenth century in contrast to Britain and the United States? The answer lies in the nature of the Spanish Monarchy and the timing of Spanish American independence.

In contrast to the United States, which obtained its independence in 1783, just in time to benefit from the insatiable demand for its products generated by the twenty years of war in Europe following the French Revolution, the Spanish world achieved emancipation after the end of the European wars. Not only did the new nations have to rebuild their shattered economies, but they also faced lack of demand for their products. The new countries did not enjoy prosperity during their formative years as the United States had. Rather, the Spanish American states had to face grave internal and external problems with diminishing resources.

The United States and the new nations of Spanish America had conflicting interests. Religion sharply divided the population of the United States and Spanish America. During the sixteenth century, the Spanish Monarchy had become the champion of Catholicism; Protestant England, although not its equal, became one of Spain's most hostile enemies. That tension continued in America after independence, although some groups tolerated religious diversity.

The United States, whose merchants engaged in legal and clandestine trade in the Caribbean, pursued an aggressive expansionist policy. As early as 1786, Thomas Jefferson declared: "Our confederacy must be viewed as the nest from [which] all America, North and South, is to be peopled. We should take care, too, not to think it for the best of that great continent to press too soon on the Spaniards. Those countries cannot be in better hands. My fear is that they [the Spaniards] are too feeble to hold . . . [their national territory] until our population can be sufficiently advanced to gain it from them piece by piece."[30]

The purchase of the Louisiana Territory from Napoleon in 1803 strengthened the North American nation. The acquisition gave the United States free navigation of the Mississippi River and the port of New Orleans, providing access to New Spain's northern territories, particularly Texas. The United States, which claimed that the Province of Texas and parts of the Floridas were included in the Louisiana Territory, sent expeditions to explore and to "liberate" if possible some northern regions of New Spain.

During the turbulent years from 1808 through 1821, the United States maintained relations with the government of Spain while simultaneously trying to acquire the northern provinces of New Spain. The North Americans also profited from the armed struggle by using New Orleans to shelter Spanish Americans who were conspiring against the royal government in New Spain; at the same time, the port became an arms market for various insurgent factions in Spanish America. Ironically, when King Fernando VII returned to power, he rewarded the United States for its ostensible support of the government in Spain. In 1819 the two nations signed the Transcontinental Treaty, also known as the Adams-Onís Treaty, whereby the Spanish Monarchy surrendered the Floridas to the North American republic. It was the second step—after the Louisiana Purchase—in America's drive to take Mexico's' northern provinces from Texas to California.[31]

While the independence of the United States had little influence on the process of Spanish American independence, the northern federation exerted great influence on the region after independence because of its political stability and economic resources, which underpinned an aggressive U.S. foreign policy.

7

Caudillos and Historians

Historians and subsequently other social scientists use the concept of the *caudillo*, a particular type of politician, to explain events that have not been adequately researched. The term *caudillo* is not unique to the Spanish language. It is *the leader* in English, *der Führer* in German, and *il duce* in Italian, and it simply means "he who directs." Nevertheless, scholars imbue the terms *caudillo* and *caudillaje* (the actions of the caudillo) with having explanatory significance when explaining the complex political events in the countries of the Hispanic world. Many scholars consider caudillaje to be a unique characteristic of Hispanic history and culture, which they identify as authoritarian. They generally associate the appearance of the phenomenon with the collapse of the Spanish Monarchy in 1808. Francisco José Moreno, for example, asserts: "Within the Spanish political tradition, caudillismo was an effort to fill the vacuum left by the removal of the symbol of institutional authoritarianism [i.e. the king]"[1]

Those who have attempted to explain the phenomenon of caudillaje advance interpretations ranging from historical determinism and authoritarian Catholic culture to psychosocial explanations. Most of these words are broad general analyses of the first decades of nineteenth-century Hispanic history, the period when the Spanish Monarchy collapsed, the great Hispanic revolutions occurred, and the new nation-states of Spain and Spanish America emerged. It is a complex era that is little studied; the only topic that has been examined in any depth is the wars of independence in Spain and in America. The political history of the time, especially the great political revolution of the Hispanic world, is in its formative stage. The new works that focus on "the new political history" demonstrate that, because of the Hispanic revolution, large numbers of men from all social groups emerged as influential political actors. Although scholars who examine popular politics emphasize this political revolution when discussing their respective topics, they, like earlier scholars, often explain events not central to their work by referring to the actions of caudillos. Thus, the older emphasis on caudillos remains strangely prominent in the new works.[2]

This essay will examine the actions of three caudillos—Rafael Riego, Agustín de Iturbide, and Antonio López de Santa Anna—to demonstrate that broad political forces shaped events and in turn determined who became the "leaders" of these movements. Using caudillaje as an analytical concept limits our ability to understand the nineteenth-century history of the Hispanic world.

THE RIEGO REVOLT

Historians of Spain and Spanish America generally explain the political transformation of 1820 by stating that the revolt led by Colonel Rafael Riego forced King Fernando VII to restore the constitution. Historians of Spain, as to be expected, provide a more nuanced account. They discuss the early conspiracies against Fernando VII, the plans of conspirators to convince the army in Andalucía to rebel rather than go to America to fight against the insurgents, the failure of the conspiracy, and Riego's decision to act. Nevertheless, historians of Spain frequently explain the transformation in terms of Rafael Riego's decisions. The British historian Raymond Carr, for example, declares: "It was Riego who gave the revolution its programme by declaring on 1 January 1820 for the Constitution of 1812: thus a single man, acting on impulse and without consulting civilians, committed liberalism to the constitution."[3] The Spanish historian Miguel Artola presents a more cautious account but also suggests that the conspirators lacked a political program. He observes that Antonio Alcalá Galiano, one of the leading civilian conspirators, wrote "the manifestos that were to be read to the troops ... [which] were not written until the last minute and were not submitted to the conspirators." Furthermore, he states, "Alcalá Galiano's manifesto is a document that lacks any doctrine .... Riego's proclamation emphasizes the dangers of embarking [in damaged ships to reconquer Spanish America] and the need to establish 'a moderate and paternal government' and 'a Constitution that assures the rights of all citizens.'" Artola continues that "after reading the manifesto cited, Riego, in front of his men, proclaimed the Constitution of 1812."[4] Thus, although with various degrees of sophistication, historians continue to accept that Riego restored the constitution in 1820.

The authors of the works discussed above failed to place the restoration of the constitution within the context of the profound political transformation sweeping the Hispanic world and the impact of the Hispanic revolution on politics at all levels. Most of the studies of popular elections for members of the governing institutions established by the Constitution of 1812—the constitutional ayuntamientos, the provincial deputations, and the Cortes—focus on America.[5] We have only a vague idea of how those institutions actually worked and how they affected the lives of millions of people in the Spanish Monarchy, or the Spanish *nation* as it was called. It is clear, however, that in 1813 and 1814 vast numbers of men participated in the new political process both in Spain and in America. This political experience would continue to influence their actions and attitudes after the abolition of the constitution in 1814.

Opposition to Fernando VII's rule began as soon as he abolished the constitution. Spanish liberals and military men formed secret societies to organize the opposition. As the liberal, military man, and mason Evaristo San Miguel later declared: "The Masonic lodges became liberal and conspiratorial juntas. The terms constitutional and mason were synonymous."[6] The revolutionaries had a variety of motives. Many merely wanted jobs. Others wanted to restore constitutional rule. Although the conspirators disliked Fernando VII's rule they did not agree on the best form of government for Spain. Some who supported the charter of 1812 condoned no change. Other liberals wanted to strengthen the executive branch or establish a two-chamber legislature to prevent radicalism. A few saw no difference between the American desire for home rule and the demand for local representative government in Spain. Indeed, one of them, Javier Mina, believed that the insurgents' struggle in America was really an attempt to restore the constitution.

The Mina Insurrection is a good example of the relationship between Spanish liberals and American insurgents. Mina was a hero of the Spanish War of Independence who, like other guerrilla leaders, could find no employment at home after the war ended. He indignantly refused the command of a division in New Spain tasked with defeating the insurgents commanded by the cura José María Morelos y Pavón.[7] Instead, he and his uncle, Francisco Espoz y Mina, rebelled in September 1814 and demanded the restoration of the constitution. The insurrection failed and the leaders fled to London.[8] At the request of Fray Servando Teresa de Mier, the exiled Javier Mina agreed to lead an invasion of New Spain. After obtaining support from various Spanish Americans, the conspirators landed in northern New Spain in mid-1816. They fought for a year, but in the end, the royalists captured and executed Mina and imprisoned Mier. Mina had hoped to restore constitutional rule in New Spain and extend it from there to Spain and other parts of the Monarchy.[9] Although the plan was implausible, it was not entirely illogical. New Spain was one of the wealthiest parts of the monarchy and, if liberated, could serve as a base for restoring the Constitution of 1812 throughout the Spanish Monarchy.

Like the renewed insurgency in America, opposition in Spain increased despite the king's attempts to end it through violent repression. Another rebellion occurred in Spain even before Mina reached New Spain. Juan Díaz Porlier, a native of Buenos Aires and a hero of the Spanish guerrilla war against the French, rebelled in La Coruña in September 1815, demanding the constitution's restitution. At first, the movement appeared successful, but strong government action triumphed. As with the case of Mina, the royalist forces prevailed, and executed Díaz Porlier. The deaths did not deter other rebels. In 1816 Vicente Richard plotted to assassinate the king in a brothel. The following year, Lieutenant General Luis Lacy rebelled in Cataluña and failed. Shortly thereafter, the Inquisition uncovered another conspiracy known as the Great Masonic Plot of 1817. In 1818 government officials thwarted an attempt to restore Carlos IV to the throne as a constitutional monarch. When this plan failed, Colonel Joaquín Vidal led an insurrection in Valencia. All these attempts to restore the constitution failed and their leaders forfeited their lives.[10]

The leaders of these rebellions, the caudillos, did not act unilaterally; they were part of larger movements that included many liberals and other discontented civilians as well as military men. Some urban groups came to realize that the Cortes had established an acceptable equilibrium between the desire for local self-government and the need for an effective national government. The growing appreciation of the constitutional structure, particularly the constitutional ayuntamientos and the provincial deputations, prompted more and more people to participate in movements to restore the constitution. However, as late as 1819, none of the insurrections had found support among the masses. If the liberals were to return to power, they had to gain wider backing.

The discontent caused by the Crown's determination to use force to subdue insurgency in America provided liberals an opportunity to gain mass support for their efforts to restore constitutional government. The war in northern South America turned against the Crown by 1819, and the expeditionary force raised to regain Buenos Aires was now preparing to fight the insurgents in Venezuela. This army had been encamped in Andalucía for months awaiting transportation to America. The delay and the soldiers' wretched living conditions increased dissatisfaction. No one wanted to participate in the bitter fratricidal struggle in the New World. Liberals exploited the troops' reluctance to leave Spain. They argued that the restoration of the constitution would eliminate the need for an American campaign. Clandestine organizations in Cádiz also attempted to convince the commanding general, Enrique O'Donnell, the Count La Bisbal, to join them. Unfortunately, La Bisbal betrayed the movement. Although the conspirators fled, a sudden outbreak of yellow fever among the soldiers prevented the government from rooting out other conspirators.[11]

Subsequently, some radicals attempted to renew efforts to turn military men against the king. Antonio Alcalá Galiano returned to

Andalucía and approached several younger officers. Colonels Antonio Quiroga and Juan O'Donojú, who had been implicated in the Great Masonic Plot, were receptive. However, it was Colonel Rafael Riego, commander of the Asturias Regiment, who acted.[12] On January 1, 1820, he raised the banner of rebellion, demanding the restoration of the constitution. As he declared in his proclamation to the troops, "The Constitution, yes, the Constitution, is sufficient to pacify our brethren in America."[13] Other units joined the movement, but rapid government action prevented the Cádiz liberals from reinforcing the military uprising. New royalist troops, dispatched to quell the rebellion, took control of the cities in the South. For nearly two months, the rebels marched throughout southern Spain hoping to obtain support, but found none.

Civilian politicians, not military insurrectionists, succeed in mobilizing the Spanish people. On February 21, 1820, urban groups in La Coruña rebelled. They immediately restored the ayuntamiento constitucional and the provincial deputation. Other northern cities and towns also restored their constitutional ayuntamientos. By March 5 even large cities such as Zaragoza and Barcelona had reestablished constitutional ayuntamientos and provincial deputations. The provincial cities and towns of Spain restored the self-government granted them by the Constitution of 1812. Liberal officers such as Quiroga, claimed success and the rest of the army hastened to join them. Even La Bisbal saw the error of his ways and returned to the liberal fold. Riego, whose uprising had been unsuccessful, became a popular hero.[14]

Only Madrid remained in government hands by March 6, 1820. Even there Henry Wellesley, the British minister, estimated that two thirds of the population sympathized with the rebels.[15] The liberal conspirators capitalized on the general disenchantment with the government to mobilize the masses in the capital. Crowds poured into the streets demanding the restoration of the constitution. Fernando VII who had no alternative ordered the Cortes to reconvene. The king appointed a junta of liberals to advise him until the Cortes met and appointed a ministry of "*presidiarios*," liberals released from prison.[16]

The six years of the restored antiguo régimen had demonstrated the value of self-government and the institutions that guaranteed representation and civil rights. Unlike the first constitutional period when local notables had been apathetic and hesitant to hold elections, in 1820 the cities immediately proceeded to organize and elect ayuntamientos constitucionales. Although the transformation of 1820 requires additional study, it is clear that the people and their civilian political leaders, and not Riego, restored the constitution.

AGUSTÍN DE ITURBIDE

Although the historiography of Mexican independence is enormous, Mexican historians are diffident about their emancipation. Currently in Mexico the government and the public, as well as those cities and towns of the United States that have large Mexican-origin populations, celebrate independence on September 15 and 16 to honor Father Miguel Hidalgo's initiation of the insurgency in 1810. Most historians accept those dates as the beginning of the eleven-year movement for independence. New Spain, however, did not separate from the Spanish Monarchy until 1821, when the royalist colonel Agustín de Iturbide proclaimed the Plan of Iguala. Although there is debate among liberal and conservative historians concerning Iturbide's actions, most give him credit for achieving independence in 1821.[17] This interpretation ignores the great Hispanic political revolution that culminated in Mexican independence.

Like most of their Spanish counterparts, most historians of Mexico have not studied the profound impact that the great Hispanic revolution had on New Spain. Instead, they have focused on the insurgency, which was defeated. Although Nettie Lee Benson noted more than sixty years ago, the significance of the popular elections and the importance of the institutions created by the Constitution of 1812, only recently have a few historians begun studying these important institutions and processes.[18] Their work demonstrates that politics was not the domain of a few elites. Indeed, the vast majority of the adult male population became active participants in politics. Moreover, it is important to note that the insurgency occurred only in some areas of New Spain, whereas the political transformations affected the entire kingdom.

Because of the collapse of the Spanish Monarchy in 1808, many *novohispanos* pursued various avenues to obtain autonomy: they aspired to home rule, participated in secret societies, and distinguished themselves as parliamentarians and constitutionalists. The autonomists, who proposed self-government in 1808, conspired to win home rule between 1809 and 1820 and grasped for political power through constitutional means in the elections of 1812, 1813, and 1814. All the while, they flirted with the insurgents. Indeed, some autonomists seriously contemplated joining an insurgent government in 1813 and 1814 when it appeared that the movement had a chance of success. They went underground in 1814 and 1815 when the Constitution of 1812 and the insurgent movement seemed doomed, remaining active in clandestine groups until the liberals in Spain restored the constitution in 1820.[19]

The restoration of the Constitution of Cádiz unleashed widespread political activity in New Spain. In the months that followed, ayuntamientos from Chiapas in the South to Béxar, Texas in the North, reported that they had sworn allegiance to the constitution in formal ceremonies and that they had restored or established constitutional ayuntamientos. Thousands of publications argued the pros and cons of the constitutional system. Although political debate attracted public attention, perhaps more than any other activity, elections politicized New Spain's society. From June 1820 until March 1821, electioneering and elections occupied the politically active population. Officials immediately held elections for the constitutional ayuntamientos of 1820 and a few months later for those of 1821. They also held two separate elections for the Cortes: one rapidly in the autumn of 1820 for the Cortes of 1821–1822 and a second for the 1822–1823 session of parliament. The electorate also selected for members of former viceroyalty's six provincial deputations.[20]

Politically active novohispanos, however, did not place all their hopes in the success of the restored constitutional order. The autonomists of New Spain embraced two strategies in their efforts to achieve home rule: the Hispanic constitutional process and, as in 1813–1814 when they had considered joining the insurgent regime, the possibility of establishing their own autonomous government. Initially, they viewed the Hispanic constitutional process as a more manageable and more attractive alternative. The autonomists gained control of the constitutional ayuntamientos and the provincial deputations and won elections to the Cortes.[21]

In Mexico City, members of the national elite, who were concerned about retaining home rule, kept in close touch with like-minded individuals in the provincial capitals. Many matters concerned them. The intense involvement of the people in the political process was new and unsettling. Some members of the military and the clergy became hostile to the constitutional system because the Cortes enacted negative measures suppressing the Jesuits and abolishing ecclesiastic and military immunity from civil prosecution. While the decrees of the Cortes intensified the disaffections of those key groups, their discontent arose from more immediate factors. The newly erected ayuntamientos rapidly seized upon constitutional guarantees to end war taxes and to prohibit royal officers from raising militia forces in their regions. Since the authorities had not paid many units for months, these units lacked supplies and equipment. Since they could not continue to operate without wartime levies, their officers viewed the restoration of the constitution as a mortal blow. Moreover, the new policies of the constitutional ayuntamientos not only weakened the institutional integrity of the royal army and eliminated the economic and political power of some officers, but also threatened many with prosecution for their earlier abuses. The impact of the restored constitution upon the clergy was less uniform, resulting in divisions within the church. The political instability of the times adversely affected many ecclesiastics, particularly the members of the monastic orders. But many other clergymen became very successful politicians. It is likely, however, that the traditional segments of the military and the clergy resented the loss of their privileged status. Once the bulwark of the state, many of them felt themselves abandoned to opportunist politicians.[22]

Perhaps most distressing to the autonomists were reports about the political disintegration of the Peninsula. Was social revolution imminent? If so, what action would protect orderly representative government in New Spain? Some spoke openly of independence! One group, which included various factions, among them discontented clergymen, army officers, and government officials as well as a large number of autonomists, concluded that independence might be necessary to retain home rule under the Constitution of 1812, that is, to establish a limited constitutional monarchy in New Spain. In 1820 and 1821 the leaders of New Spain followed two paths in their efforts to achieve home rule: the constitutional process and other "extra legal means."[23]

In 1820 José Mariano Michelena, a substitute deputy to the Cortes from Michoacán, a military man and a liberal, proposed a plan that combined elements of the widely discussed proposals for American autonomy with the new system of constitutional government. He and other American substitute deputies discussed the project at a series of meetings in Madrid, obtaining support from the proprietary (elected) deputies when they arrived in 1821. The proprietary deputies from New Spain were aware of Michelena's proposal because he had been in communication with colleagues in Michoacán and other regions of New Spain. The Michelena plan proposed dividing the New World into three kingdoms: New Spain and Guatemala; New Granada and the provinces of *Tierra Firme* (Venezuela); and Peru, Chile and Buenos Aires. Each kingdom would possess its own cortes that would function under the Constitution of 1812. A Spanish prince or a person appointed by the king would preside over each kingdom. Spain and the American kingdoms would maintain special commercial, diplomatic, and defense relationships. Finally, the new realms would pay a portion of Spain's foreign debt.[24]

The representatives from New Spain, who constituted the overwhelming majority of American deputies, were determined to win concessions from the Cortes. They possessed instructions from their provinces demanding greater autonomy and insisting on provincial deputations for every former intendancy in the New World. Their successful proposal doubled the number of provincial deputations from New Spain, and the Cortes granted provincial deputations to every former intendancy in America. It also appointed a committee of four Spaniards and five Americans—novohispanos Lorenzo de Zavala, Lucas Alamán, Francisco Fagoaga, and Bernardino Amati, and the Venezuelan Fermín Paul—to consider the Michelena proposal and other American questions. In addition, Michelena and his novohispano colleague Miguel Ramos Arizpe, a prominent liberal clergyman, managed to have Juan O'Donojú appointed captain general and superior political chief of New Spain, the office that replaced the viceroy under the constitution. The new official, a distinguished military man, liberal, and supposedly a member of a secret society, had served as minister of war during the first constitutional period, and had conspired against the monarch in 1818 and 1819, then serving as Political Chief of the Province of Sevilla.[25]

The Americans were ecstatic; Ramos Arizpe declared:

Madrid and the entire Peninsula constitute a glorious spectacle. It is an entirely free theater where the most important questions of practical politics relative to the future of Spain's America are treated. Questions, which a few years ago were a crime to mention in the most private of conversations, today are openly discussed with the most absolute liberty. They are debated in *tertulias* [social gatherings], in the public patriotic societies, in speeches and very sound public addresses, in the public papers, in the meetings of deputies, and in a publicly named special commission of the Cortes cordially attended by the honorable secretaries of state and by many Spanish American deputies. And, [there are those who] assure that the ministers of the King, the good King Fernando VII, have been authorized to inform the commission of the Cortes, that H. M., aware of the state of Spanish America . . . recognized that it was now time to seriously address the nature of its government and adopt radical measures [if necessary] . . . . Therefore, he authorized the ministers to attend the discussion of the commission of the Cortes that was concerned with such an important object.[26]

O'Donojú was well aware of the aspirations of the novohispanos. Michelena and Ramos Arizpe had discussed with him their plan for regencies for America. With the project's apparent support from the government as well as the American deputies, O'Donojú departed for New Spain. Clearly, the new superior political chief left the Peninsula believing he had the responsibility of strengthening the constitutional order in New Spain and that, in all likelihood, he would also introduce the new system of American regencies.[27]

Concerned that Spain would not grant them the full autonomy they sought, some autonomists in New Spain pursued an alternative means of achieving home rule. Although they gathered to discuss their country's future in a variety of places, one of the most prominent was the Mexico City salon of María Ignacia Rodríguez de Velasco, popularly known as *la Güera Rodríguez* (the blonde Rodríguez). With her help, they convinced an efficient and ruthless royalist officer, Colonel Agustín de Iturbide, to accept their plan for autonomy, which resembled the proposal presented to the Cortes. In early 1821 he began coordinating his activities with the leading civil, clerical, and military leaders of the viceroyalty. With their help, he formulated a program that he issued at the village of Iguala on February 24, 1821. A carefully crafted compromise document, the Plan de Iguala, like the proposal to the Cortes, combined the long-discussed autonomous regency with the constitution. In addition, the Plan de Iguala offered protection to the clergy, the army, and the Europeans. It imposed the Roman Catholic faith as the official religion "without any tolerance for any other [religion]," proclaimed "the absolute independence of this realm," established a constitutional monarchy, and invited Fernando VII or a member of his family to govern. The Plan de Iguala retained representative constitutional government that did not preclude reconciliation with the Spanish Monarchy. Following Hispanic traditions and practices introduced in 1808, the plan proposed establishing a governing junta until a Mexican cortes convened.[28]

Iturbide later claimed that "I formed the plan known of as Iguala; it is mine because I alone conceived it, elaborated it, published it, and executed it."[29] It is evident, however, that the document had a complicated history. Contemporaries attributed authorship of the plan to various individuals, among them Matías Monteagudo, rector of the university and canon of the metropolitan cathedral; Antonio Joaquín Pérez, former deputy to the Cortes de Cádiz and then bishop of Puebla; and the prominent lawyers Juan José Espinosa de los Monteros, Juan Francisco Azcárate, José Zozaya Bermúdez, and Juan Gómez de Navarrete, former members of the secret society of Guadalupes. Later, while attempting to unravel these events, Carlos María de Bustamante concluded that all those individuals took part in framing the document.[30]

The plan evolved over time. It is likely that, as traditional historiography asserts, clergymen and *serviles* (reactionaries) formed the initial proposal in the former Jesuit oratory of San Felipe Neri, known as *La Profesa*, to prevent the restoration of the constitution in 1820. Monteagudo and Pérez, the reputed authors of the proposal, had compelling reasons to oppose the restoration of constitutional order. Monteagudo played a central role in the 1808 overthrow of Viceroy José Iturrigaray due to his opposition to many of the Cortes's reforms. The latter, despite having participated in writing the Constitution of 1812, earned the hostility of the supporters of the restored charter because he was one of the *Persas*, deputies to the Cortes of 1814 who had welcomed the return of Fernando VII and his restoration of the antiguo régimen. The conspirators selected Iturbide to carry out the operation, a fact upon which both his friends and enemies agreed. However, as Lucas Alamán reminds us, the plan's adherents abandoned the project when the viceroy implemented the constitution.[31]

The restoration of the Constitution of Cádiz nullified the plan of La Profesa. However, the proposal remained attractive to Colonel Agustín de Iturbide, a royalist officer who was relieved of his command in 1816 for his ruthlessness and cruelty toward prisoners and their wives and children during the counterinsurgency. This nullified his military fuero, making him eligible for trial in a civil court for his illegal actions; if convicted, he faced imprisonment. Despite the fact that "until then he had led a private life without any desire to be involved in any public endeavor," the disgraced officer saw an opportunity to salvage his career.[32] Determined to act, he consulted with civilian leaders in the capital. They dissuaded him from his initial plan to capture the viceroy, and after four years, the viceroy—who needed officers with counterinsurgency experience—appointed Iturbide commander of the South in 1820. Subsequently, the Güera Rodríguez approached him with an alternative proposal crafted by autonomists to attract Europeans and Americans, the clergy and the military, and serviles as well as liberals. While La Profesa's proposal sought independence to preserve the antiguo régimen, the new plan would maintain the constitutional system through independence. The commander agreed to lead the movement.

Iturbide pursed two strategies: he attempted to obtain the support of leading civilians and military men in the viceroyalty and seek assistance in formulating a program for autonomy. He accomplished his first goal by corresponding with prominent military, ecclesiastic, and government leaders and by dispatching trusted emissaries to discuss the project with influential novohispanos. Iturbide wrote letters to each potential supporter emphasizing how the proposal would serve their personal interests while maintaining, to the degree possible, the status quo. At the same time, he consulted a number of individuals, among them Zozaya Bermúdez, Espinosa de los Monteros, Monteagudo, Gómez de Navarrete, and Gómez Pedraza, asking them to suggest changes to a written proposal.[33]

Satisfied with his preparations, Iturbide issued the pronouncement at the village of Iguala on February 24, 1821. Despite his efforts to gain adherents, most of the kingdom's civil, military, and ecclesiastic authorities initially rejected the plan. In the months that followed, however, various groups in the provinces joined Iturbide's movement. During April, May, and June large parts of the Bajío and Nueva Galicia gradually accepted the Plan of Iguala. Royal officers including Luis Quintanar and Pedro Celestino Negrete, as well as former insurgents, such as Guadalupe Victoria and Nicolás Bravo, joined the movement. The most important victory, however, occurred in Puebla at the end of July. Provincial leaders, particularly those in Puebla's constitutional ayuntamiento, negotiated with the new insurgents and pledged to support the movement in exchange for the creation of a provincial deputation. Once Iturbide reached the accord, he entered Puebla in triumph on August 2, 1821.[34]

When O'Donojú arrived in Veracruz at the end of July, large parts of New Spain were in rebel hands and, in the capital, Spanish troops had overthrown the legally constituted authorities. He faced a delicate task. As a Spaniard, he was committed to maintaining ties between the Peninsula and New Spain, and as a liberal, he was determined to ensure the restoration of constitutional rule. Under the circumstances, the only course open to him was to begin negotiations with Iturbide. The two men met in the city of Córdoba on August 23, 1821. The following day the two officers signed a treaty recognizing the independence of New Spain. They reached an accord quickly because the Plan of Iguala was essentially the same as the Michelena proposal that O'Donojú believed the Cortes had already ratified. As Iturbide later declared, the Spaniard accepted his proposal "almost as if he had helped me write the plan."[35]

O'Donojú acted immediately to implement the agreement. He informed his government of the accord and urged its rapid approval. Then he arranged for the troops in the capital to recognize him as captain general and superior political chief of New Spain. In Puebla, O'Donojú and Iturbide agreed on the composition of the transitional government. They expanded the regency from three to five men and increased the size of the governing junta to thirty-eight members. The body consisted of the most important men of the kingdom, among them the leading autonomists, constitutionalists, former Guadalupes, and a few servile clergymen and military men.[36]

On September 22, 1821, the members of the Sovereign Governing Junta convened in Tacubaya, outside Mexico City, where they swore to fulfill their responsibilities. At its second meeting, the body voted unanimously "that the Junta will possess the exclusive exercise of the national representation until the [Mexican] Cortes meets." It also arrogated to itself "all the governing powers established for the [Hispanic] Cortes by the Political Constitution of the Spanish Monarchy." Following the precedent of the Cortes of Cádiz, the junta declared that it was *sovereign* and was to receive the treatment of *majesty*.[37]

Captain General and Superior Political Chief Juan O'Donojú entered the capital on September 26 to the sound of bands, the ringing of bells, and the firing of cannon. The following day, under Iturbide's command, the Army of the Three Guarantees entered Mexico City. That evening, the ayuntamiento welcomed the heroes of independence at a lavish dinner in the palace. After many toasts and speeches, Regidor Sánchez de Tagle read an ode in which he declared that the people of America thanked O'Donojú, that "super human mortal . . . who assures us peace."[38]

At its first session in Mexico City, on September 28, the Sovereign Governing Junta signed the declaration of independence. Then the body, together with other corporations, attended a Mass of Thanksgiving at the cathedral. That evening the Sovereign Governing Junta reviewed and approved the participation of the members present. O'Donojú could not attend because he was ill. The junta then selected the five individuals who would compose the Council of Regency. Without opposition, Iturbide was selected first regent and president of the Council of Regency and O'Donojú, second regent. The junta elected three other regents from a list of fifteen candidates. While the Sovereign Governing Junta granted Iturbide a significant honor by naming him president of the Council of Regency, it did not grant him the power to act independently. As the Sovereign Governing Junta made clear at the outset, in accord with Hispanic precedent, sovereignty resided in the legislative branch. The executive branch was required to implement the mandates of the legislature.[39]

Although New Spain had achieved its independence, tensions existed between civilians and the military, both of which considered emancipation their triumph. Two opposing political traditions emerged between 1808 and 1821; one forged in the crucible of war emphasized executive power and the other, based on civilian parliamentary experience, insisted upon legislative dominance. It is possible that an experienced administrator and a committed liberal like O'Donojú would have peacefully resolved those tensions. Unfortunately, he died of pleurisy on October 8. It is clear, however, that civilian politicians—not Iturbide—orchestrated the independence of Mexico.

ANTONIO LÓPEZ DE SANTA ANNA

Antonio López de Santa Anna, known popularly as Santa Anna, became a symbol for the political instability of early nineteenth-century Mexico. Lucas Alamán, perhaps the country's foremost historian, labeled the period "The Age of Santa Anna" in 1852. Others have followed. Wilfred H. Calcott entitled his 1936 biography, *Santa Anna: The Story of an Enigma Who Once Was Mexico*. In 1993 Enrique González Pedrero called his study of the period, *País de un solo hombre: El México de Santa Anna* (A Country of one man: Santa Anna's Mexico). Recently, Will Fowler published a biography entitled *Santa Anna of Mexico* that portrays the military man as the most important political leader of the period.[40] Santa Anna has become the leitmotiv of nineteenth-century Mexico. These works demonstrate the lack of studies focusing on the politics and political processes of the first half of the nineteenth century that would allow scholars to place his actions within the broad context of Mexican political development.

An examination of the Revolution of 1832, the movement that culminated in Santa Anna's first presidency, illustrates clearly that these "Great Man" explanations distort actual events. Historians portray the upheaval as typical of the many *pronunciamientos* (proclamations) that plagued the first half of the nineteenth century. However, despite Santa Anna's role as titular head of the movement, the January 1832 Plan de Veracruz that initiated the struggle was part of a broader opposition to the administration of Vice President Anastasio Bustamante. The focus on the success of the Veracruz caudillo obscures the actions of other opponents to the regime, especially a clandestine group of Mexico City politicians who sought to oust a government that they characterized as oppressive and illegitimate. The actions of these men are particularly significant because they are representative of a pattern of opposition politics that emerged during the independence period.

Clandestine opposition groups originally emerged during the post-1808 period because the viceregal government used its coercive power to hamstring the opposition. Those who favored autonomy began to form secret and loosely-organized groups. They developed a pattern of opposition politics based on shifting coalitions formed to attain specific purposes. Since these groups were by their very nature secret, and since membership in these coalitions varied, depending on the time and the issue involved, it is difficult or perhaps impossible to identify all the participants and futile to assign to them a consistent political role. When their interests diverged, they either withdrew from the group or changed sides.[41] The political patterns that emerged in the independence period continued in the 1820s and 1830s. During the 1820s, political groups coalesced around Masonic lodges. The *escoceses* in the Scottish-Rite lodge generally represented the conservative faction, while the *yorkinos* in the York-Rite lodge attracted liberal and radical members. These groups, of course, only reflected tendencies. They did not constitute embryonic political parties.[42]

The presidential succession of 1828 set the stage for the turbulent politics of 1830s. The election to replace Mexico's first president, Guadalupe Victoria, occurred in the midst of a major political and constitutional crisis. Although a number of questions, from national finances to church-state relations preoccupied the public, the expulsion of the Spaniards dominated public debate and shaped opinion. After months of heated discussions, the yorkinos had enacted federal laws to expel Spaniards from Mexico. On December 23, 1827, three days after the passage of the expulsion law, leading escoceses including Vice President Nicolás Bravo rebelled. The government reacted decisively, dispatching a large army under General Vicente Guerrero, a prominent yorkino, to quell the rebellion. The victorious president Guadalupe Victoria exiled the rebels.

The defeat of the escoceses left the yorkinos to dispute the presidency among themselves. Two factions emerged: the moderates, who championed Minister of War Manuel Gómez Pedraza, and the radicals, who favored General Guerrero. After a heated campaign in which secret societies played an important role, Gómez Pedraza won eleven states to Guerrero's seven in the elections of September 1828. The radicals sought to overturn the election by asserting that Gómez Pedraza would not enforce the expulsion laws. Mass demonstrations supporting the radicals' demands erupted in Mexico City. When General Guerrero joined the rebels, President-elect Gómez Pedraza resigned on December 4, and fled the country rather than precipitate a civil war. In January 1829 congress annulled the election and selected Guerrero, who had received the second highest number of votes, as president, and General Anastasio Bustamante, who placed third, as vice president.[43]

The Guerrero administration, facing both internal and external crises, quickly collapsed. Forced to cope with mass politics and high public expectations at a time when the government was virtually bankrupt, the new president also confronted in the summer of 1829 a Spanish attempt to reconquer Mexico. Poor leadership, bad luck, and disease defeated the Spanish force, which surrendered on September 11, but the victory provided the Guerrero administration only a short respite. In November, discontented groups rebelled against the government. Guerrero's attempts to negotiate with the rebels failed when Vice President Bustamante joined the insurgents on December 4, 1829, alleging that the administration had failed to maintain order. Thus, for the second time in as many years, a vice president took up arms against his chief executive. On this occasion, however, the president proved incapable of quelling the uprising and eventually abandoned his office.[44]

Once again, congress ratified the change, recognizing Vice President Bustamante as the new chief executive. Many moderates and conservatives, who deplored insurrection in principle, accepted the transfer of power because they believed that Guerrero had abused his office by favoring popular democracy and because they hoped the new government would restore order and tranquility.

It soon became evident that the price of stability would be high. Not content merely to purge radical yorkinos and alleged malcontents from public life, in the months that followed the new regime became authoritarian, elitist, and proclerical. More importantly, it sought to transform the federal system with a dominant national government. Predictably, the states opposed such changes. Regional insurrections erupted, but most were rapidly overwhelmed because the Bustamante regime controlled the army. In February 1831 the government captured and executed ex-president Guerrero. The following month, Juan Alvarez, the last remaining insurgent leader, surrendered and agreed to cooperate with the Bustamante administration.

By mid-1831, only a small group of congressmen in the capital continued to oppose the regime. Led by Senators Antonio Pacheco Leál and Manuel Crescencio Rejón, and Deputies Andrés Quintana Roo and Juan de Dios Cañedo, the legislators braved threats and assaults to criticize the government. They attacked the administration in newspaper articles and pamphlets, insisting that only the return of Gómez Pedraza to the presidency would restore constitutional government in Mexico. Angered by these statements, the Bustamante administration fined opposition papers for violating press laws, thus driving many antigovernment periodicals out of business. In the ensuing months, the authorities continued the campaign to stifle dissent by imprisoning or exiling countless newspapermen and other critics.[45]

As arrests and repression increased, moderates began to protest. In August 1831 Carlos María de Bustamante's *Voz de la patria* demanded that individuals in custody be tried, insisting that the state dispense prompt and impartial justice. The administration applied economic sanctions against the *Voz de la patria*, forcing the newspaper to cease publication on October 18, 1831.[46] The demise of Carlos María de Bustamante's paper did not signify an end to press opposition. Senator Rejón founded *El Tribuno del pueblo mexicano*, a paper devoted to "legal opposition." The periodical inflamed public opinion in the capital when it reported that the federal government had concentrated an army of two thousand men in Orizaba, had assembled soldiers in Veracruz, and was possibly planning further troop concentrations, to attack the states. On October 29, soldiers ransacked the offices of *El Tribuno*. The following month, recognizing that their tactics had failed to prevent the paper's publication, several officers attacked Rejón with drawn sabers. The senator escaped. When an outraged congress demanded to know why the military had violated the legislator's immunity, Minister of Interior Alamán "appeared in Congress . . . to say that Rejón's senatorial immunity had not been violated, since the soldiers assaulted Rejón the writer, not Rejón the senator."[47] Although Minister of War José Antonio Facio assured congress that the government would apprehend the culprits, the case remained unsolved. Fearing further attacks, Rejón ceased publication of *El Tribuno*.

The continuing excesses of the Bustamante regime, and its dismissive attitude toward congress, convinced a growing number of influential moderates that they could no longer tolerate the progressive destruction of civil liberties. Following traditional political practices, they formed a secret society. In mid-November, Quintana Roo, Rejón, Pacheco Leál, Mariano Riva Palacios (son-in-law of the late Vicente Guerrero), and Juan Rodríguez Puebla founded a junta to unite former moderate escoceses, yorkinos, and other antigovernment forces. Believing that the nation's constitutional process could not survive unless the constitution was strictly enforced, junta members decided to demand the return of Gómez Pedraza to the presidency. They also agreed to coordinate congressional opposition with antigovernment activity in the states.[48]

The Mexico City junta immediately initiated an antigovernment propaganda campaign. They purchased a printing press, established a new antigovernment newspaper—*El Fénix de la libertad*—and convinced other critics of the government to publish pamphlets against the regime. Through contacts with regional leaders, the junta urged the states to raise forces to fight the Bustamante regime. Although some states, such as Zacatecas, had formed powerful militias, it became evident that the dissidents needed the support of a number of regular army commanders before they could overthrow the government. A few junta members hesitated to take such a step, fearing that once involved, the military might seize the presidency. In spite of these concerns, however, most believed that Bustamante could not be removed without the assistance of the leading army commanders. Therefore they decided to approach key officers in the hope of winning them to their side.[49]

Although successful in arousing antigovernment activity, the junta failed to convince any of the leading military men to rebel. Fortunately for the conspirators, the regime played into the hands of the opposition. Fearful that the growing discontent in Veracruz would cause the senior commanders to betray the administration, the minister of war decided to remove a number of the state's military hierarchy. The Mexico City junta used this information to convince senior officers in Veracruz to oppose the government. On January 2, 1832, General Ciriaco Vázquez, commander of the Veracruz garrison, and other senior officers promulgated the Plan de Veracruz, which called for changes in the government of Vice President Bustamante and invited General Antonio López de Santa Anna, a popular native of Veracruz who would likely obtain local support, to assume command of the movement.[50]

After taking command of the Veracruz movement, Santa Anna tried to compromise with the national government, informing Vice President Bustamante that the army demanded that the government rescind orders modifying the Veracruz command structure and that it restructure the cabinet. Santa Anna proposed that moderates and liberals replace conservative ministers. He suggested Sebastian Camacho as minister of interior and foreign relations, Valentín Gómez Farías as minister of justice and ecclesiastic affairs, Melchor Múzquiz as minister of war and marine, and Francisco García as minister of finance.

Santa Anna believed that changing the ministers would satisfy the opposition in the capital. Although the vice president's cabinet presented its resignation to provide the chief executive freedom of action, the gesture proved meaningless because, despite the distinguished new cabinet proposed by Santa Anna, the members of the Mexico junta refused to accept any solution that would allow Bustamante to remain in office. Their intransigence convinced Santa Anna that no compromise was possible, and in February 1832, Santa Anna reluctantly prepared to oust the Bustamante administration. In the months that followed, the opposition in Mexico City escalated their criticism of the government, openly endorsing armed resistance. In Tamaulipas, General Francisco Moctezuma, one of Guerrero's former ministers, joined the struggle against the government.[51]

As late as May 1832, the Bustamante regime hoped to defeat the rebels. Despite widespread disaffection, most states had not openly taken the field against the vice president. Only in the coastal states of Veracruz and Tamaulipas were insurgents fighting the national government. Initially, it appeared that federal forces would crush Veracruz and Tamaulipas rebels, but the administration's hopes for an easy victory collapsed on May 13, 1832, when General Moctezuma won the first major antigovernment battle by defeating a federal army at Tampico. Threatened by the debacle in the North, the other federal forces abandoned their siege of Veracruz.[52]

The events on the coast prompted Bustamante to seek negotiations with the opposition. However, the Mexico City junta opposed any compromise. Although the government maintained rigid authority in the capital, it rapidly began losing control of the states. In the months that followed, new provincial leaders arose to oppose Bustamante and the insurgent armies began to converge on Mexico City. Santa Anna's forces advanced from the east, Moctezuma from the northeast, García—the governor of Zacatecas—from the north, and Alvarez from the southwest. On September 18, the situation appeared to change when General Bustamante defeated Moctezuma and García's forces at the bloody battle of Gallinero, an hacienda near San Miguel Allende. The government's recovery was short-lived. Santa Anna defeated federal forces near Puebla at the end of the month and accepted the city's surrender on October 5. Unable to fight on all fronts, Bustamante concentrated his forces in the states of Puebla and Mexico. His tactic failed. On December 5, he was decisively defeated. Three days later, he sued for peace. Bustamante and his leading officers met with Santa Anna, Gómez Pedraza, and other opposition leaders at Zavaleta, an hacienda near the city of Puebla. They reached an agreement on December 23 that allowed Bustamante and his officers to go into exile and Gómez Pedraza to assume the presidency and oversee state and national elections.[53]

The Treaty of Zavaleta resulted in an ambiguous victory for the Mexico City opposition junta. Since the agreement returned Gómez Pedraza to the presidency, the group believed that they had restored political legitimacy to the office. However, despite their prominent role in undermining the Bustamante regime, only a few members of the junta were well-known opposition leaders. The junta itself was a secret group that remained unknown to the public. Despite the presence of men such as Gómez Pedraza at the negotiations, contemporaries as well as later historians generally assumed that Santa Anna had been the individual responsible for the overthrow of the Bustamante regime, in part because the junta's propaganda had depicted him as a hero. As some members of the junta had feared, the military leader's public role in Bustamante's ouster made him one of the most popular men in Mexico. The voters elected him president in 1833.

CONCLUSION

An analysis of Riego's, Iturbide's, and Santa Anna's political activities demonstrates that these caudillos did not impose their will upon a passive people. Instead, the circumstances of the time and broad political forces shaped their public trajectories. Recent studies of the great Hispanic political revolution reveal that that revolution introduced mass politics to Hispanic society. The people emerged as a new political force in 1808. However, it was the institutions created in Cádiz—the constitutional ayuntamientos, the provincial deputations, and the Cortes—which provided the mechanisms for the political expression of the people's wishes. With the rise of popular politics, there also emerged populist leaders, among them curas, lawyers, functionaries, and military men. They represented a variety of political positions and interests that frequently conflicted with those of their corporations. Although on occasion they supported the interests of the higher clergy and the military, it would be a mistake to assume that their political positions are evidence of clerical and military influence or domination within the political system.

The clergy in general and the parish priests in particular played a significant role in the political life of the Hispanic world. They constituted a literate and educated group, which understood the needs and concerns both of the local community and the larger society. The crisis of 1808 opened a tremendous opportunity for ecclesiastics to enter politics in new and broader arenas. As politicians, they participated at all levels from the parish and the province to the monarchy. Like their secular brethren, they shaped the evolving political system.

As in the case of their clerical colleagues, the Hispanic revolution provided the military a unique opportunity to enter politics. This did not mean that the army as an institution determined the nature of politics. Rather, it meant that military commanders made good popular politicians. They were charismatic figures who captured the popular imagination. Moreover, military men were attractive to people of various opinions because the military, like their civilian counterparts, held a broad range of political views. Since they could galvanize popular support, military politicians emerged as the new political leaders (caudillos) that subsequently fascinated historians and social scientists. However, they constituted only one, albeit a prominent, element of the new Hispanic political order.

Because of the great political revolution of the Hispanic world, the people of Spain and Spanish America forged a new political legitimacy. Despite numerous political upheavals, most Hispanic people believed in the principles of popular sovereignty, local rights, and civilian constitutional government that had crystallized in the Cortes de Cádiz. If we wish to understand the politics of that period, it is necessary for historians to stop focusing on the role of caudillos to explain events. Instead, we must study the actions of el pueblo and the role of politicians—civilian, clerical, and military—within the context of the politics and political processes of the era.

8

New Directions and Old Questions

There have been many "new histories" in the long history of the discipline. In 1932 writing about the new history of the time, Carl Becker argued that the difference between the new and the old was what he called a "climate of opinion." He noted in his book, *The Heavenly City of the Eighteenth-Century Philosophers*, that although "the eighteenth century was preeminently the age of reason . . . the *Philosophes* were nearer the Middle Ages, less emancipated from the preconceptions of medieval Christian thought, than they quite realized or we have commonly supposed."[1] Much of their work was new in the sense that it utilized a different climate of opinion; that is, it employed fashionable terminology. Becker's insight is useful when analyzing contemporary new histories.

Two new types of Latin American political history have emerged in the last four decades. The first concerns itself primarily with gender and cultural issues and tends to be "postmodern." This form, which is frequently called the "new cultural history," is particularly prominent in the literature published in English. The second type reexamines the nature of political institutions and processes and is particularly significant among scholars writing in the Romance languages—Spanish, Portuguese, French, and Italian—and in German. This discussion will focus on English-language works since the new Latin political history centers on politics, political culture, and the political process.

The first part of this presentation, which summarizes the evolution of Anglophone history during the second half of the twentieth century, provides context for the subsequent discussion of the new Anglophone cultural history of Latin America. After World War II, scientific social science and analytical philosophy dominated the Anglo-American academic world, emphasizing careful empirical research while rejecting systematic theories about the nature of man and society. That comfortable intellectual world was shaken in the late fifties, sixties, and seventies by questions regarding the validity of the scientific method and by the rise of grand theorists, first in continental Europe and then in the citadels of Anglo-American empiricism, the United Kingdom and the United States.

One of the earliest and most influential attacks on science was *The Structure of Scientific Revolutions*, which appeared in 1962. Its author, Thomas S. Kuhn, already had distinguished himself in his 1957 volume *The Copernican Revolution*, in which he introduced the concept of a "paradigm shift" to explain that great transformation in scientific thought. Kuhn's "paradigm" at first seems analogous to Becker's "climate of opinion." *The Structure of Scientific Revolutions*, however, went much further because, unlike Becker's climate of opinion that incorporated earlier forms of thought, Kuhn's paradigms are mutually exclusive. He argues that since a paradigm shift means complete abandonment of an earlier paradigm, there is no common standard to judge scientific theories developed under different paradigms. Therefore there are no ways to validate or invalidate a theory. In his criticism of Kuhn's work, Nobel Prize winner Steven Weinberg notes: "If scientific theories can only be judged within the context of a particular paradigm, then in this respect scientific theories of any one paradigm are not privileged over other ways of looking at the world, such as shamanism or astrology or creationism."[2] A group of philosophers and sociologists at the University of Edinburgh adopted and developed Kuhn's views. One of them, David Bloor, advanced what he called "the strong programme" that considers scientific "facts" nothing but "social constructions." Indeed, he argued that it was is unclear whether there was a "reality" out there to study.[3]

Other criticisms of science, the scientific method, and objectivity emerged from a variety of sources. In the United States, the civil rights, anti-Vietnam war, and women's movements of the 1960s raised a number of questions about the nature of knowledge, its acquisition, and its uses. The civil rights and women's movements also emphasized the role of minority groups and women, segments of society frequently omitted from historical works. The new social history that emerged from the French *Annales* School and from British historians such as E. P. Thompson emphasized history "from the bottom up."[4]

In the 1970s English-speaking academics became aware of European— primarily French—intellectuals who raised profound questions about the nature of knowledge. These observers frequently considered the theorists a single group that they labeled as "structural Marxists, "Post-Structuralists," and "Postmodernists." However, individuals such as Louis Althusser, Michel Foucault, Jacques Derrida, Pierre Bourdieu, Jacques Lacan, Antonio Gramsci, and Jürgen Habermas—to mention some of the most prominent—did not form a unified school and often disagreed with one another. Still, they did challenge the older belief in "objectivity" and raised new questions about society. Much of their work utilizes obscure terminology and an overly complex writing style. Althusser exercised great influence at the University of Birmingham and its Center of Cultural Studies. Derrida became the guru of Yale University's "school of literary criticism," where Paul de Mann and J. Hillis Miller established themselves as the most prominent U.S. "post-modernists." After de Mann's death, Miller and Derrida migrated west to the University of California, Irvine. As one critic noted: "By the early 1980s both groups were in the ascendancy in their own areas but remained confined to a fairly narrow range of subjects: literary theory, communications theory and media studies, all places where the practitioners could make a lot of noise but do little damage to anything further afield."[5]

The European theorists also affected the discipline of history. A new Anglophone cultural history was emerging as the 1985 volume, *The Return of Grand Theory in the Human Sciences* edited by Quentin Skinner, noted.[6] Although historians in the United States investigated a variety of "new topics, such as slaves, women, immigrants, workers, and homosexuals," they remained unwilling to believe that there was no difference between truth and fiction. For example, Peter Novikc's volume, *That Noble Dream*, which examined the decline in the belief in "objectivity" among historians of the United States, relied on careful empirical research and did not treat facts as though they were relative.[7] Only a few historians—such as Joan Wallach Scott, who studied feminist politics—argued that scholars should employ "a more radical epistemology," such as the approaches advanced by Foucault and Derrida, which made the status of all knowledge relative.[8]

Latin Americanists were slow to enter the debate. Once again, literary theorists took the lead. They were members of a movement that called itself the "New Historicism." Unlike those identified with the Yale School and with Derrida, these literary theorists moved into the fields of history and the social sciences. Taking advantage of the quintcentennial, they published the volume *New World Encounters*, edited by one of their leaders, Stephen Greenblatt.[9] Other members of the group examined pre-Hispanic history, offering new and controversial views of native society, religion, and pre-Hispanic gender relations. Literary critics and anthropologists took up the new approaches, broadly called "postmodernist," even though the label included different points of view.

Latin American historical research lagged behind other fields. As I have argued elsewhere, history is not written by the victors—as commonly asserted—but by the rich. It takes resources to establish libraries and archives and to create universities and other academic centers that may employ research historians. During the nineteenth century, a time of Iberoamerican decline, the wealthy nations of Western Europe and the United States published large collections of documents, studied their institutions extensively, and established their national histories. During the twentieth century, they had the luxury not only to refine and reinterpret those histories, they also explored new aspects of their past. In Mexico, as in much of Latin America, political historians such as Lucas Alamán, published grand narratives designed to create a national history. Unlike their colleagues in the rich nations, they lacked the resources and the institutions to publish great document collections and undertake detailed institutional studies that would allow future generations of historians to develop nuanced interpretations of the national experience.[10]

Anglophone historians, particularly in the United States, began by studying diplomatic relations between their country and Latin American nations. They examined colonial institutions and wrote "traditional" political history. That changed in the 1960s and 1970s. They turned first to economic history and then to social history in response to the movements focusing on civil rights, women and other minorities, and the opposition to the Vietnam War and U.S. engagement with the world. The theories that influenced these economic and social historians tended to be variants of developmentalism, Marxism, structuralism, and dependency. Subsequently, in the late 1970s and 1980s, cultural history emerged as an important new research topic.

Although some historians including Nettie Lee Benson at the University of Texas, Austin continued to focus on political history, many younger historians dismissed the field as outmoded. However, she devoted her research and teaching to an examination of representative government in the Hispanic world and developed a new interpretation of politics within this field. In 1946 she had published an article entitled "The Contested Mexican Election of 1812," in which she demonstrated that the Constitution of 1812 provided representative government for the entire Hispanic world and argued against the views of the Audiencia of Mexico, Lucas Alamán, and later critics who maintained that those contested elections demonstrated that novohispanos were not prepared to govern themselves. As she concluded: "The election was far from ideal, it is true; but it is *not* true that it was all confusion, disorder, and dishonesty, nor that it proves that Mexico was not prepared for democratic government in 1812."[11] Three years later, she completed her PhD thesis, published in 1955 as *La Diputación Provincial y el federalismo mexicano.*[12] In that work, Benson observed that regional interests and the public's identification with their localities in New Spain had evolved over time and the institution created by the Constitution of 1812 to represent the provinces within the Spanish nation was the direct precursor of Mexico's federal system.[13] Based on this research, she maintained that those who claimed that Mexican federalism was a copy of the U.S. system were wrong.[14]

Mexico and the Spanish Cortes, 1810–1822, a 1966 volume growing out of one of her seminars, advanced our understanding of the nature of Hispanic liberalism and representative government.[15] Chapters of that book focus on questions that later became the nucleus of the new Latin American political history—representation, citizenship, and constitutionalism as well as freedom of the press, economic and social reform and the status of the church and the military. Although her students wrote the eight essays, they represent Benson's path-breaking views and utilized material she originally located; the sources include materials from the Archivo General de la Nación de México, the Archivo General de Indias in Seville, and the fabled library at the University of Texas, Austin that bears her name. She guided her students' work, defining the topics and the period. The last point is important because she was the only person who considered the first and the second constitutional periods—from 1810 to 1814 and from 1820 to1822—to constitute a single process. Most students of the period then and now instead focused on the Cortes of Cádiz and examined the trienio constitucional (the three constitutional years of 1820 to 1822) separately. Ironically, none of the eight participants in that volume later wrote their doctoral theses on those or related topics. She did not create a school; it was not until the late 1980s that other researchers began to analyze the period.[16] Although she was a pioneer of the new political history, Benson had little impact on Anglophone historians, who ignored her scholarship. Charles A. Hale, for example, dismissed Benson's work and ignored Hispanic constitutionalism in discussing early Mexican liberalism. Instead, he focused on José María Luis Mora's thought, which he considered to have been strongly influenced by Benjamin Constant.[17]

At the end of the 1980s and the beginning of the 1990s, a new cultural history emerged in the United States. Although two of its leaders, Gilbert Joseph and Florencia Mallon, are graduates of Yale University, they were not products of the "Yale School" of literary criticism; rather, Marxism and dependency theory influenced their work. They drew their inspiration from scholars working on other third world areas.

At a symposium on "Rebellions in Mexican History" held at the University of California, Irvine in 1989, Joseph presented an early analysis of the work of the Indian historian Ranajit Guha and argued that his approaches were applicable to Latin American history.[18] Later, Joseph obtained a professorship at Yale University and established ties with scholars at Duke University, the institution that became the epicenter of U.S. postmodernism. He subsequently coordinated a number of volumes published by Duke University Press that spread the new orthodoxy, including *Reclaiming the Political in Latin American History: Essays from the North*, a book by Yale graduates that aroused the ire of John Womack.[19]

Far from the eastern universities of Yale and Duke, in the hinterland of the University of Wisconsin, Florencia E. Mallon launched a challenge to Latin Americanists in the pages of the venerable *American Historical Review*. In the 1994 article entitled "The Promise and Dilemma of Subaltern Studies: Perspectives from Latin American History," Mallon noted: "This is not an easy time for scholars who work on Latin America. Over the past five years or so, many of our most important inspirational historical narratives have come undone." The Cuban Revolution was "dying a slow death;" the Soviet Union had collapsed; the Sandinistas had lost control in Nicaragua; "the post-Pinochet Christian democrats" were following the Chilean dictator's economic policies; and Sendero Luminoso in Peru, despite having gone berserk and killed "an astounding number of people," had "reached an agreement with an authoritarian, free market-oriented president . . . . what is a progressive scholar to do?" The answer, she declared, was subaltern studies, "formulated by a group of intellectuals based in the 'Third World,' anticolonial and politically radical yet conversant with the latest textual analysis and postmodern methods: what more could a cautious, progressive scholar hope for."[20] The following year, Mallon published *Peasant and Nation: The Making of Postcolonial Mexico and Peru*, which used or reflected some of new scholarship. Significantly, Dipesh Chakrabarty, a prominent member of the subaltern school, but not known to be a specialist in either Mexico or Peru, praised her book on the back cover, declaring "scholars of subaltern histories elsewhere will find her work enormously helpful."[21]

As noted at the beginning of this chapter, anti-scientific approaches elicited criticism from the outset. In 1965 the philosopher Paul Feyerabend described Kuhn's work as a defense of irrationality in science. Later, Stephen Weinberg asserted that Kuhn's study was "The Revolution That Didn't Happen."[22] In the end, even Kuhn repudiated the misuse of his theoretical constructs. In 1991 Kuhn, in referring to the group at the University of Edinburgh, declared: "I am among those who have found the claims of the strong program—which criticized science—absurd, an example of deconstruction gone mad." The following year, he insisted that he was not a "Kuhnian."[23]

Other scientists criticized the large group of intellectuals who espoused so-called postmodernist views. The New York University physicist Alan Sokal became the most notorious of these critics. Concerned by what he called "an intellectual current characterized by more-or-less explicit rejection of the rationalist tradition of the Enlightenment, by theoretical discourse disconnected from any empirical test, and by a cognitive and cultural relativism that regards science as nothing more than a 'narration,' a 'myth' or a social construction among many others," he decided to submit a parody of that type of analysis to the prominent "postmodernist" journal published by Duke University Press, *Social Text*. Sokal later described his article, "Transgressing the Boundaries: Toward a Transformative Hermeneutics of Quantum Gravity," as "chock-full of absurdities and blatant non-sequiturs."[24] The article was not only accepted, but also published in a special issue "devoted to rebutting the criticisms leveled against postmodernism and social constructivism by several distinguished scientists." When Sokal later revealed the hoax, he created an international scandal that resulted in severe repercussions in the U.S. academic world from Duke and Yale to Irvine. For example, when Stanley Fish, one of the leaders of postmodernist criticism, the director of the journal *Social Text*, and a professor at Duke University was under consideration for the position of Dean of Humanities at the University of California, Irvine, an important group of professors led by scientists opposed his appointment. Their successful action was unprecedented; professors in one faculty had intervened in the administration of another. Subsequently, in 1997, Sokal and the Belgian theoretical physicist Jean Bricmont published a volume in France entitled *Impostures intellectuelles*, which systematically exposed the ignorance, misunderstanding, and misuse of science by some of the country's leading intellectuals.[25]

Historians also entered the fray. In 1987 the conservative historian Gertrude Himmelfarb challenged the new tendencies in a volume entitled *The New History and the Old*. She argued that social history had "devaluated the political realm." Instead, she argued, it was more interested in the irrational and non-rational aspects of life.[26] The following year, Lynne V. Cheney, then chairwoman of the National Endowment for the Humanities, reported to Congress that the new social history undermined both education and society. By 1994 even distinguished historians—practitioners of social and cultural history—had become concerned with the impact of postmodernism on the profession. Joyce Appleby, former president of the American Historical Association and an expert on eighteenth- and early nineteenth-century U.S. history, along with Lynn Hunt, also a former president of the American Historical Association and Margaret Jacob—both distinguished historians of eighteenth- and early nineteenth-century France— published *Telling the Truth About History*, in which they discussed the new approaches and carefully criticized postmodernist tendencies. They concluded by reasserting their belief that there was a truth to be told about the past.[27]

Alan Knight was among the first Anglophone Latin American historians to participate in the debate when he published a highly critical review of Mallon's *Peasant and Nation*. He focused primarily on her use of jargon and her misuse of language.[28] The most extensive criticism, however, came in a 1997 essay by Stephen Haber entitled "The Worst of Both Worlds: The New Cultural History of Mexico," which appeared in *Mexican Studies/Estudios Mexicanos*. He criticized the new cultural history because its practitioners rejected "the notion that there are objective facts that can be established regardless of the subjective beliefs of the observer." Like Knight, Haber was especially critical of Mallon. He noted that she and others used concepts such as discourse, hegemony, space, and subaltern in confusing, misleading, and contradictory ways. For example, he asked, "What is a discourse?" And he observed, "Rituals contain discourse, as do works of art, drama, or, for that matter, the way people dress. The problem is that one can assert that any kind of discourse exists and there is no way that I can find in the literature," to determine if that proposition is true or false. To make his point, he quoted Mallon to the effect that "hegemony is a hegemonic process: it can and does exist everywhere at all times . . . . Hegemony is [also] an actual end point, the result of hegemonic processes." Similarly, he observed that according to the new historians "the subaltern is not one thing. It is . . . a mutating, migrating subject." One article stated that the subaltern is "defined very broadly as anyone who is subordinated 'in terms of class, caste, age, gender and office or in any other way." "Who then, asked Haber, is not subaltern?"[29]

In 1999 the *Hispanic American Historical Review*, then at Yale University under the direction of Gilbert Joseph and Steward Schwartz, published a special issue on the new cultural history.[30] Eric Van Young, William French, and Mary Kay Vaughan wrote articles defending the new cultural history in their respective fields—colonial, nineteenth-century, and twentieth-century history. Haber revised and expanded his earlier broadside and Mallon defended herself as well as the new cultural history. Claudio Lomnitz presented a mild defense of the approach, and Susan Socolow criticized it. Despite convoluted and sometimes obscure "theoretical" discussions, the three proponents of the new cultural history essentially maintained that it is good to study culture because all history is essentially cultural history. No one, not even Mallon, relied on so-called postmodernist arguments, which Haber had criticized so effectively. Indeed, her principal defense was that she really was an empirical historian. It had been, it appeared, a tempest in a teapot.

An analysis of the writings of the new cultural historians, with few exceptions, demonstrates that most have not practiced what they have preached in their more passionate moments. Most essentially remain "traditional," "regular," "standard" historians who believe it is important to study society and politics from a cultural perspective. They do not use the postmodernist epistemology, although their writing is frequently obscure and incorporates ill-defined concepts and terms. While some new cultural historians insist that they are capable of giving voice to people who left no record such as women, workers, and peasants, they generally do not carry their arguments to their logical conclusions. They employ terms such as "subalterns," but generally do not use Guha's methods. They are asking new questions, exploring new themes, and using new terminology, but the dreaded European intellectual disease broadly known as "postmodernism" does not overwhelm them. They exhibit many of the characteristics Carl Becker describes in his discussion of the new history. They are less radical than either they or their critics believe. The new Anglophone cultural historians generally focus on history from the "bottom up." Elites and so-called elite institutions do not attract them. In their defense of the so-called subalterns, they often caricature the old oligarchies, elites, and the rich and powerful who may be called "overalterns." Instead, new actors appear and seem to be in charge—in the new language, they possess "agency." Women are in control, peasants determine national politics, and, in one case, prostitutes and the insane not only reject the practices of the asylum, but also "fully participated . . . in the very creation of medicalized discourses within the hospital and the insane asylum."[31]

Despite claims to "put politics back in," the new Anglophone cultural history does not place the new actors within the broader political processes and institutions. Instead, it is concerned with the state and with the relations between some segments of "civil society" and the state. Equally problematic with the new Latin American cultural history is that it is carried out in nations where fundamental facets of the political system have not been well studied. Here it is worth returning to a point made earlier. The rich nations of the North Atlantic have studied their political institutions and processes extensively. Therefore, when historians in those countries expand their national histories to include new groups, their activities can be placed within well-understood processes. The historians of the rich nations can afford to examine subtle new aspects of their national experience.

Unfortunately, when the current new Anglophone cultural historians of Latin America eagerly imitate the latest analytical approaches emanating from Paris and elsewhere, they do so within the context of an underdeveloped political historiography. Today too many historians are busy making the icing when we have virtually no cake. In Mexico, as in all of Latin America, there are immense gaps in our knowledge. We do not know how most of the institutions of government actually worked. Although institutional scholars have examined many institutions, much remains unstudied. We have a sense of the broad outlines but have little or no idea of how municipal government, the courts, congresses, etc. actually worked. As a result, there is a tendency to generalize from too few instances. Most scholarly works on the history of the first half of nineteenth-century Mexico examine their topic from the perspective of the capital even though we have known for at least half a century that at that time power resided in the regions. Fortunately, the new Latin American political historians are undertaking the detailed state, regional, and institutional and political studies that are necessary to understand the complex political, social, and economic relationships among the elites and the popular groups.[32] History from the bottom up depends upon understanding the broader context.

SOURCE ACKNOWLEDGMENTS

The chapters herein were originally published in a Spanish collection of articles entitled *"Lo politico" en el mundo Hispánico* by Jaime E. Rodríguez O. (Zamora: El Colegio de Michoacán, 2015).

Chapter 1 previously appeared as "La naturaleza de la representación en la Nueva España y México," *Secuencia: Revista de historia y ciencias sociales* 61 (enero-abril 2005): 6–32.

Chapter 2 previously appeared as "Los Orígenes de la Revolución de 1809 en Quito," in *Soberanía, lealtad e igualdad: Las respuestas americanas a la crisis imperial hispana, 1808–1810*, edited by Ana Buriano and Johanna von Grafenstein, 199–227 (Mexico City: Instituto Mora, 2008).

Chapter 3 previously appeared as "La cultura política clerical en el Reino de Quito y Ecuador," in *Religiosidad y Clero en América Latina: La época de las Revoluciones Atlánticas (1767–1850)—Religiosity and Clergy in Latin America (1767–1850)—The Age of the Atlantic Revolutions*, edited by Peer Schmidt, Sebastian Dorsch, and Hedwig Herold-Schmidt, 285–306 (Cologne: Böhlau-Verlag, 2011).

Chapter 4 previously appeared as "Ciudadanos de la Nación Española: Los indígenas y las elecciones constitucionales en el Reino de Quito" in *La mirada esquiva. Reflexiones históricas sobre la interacción del Estado y la ciudadanía en los Andes*, edited by Marta Iroruzqui, 41–64 (Bolivia, Ecuador y Perú), Siglo 19 (Madrid: Consejo Superior de Investigaciones Científicas, 2005).

Chapter 5 previously appeared in "The Emancipation of America," *American Historical Review* 105, no. 1 (February 2000): 131–52.

Chapter 6 previously appeared as "Sobre la supuesta influencia de la independencia de los Estados Unidos en la independencia de Hispanoamerica," *Revista de Indias* 70, no. 250 (septiembre-diciembre 2010): 691–714.

Chapter 7 previously appeared as "Los caudillos y los historiadores: Riego, Iturbide y Santa Anna," in *La construcción del héroe en España y México, 1789–1847*, edited by Manuel Chust and Víctor Minguez, 309–35 (Valencia: Universitat de Valencia, 2003).

Chapter 8 was originally presented at the coloquio Internacional "Los Caminos de la democracia en América Latina" held at El colegio de México, November 26–28, 2003.

NOTES

INTRODUCTION

1. Carlos A. Forment, for example, has recently argued that Catholic culture is essentially irrational and that Latin Americans were colonial peoples and "were two passionate to be able to exercise their rational faculties." Therefore they could not govern. Forment, *Democracy in Latin America*, 51.

2. Cartledge, "Greek Political Thought," 11.

3. Flower, *Roman Republics* and Wiedemann, "Reflections of Roman Political Thought," 517–31. The English term *filibuster* is derived from the Dutch *vrijbuiter* (privateer, pirate, robber). The Spaniards converted it into *filibustero* to refer to the Dutch, English, and French attackers and thieves in the Spanish world. In the 1850s, the Spanish term was applied to U.S. privateers then operating in Central America and the Spanish West Indies such as William Walker. Apparently, the term was used first used in 1853 by Representative Albert G. Brown when referring to Abraham Watkings' speech against "filibustering" intervention in Cuba. Subsequently, it has been used as a dilatory tactic.

4. Blythe, *Ideal Government*.

5. O'Callaghan, *The Cortes of Castile-León*.

6. Van Zanden, Buringh, and Bosker, "The Rise and Decline of European Parliaments," 1–28.

7. Maravall, *Las comunidades de Castilla*.

8. Skinner, *Foundations of Modern Political Thought*, 2:159, 347. See also: Quijada, "From Spain to New Spain," 185–219.

9. Skinner, *Foundations of Modern Political Thought*, 2:114.

10. Stephen E. Lucas asserts: "Of all the models available to Jefferson and the Continental Congress, none provided as precise a template for the Declaration as did the Plakkant." Further, he declares "When you look at the two documents side by side, you cannot avoid noticing that the American Declaration more closely resembles its Dutch predecessor than any other possible." Lucas, "The 'Plakkant van Verlatinge,'" 189–207.

11. Israel, *The Dutch Republic*; and Van Gelderen, *Political Thought of the Dutch Revolt*.

12. Van Gelderen, "'So Merely Humane,'" 149–70.

13. Skinner, *Foundations of Modern Political Thought*, 2:184.

14. Brett, *Liberty, Right and Nature*, 165–235. See also Quijada, "From Spain to New Spain," 192–204.

15. Skinner, *Foundations of Modern Political Thought*, 2:347–48.

16. Burkholder, "Spain's America: From Kingdoms to Colonies," 1–29. The rights of the New World realms were codified in the *Leyes y Ordenanzas Reales de las Indias del Mar Oceano* by Alonzo Zorita, 1574.

17. Rodríguez O., "Introducción a las Reales Ordenanzas," 256–310. The earliest audiencia was established in New Spain in 1527. Subsequently, it was conformed to the Ordenanzas de Monzón de Aragón.

18. Marchena Fernández, "Obedientes al rey," 143–208.

19. Mier, "Idea de la Constitución", 31–91.

20. Lempériere, "La questión colonial."

21. Horsman, *Race and Manifest Destiny*. See also Madley, "Reexamining the American Genocide Debate," 98–139.

22. Kimmel quotes Bowsma in his Absolutism and its Discontents, 15. See also: Henshall, *The Myth of Absolutism*.

23. Henshall, "Early Modern Absolutism" 25-53; and Thompson, "Absolutism, Legalism and the Law," 185–228.

24. Rodríguez O.,"*We Are Now the True Spaniards,*" 7–9.

25. Rodríguez O., *Independence of Spanish America*, 59–74; and Chust, *1808: La eclosión juntera.*

26. Deputies had to be natives of the region. Rodríguez O., "*We Are Now the True Spaniards,*" 97–148.

27. Rodríguez O., *Independence of Spanish America*, 82–92.

28. Guerra, "El soberano y su reino," 45.

29. Rodríguez O., *Independence of Spanish America*, 93–107.

30. Rodríguez O., "*We Are Now the True Spaniards,*" 166–94.

31. Rodriguez, *The Cádiz Experiment*, 106–23; Dym, *From Sovereign Villages*, 127–56; and Avendaño Rojas, *Centroamérica*, 87–107.

32. Almer, "The Spanish Constitution."

33. Rodríguez O., *La revolución política*, 79–88.

34. The Constitution of Cádiz placed the great southern coastal province of Guayaquil under the authority of the Provincial Deputation of Peru.

35. Rodríguez O., *La revolución política*, 79–88.

36. Rodríguez O., "De la fidelidad a la revolución," 35–88.

37. Peralta Ruíz, *La independencia*, 243–69 and Peralta Ruíz, "Los inicios del sistema," 65–92. See also: Núñez, "La participación electoral indígena," 361–94.
38. Peralta Ruíz, "Los inicios del sistema," 89–91.
39. Irurozqui, "Huellas, testigos y testimonios," 157–78.
40. Mirow, "The Constitution of Cádiz in Florida," 271–329; Ruiz Alemán, "Los municipios cubanos," 379–87; and Gómez Vizuete, "Los primeros ayuntamientos," 581–615.
41. Rodríguez O., *Independence of Spanish America*, 103.
42. Rodríguez O., *Independence of Spanish America*, 107–68.
43. Rodríguez O., "Los caudillos y los historiadores," 309–35..
44. The decree and other instructions arrived in Quito on September 4, 1820. Archivo Nacional de Historia, Quito (hereafter ANHQ): Presidencia de Quito (hereafter PQ), vol. 579, fols. 18–47.
45. D.U.L.A., *Idea general de la conducta política*; Cañedo, *Manifiesto a la nación española*; Vidaurre, *Manifiesto*. Extensive documentation on the American arguments for greater representation is located in AGI: Indiferente, 1523.
46. Rodríguez O, *"We Are Now the True Spaniards,"* 235–67.
47. Mirow, "The Constitution of Cádiz in Florida"; Ruiz Alemán, "Los municipios cubanos"; and Gómez Vizuete, "Los primeros ayuntamientos."
48. Rodríguez O, *La revolución política*, 93–97.
49. "Actas del Cabildo Colonial de Guayaquil, vol. 29, 1817–1820," September 10, 13 and 29, 1820.
50. Rodríguez O, *De la fidelidad a la revolución*, 93–108.
51. "Actas del Cabildo Colonial de Guayaquil, vol. 29, 1817–1820," 93–101.
52. "Actas del Cabildo Colonial de Guayaquil, vol. 29, 1817–1820," 199.
53. Almer, "'La confianza que han puesto en mi,'" 365–95.
54. Anna, *The Fall of Royal Government*, 163–83.
55. Sala I Vila, "El Trienio liberal," 693–728.
56. Rodríguez O, *Independence of Spanish America*, 199–202; and Frasquet Miguel, *Las caras del águila*.
57. Rodríguez O, *"We Are Now the True Spaniards,"* 268–334.
58. Rodríguez O., *La revolución política*, 179–86.
59. Rodríguez O., *Independence of Spanish America*, 238–46.
60. Rémond, *Pour une histoire politique*.
61. On the nature of mass political participation in rural Mexico, see Escobar Ohmstede, "Del gobierno indígena," 1–26; Ducey, "Village, Nation and

Constitution," 463–93; Guarisco, *Los indios del valle de México*, 129–90; Guardino, *Peasants*; and Guardino, *The Time of Liberty*; and Caplan, "The Legal Revolution," 255–93. On the same process in urban Mexico see: Guedea, "El pueblo de México," 27–61; and Warren, *Vagrants and Citizens*. For a different interpretation than mine see Eric Van Young's magisterial work, *The Other Rebellion*, and his "Etnia, política local e insurgencia," 143–69.

62. According to Jean Piel, "At Junín and Ayacucho, the Peruvian soldiers on the two sides, that of the Crown and that of Independence, killed each other without a thought. To the majority, the idea of an independent Peru meant nothing," Piel, "The Place of the Peasantry," 116. Some historians, such as Eric Van Young, have held, for example, that the Indians neither knew nor understood the nature of the new elite politics. Moreover, they maintain that the natives' vision of the world was limited to the confines of their village and they were not interested in events beyond the sound of their church bell. Van Young, *The Other Rebellion*.

1. THE NATURE OF REPRESENTATION

1. The Spanish term *los pueblos* in plural referred to the cities while the word *el pueblo* later came to mean the people.

2. The Spanish terms *ciudad, villa, aldea* and *lugar* refer to different types of urban centers. A ciudad was an independent urban center with its own city government, generally called ayuntamiento or cabildo, and supervised extensive rural lands. Although a villa had a secondary status, it possessed its own ayuntamiento. An aldea or lugar was a small settlement within the boundaries of a city. Nader, *Liberty in Absolutist Spain*, xv-xvi. See: O'Callaghan, *The Cortes of Castile-León*; González Antón, *Las Cortes en la España*; Dios, "Corporación y nación," 198–298; and Artaza, *Rey, reino y representación*.

3. On a detailed study of cities and pueblos see: Nader, *Liberty in Absolutist Spain*.

4. Blythe, *Ideal Government*.

5. Altamira, *Historia de España*, 3:316.

6. Lohmann Villena, "Las Cortes en Indias," 650.

7. Although *representation* was demanded by the elites, they did not struggle only for their interests. The Hispanic tradition of *buen gobierno* (good government) required that they represent all they people in the jurisdiction of

their city. Similarly, *mixed government* required that those who govern represent the interests of those people within their jurisdiction.

8. According to Manuel Giménez Fernández, "The *pronunciadores* (those who pronounced) restored a traditional Spanish doctrine . . . and proclaimed . . . that the true jurisdiction corresponded to the ordinary authority (an action) founded on the wellbeing of the pueblo or the political community." Giménez Fernández, "Hernán Cortés y su revolución," 1–144, quote 105. See also: Zavala, "Hernán Cortés," 39–61; and Nader, *Liberty in Absolutist Spain*, 94–97.

9. *Actas del Cabildo de la ciudad de México*, 183. Alamán, *Disertaciones*, 2:269–70.

10. Ramos, "Las ciudades de Indias," 170–85; and Miranda, *Las ideas y las instituciones*, 141, note 228.

11. Lohmann Villena, "Las Cortes en Indias," 656. Emphasis in the original.

12. Betancourt, "Orígenes españoles," 360–62; Altamira, *Historia de España*, 3:316; Casariego, *El municipio y las Cortes*, 100.

13. Lohmann Villena, "Las Cortes en Indias," 655.

14. Lohmann Villena, "Las Cortes en Indias," 657–662.

15. "Libro III, Título VIII, Ley ij," *Recopilación de leyes*, 2:25.

16. Maravall, *La comunidades de Castilla*.

17. Miranda, *Las ideas y las instituciones*, 51. Góngora, *El estado en el derecho indiano*; and MacLachlan, *Spain's Empire*, 21–44.

18. Pérez Prendes y Muñoz de Arracó, *La Monarquía indiana*, 167–68. Unfortunately, today most scholars mention the first part, "obey but not to enforce," but ignore the reasons why those warrants should not be enforced as well as the requirement that "at the first opportunity they [the authorities] must notify us [the king] of the reason why they did not implement them."

19. Lavallé, *Quito y la crisis de la alcabala*.

20. Phelan, *The People and the King*, xviii.

21. Elliott, "Empire and State" 365-382; and Annino, "Comentario," 445–56.

22. Viroli, *For Love of Country*, 18–40.

23. Borah, *Justice by Insurance*; Oswensby, *Empire of Law*.

24. Phelan, *The People and the King*, 34–35.

25. Garrido, *Reclamos y representaciones*.

26. Quoted in Elliott, "Empire and State," 369. See also: Brading, *The First America*, 215–27.

27. Mier, "Idea de la Constitución," 31–91.

28. Rodríguez O., *Independence of Spanish America*, 16.

29. Rodríguez O., *Independence of Spanish America*, 26–33. See also: Cañizarez-Esguerra, *How to Write the History of the New World*, 204–61.

30. Lempérière, "La representación política," 55–71.

31. Rubio Fernández, *Elecciones en el antiguo régimen*, 46.

32. Lierh, *Ayuntamiento y oligarquía en Puebla*, 1:100.

33. Guerra, *Modernidad e independencias*, 192. In note 48 in the same page, he states: "We find a *síndico personero del común* in [the cities of] Querétaro, Puebla, Zacatecas, Guanajuato, San Luis [Potosí] and Veracruz and *four diputados del común* in Zacatecas, Guanajuato, Veracruz and also in Mexico City."

34. "Lista de los Vecinos que compusieron la Junta y votaron para Síndico Personero de esta Villa de Yxtlahuaca," Archivo General de la Nación de México (hereafter AGN): Ayuntamientos, vol. 141.

35. Lempérière, "La representación política, 65.

36. Ladd, *The Making of Strike*; Moreno "Instituciones de la industria minera novohispana," 69–64; Moreno, "Régimen de trabajo," 242–67. See also: González,. Título décimo Quinto.

37. On the status of New Spain's economy at the end of the century see: Miño Grijalva, *El mundo novohispano*, 381–410. On the financial contributions to the Monarchy see: Marichal, *La bancarrota del virreinato*.

38. Flores Caballero, *La contrarrevolución*, 28–65; Hamnett, "Appropriation of Mexican Church Wealth," 85–113; Lavrin, "The Execution of the Law," 27–49; Von Wobeser, *Dominación colonial*; and Marichal, *Bankruptcy of Empire*, 132–53.

39. "Testimonio de la sesión celebrada," in García, *Documentos históricos*, 2:7.

40. Guedea, "El pueblo de México, 36–37. Her "Criollos y peninsulares en 1808" remains the best study of these events.

41. Rodríguez O., *Independence of Spanish America*, 59–64.

42. Benson, "The Elections of 1809," 1–20.

43. Rodríguez O., *Independence of Spanish America*, 63.

44. Rodríguez O., *Independence of Spanish America*, 63–64.

45. Quoted in Rodríguez O., *Independence of Spanish America* 76–77.

46. Berry, "The Election of the Mexican Deputies," 10–16.

47. Rodríguez O., "Las elecciones a las Cortes," 79–110.

48. Rodríguez O., "The Struggle for Dominance, 205–28; "Las Cortes mexicanas," 285–320; and *"We Are Now the True Spaniards,"* 305–34.

49. Mora, "Sobre la necesidad de fijar," 633.

2. ORIGINS OF THE QUITO REVOLUTION

1. Coronel F., "La contra-revolución," 105–11.
2. Terán Najas, *Los proyectos del imperio borbónico*; Porras P., *La Gobernación y el Obispado*; and León Borja and Szászdi, "El problema jurisdiccional," 13–146.
3. Andrien, *Kingdom of Quito*, 15.
4. Estupiñan Viteri, *El mercado interno*. On the textile industry see: Tyrer, *Historia demográfica*.
5. Andrien, *Kingdom of Quito*, 29–32.
6. Céspedes del Castillo, *Lima y Buenos Aires*; and Borchard de Moreno, *La Audiencia de Quito*, 99–209. See also Andrien, "Economic Crisis," 104–17, for an assessment of Quito's economic crisis.
7. Herzog, *Upholding*, 105–20, 140–59.
8. Federico González Suárez provides a thorough account of politics in the city of Quito; see: *Historia general*, 2:926–1180. In recent times, Luis Javier Ramos Gómez has written most extensively about these questions; see: "La estructura social quiteña," 25–56; "La pugna por el poder local en Quito," 179–96; and "La acusación contra el presidente," 249–77; and Andrien, *Kingdom of Quito*, 165–80.
9. On this complex matter see: Lavallé, *Quito y la crisis de la alcabala*.
10. González Suárez, *Historia general*, 2:926–1180; and Minchom, *The People of the Quito*, 201–10.
11. McFarlane, "The 'Rebellion of the Barrios,'" 283–87; Andrien, "Economic Crisis," 110–20. See Minchon for a careful analysis of the informal economy: *People of Quito*, 101–15.
12. McFarlane, "The "'Rebellion of the Barrios,'" 289–92.
13. In his *Política indiana*, published in 1649—after nearly two decades of experience in the Indies—Solórzano Pereira maintained that the territories of the New World were kingdoms of the Spanish Monarchy that "must be administered and governed as though the king who holds them together was the sole ruler of each one of them." Solórzano Pereyra, *Política indiana*, 2:1639.
14. McFarlane, "The 'Rebellion of the Barrios,'" 293–300.
15. On the alcabala see: Fernández Martínez, *La alcabala en la Audiencia de Quito*.
16. "Relación sumaria de las dos sublevaciones de la Plebe de Quito," 102–16. Minchon argues that the tax on "babies" was considered by the people of

the barrios as an indirect method of subjecting the plebians with tribute. Minchon, *People of Quito*, 230.

17. González Suárez, *Historia general*, 2:1127.

18. The best account of these events is McFarlane, "The 'Rebellion of the Barrios,'" 300–308. An interesting account by a contemporary is Velasco, *Historia del Reino de Quito*, 2:509–11.

19. The term *chapetón* was used to refer to a European Spaniard residing in Quito. It is comparable to the Mexican word *gachupín*.

20. They were described as "la ínfima pleba" that included men, women and children who were mestizos, urban Indians, and a few criollos. Minchon, *People of Quito*, 232.

21. For contrasting interpretations of these events see: McFarlane, "The 'Rebellion of the Barrios,'" 312–17; and Andrien, "Economic Crisis," 125–29. See also Minchon, *People of Quito*, 227–33, for an analysis of eyewitness accounts.

22. On this question see: Tamar, *Defining Nations* and Rodríguez O., "La ciudadanía y la Constitución," 39–56.

23. The sources mention large numbers, from four to ten thousand people in the Plaza Mayor. However, because of the topography of the city, the "plaza mayor" of Quito is one of the smallest plazas in the city. It is unlikely that more than one or, at most, two thousand could fit there.

24. González Suárez, *Historia general*, 2:1131–1141; McFarlane, "The 'Rebellion of the Barrios,'" 313–30; Andrien, "Economic Crisis," 125–31; Minchon, *People of Quito*, 222–32.

25. José García de León y Pizarro to Ministro José de Gálvez, Quito, June 18, 1779, in González Suárez, *Historia general*, 2:1199–1201. On the impact of the "libre comercio" see: Washburn, "The Bourbon Reforms," 107–17; and Tyrer, *Historia demográfica*, 237–60.

26. González Suárez, *Historia general*, 2:1202–1203; and Andrien, *Kingdom of Quito*, 192–93.

27. González Suárez, *Historia general*, 2:1205–1215; and Andrien, *Kingdom of Quito*, 203–10.

28. Andrien, *Kingdom of Quito*, 202.

29. Meisel, "El situado de Cartagena," 193–211.

30. Kuethe, *Military Reform and Society*, 120–27, and Table 5 on page 198. See also: Büchges, *Familia, honor y poder*, 194–96.

31. Kuethe, *Military Reform and Society*, 182. On the nature of the revolt see: Moreno Yañez, *Sublevaciones indígenas*, 297–338.

32. Molina Martínez, "Conflictos en la Audiencia," 153–73.

33. Washburn, "The Bourbon Reforms," 156–59; citation on 157–59.

34. On Carondelet see: Fiehrer, "The Baron de Carondelet." For a detailed account of the earthquake see: González Suárez, *Historia general*, 2:1286–1294.

35. Fiehrer, "The Baron de Carondelet," 620–621. See also: Larrea, *El Barón de Carondelet*, 55–67. See also Coronel Feijóo, "Poder local en la transición," 199–222.

36. Keeding, *Surge la nación*, 515–68; Shafer, *Economic Societies in the Spanish World*, 168–77. On Espejo's thought see: Roig, *Humanismo*.

37. Larrea, *El Barón de Carondelet*, 83–101.

38. "Comunicación importante del Presidente de Quito," in Larrea, *El Barón de Carondelet*, 173–88.

39. "Actas del Consejo, 1808," Archivo Municipal de Quito (hereafter AMQ), fols. 30v-31r.

40. Borrero, *La revolución quiteña*, 21–22.

41. Ramos Pérez, *Entre el Plata y Bogotá*, 171–72.

42. Jijón y Caamaño, *Influencia de Quito*, 12–13.

43. Ponce, "Alegato de [Rodríguez de] Quiroga," 62–100. On the letter from the king see Ramos Pérez, *Entre el Plata y Bogotá*, 182–84. See also Morelli, "La revolución en Quito," 335–56.

44. Torre Reyes, *La revolución de Quito*, 181–96. José Gabriel Navarro suggests that the Conde Ruiz de Castilla accepted "a large sum of money" to arrange the acquittal. Navarro, *La revolución de Quito*, 49.

45. "Actas del Cabildo Colonial de Guayaquil, 1807–1810," Archivo de la Biblioteca Municipal de Guayaquil (hereafter ABMG), 121–23; "Actas del Consejo, 1809–1814" AMQ; Chacón Zhapán, *Libro de Cabildos de Cuenca (1806–1810)*, 1:400–404.

46. "Actas del Cabildo Colonial de Guayaquil," 128–29.

47. "Actas del Consejo, 1809–1814," AMQ, fols. 23–24v. On elections to the Junta Central see; Rodríguez O., *La revolución política*, 65–70 and 134–38 and Almarza Villaloboa and Martínez Garnica, *Instrucciones para los diputados*.

48. "Manifiesto del Pueblo de Quito," 430.

49. Gilmore, "Imperial Crisis," 8–9; "Actas del Consejo, 1809 a 1814 (January 9, 1809), AMQ.

50. "De los procesos seguidos contra los Patriotas del 10 de Agosto de 1809," 18–40.

51. The Acta is cited in Torre Reyes, *La revolución de Quito*, 208–9.

52. The poderes are published in Andrade, *Historia del Ecuador*, 2:417–26. Unfortunately, the poderes and lists of male and female members of the clergy are included without any distinction. This makes one question the reliability of the poderes.

53. Torre Reyes, *La revolución de Quito*, 207–14.

54. "Manifiesto de la Junta Suprema de Quito," 136–39.

55. "Manifiesto del Pueblo de Quito," 142–44.

56. See Rodríguez O., "Revolución de 1809," 57–58; Torre Reyes, *La revolución de Quito*, 231; and Ramos Pérez, *Entre el Plata y Bogotá*, 174–78.

57. Rodríguez O., "Revolución de 1809," 61–62; 73.

58. "Acusación del Fiscal Tomás de Aréchaga," 37–65. See also: Coronel F., "La contra-revolución," 105–11; and Ponce Ribadeneira, *Quito, 1809–1812*, 136–41.

59. Ponce Ribadeneira, *Quito, 1809–1812*, 139–89; and Navarro, *La revolución de Quito*, 79–159.

3. CLERICAL CULTURE

1. There was one significant exception: the defeated Muslims were permitted to retain their religion until the beginning of the seventeenth century, when they too either had to convert or leave.

2. Quoted in Herzog, *Defining Nations*, 247, note 6.

3. Herzog, *Defining Nations*, 121.

4. Villarroel, *Gobierno eclesiástico pacífico*.

5. Adams, *The Works of John Adams*, 10:145.

6. Quijada, "From Spain to New Spain," 185–219. From the vast literature on the Catholic Church in the Hispanic world see: Fernández Albaladejo, "Católicos antes que ciudadanos," 103–27; Morgado García, *Ser clérigo*; Payne, *Spanish Catholicism*; Fields, *King and Church*; and Taylor, *Magistrates of the Sacred*. Perhaps the best work on Ecuador is: Tobar Donoso, *La iglesia, modeladora de la nacionalidad*.

7. Terán Najas,; Porras P., *La Gobernación y el Obispado*; and León Borja and Szászdi, "El problema jurisdiccional," 13–146.

8. Andrien, *Kingdom of Quito*, 15. Estupiñan Viteri, *El Mercado interno*. On the textile industry see: Tyrer, *Historia demográfica*.

9. Tobar Donoso, *La iglesia*, 200–240; and Tobar Donoso, *Las instituciones*, 121–53.

10. See, for example, Cushner, *Farm and Factory*.

11. Estupiñan Viteri, *El Mercado interno*; Tyrer, *Historia demográfica*. See also Andrien, *Kingdom of Quito*, 29–32. Borchard de Moreno, *La Audiencia de Quito*, 99–209. See also Andrien, "Economic Crisis," 104–17 for an assessment of Quito's economic crisis.

12. See Condamine, *Diario del viaje al Ecuador*; Zuñiga, *La expedición científica de Francia*; and Keeding, *Surge la nación*, 113–20.

13. Paladines, *Pensamiento ilustrado*, 36–39.

14. See, for example, the arguments of Carbajal, "Tesis de Filosofía," 139–56.

15. "Estatuto de la Real Universidad," 93–159. See also: Tobar Donoso, *La iglesia*, 240–42 and Keeding, *Surge la nación*, 305–23.

16. Velasco, *Historia del Reino de Quito*. See also: Roig, *Humanismo: Primera Parte*.

17. Minchom, *People of Quito*, 235. The following are a representative sample of recent scholars who consider Espejo the "Precursor": Paladines, *Pensamiento ilustrado*, 40–50; Keeding, *Surge la nación*; and Astuto, *Eugenio Espejo*, 145–53. However, Roig, in *Humanismo: Segunda Parte* considers Espejo a humanist reformer.

18. Shafer, *Economic Societies in the Spanish World*.

19. Astuto, *Eugenio Espejo* 60–67; Keeding, *Surge la nación*, 515–30; and Cardozo Galué, *Michoacán*, 93–94.

20. Minchom, *People of Quito*, 237.

21. "Actas del Consejo, 1808," AMQ, fols. 30v-31r.

22. Ortiz, "Notas para la biografía del obispo José Cuero y Caicedo," 111–61; and Albornoz Peralta, *Páginas de la Historia Ecuatoriana*, 171–77.

23. According to William B. Stevenson, who served as Ruiz de Castilla's secretary: "The Bishop of Quito was elected vice-president, but refused to assist at this [the first meeting of the new government] or any subsequent meeting." *Historical and Descriptive Narrative*, 3:13.

24. "El Ilmo. Cuero y Caicedo Obispo de Quito en el Proceso contra los patriotas del 10 de Agosto de 1809," 16–32; Rodríguez O., "La revolución de 1809," 72–73; and Valencia Llano, "Élites, burocracia, clero," 82–84.

25. "Acusación del Fiscal Tomás de Aréchaga," 37–65; and Ponce Ribadeneira, *Quito, 1809–1812*, 136–41.

26. Ponce de Andrade, *Carta del Ilmo. Sr. Don*; Silva y Olave, *El Excelentísimo Señor doctor*; "La ciudad de Quito, Al Excmo. Sor. D. D. José de Silva y Olave Diputado Representante del Virreynato del Perú en la Suprema Junta Central," Archivo General de Indias (hereafter, AGI): Estado, 72.N.64\15\; and "El Ilmo. Cuero y Caicedo," 16–32.

27. "El Proceso de la Revolución de Quito de 1809," AMQ. "El proceso" is carefully analyzed by Torre Fuentes, *La revolución de Quito*, 343–506.

28. Although the majority of historians who have read Stevenson assert that 300 persons died, the number of deaths that he mentions is closer to 400. Stevenson mentions 72 who died in prison and 300 in the streets. Stevenson, *Historical and Descriptive Narrative*, 3:28–29.

29. Stevenson, *Historical and Descriptive Narrative*, 3:28–30; and Minchom, *People of Quito*, 246–49.

30. Quotes in Stevenson, *Historical and Descriptive Narrative*, 3:32–33. See also: Minchom, *The People of the Quito*, 246–50 and Borrero, *La revolución quiteña*, 240–47.

31. Borrero, *La revolución quiteña*, 278.

32. Borrero, *La revolución quiteña*, 281.

33. Valencia Llano, "Élites, burocracia, clero," 82–87; and López-Ocón Cabrera, "El protagonismo del clero en la insurgencia quiteña," 124–25.

34. Ramos Pérez, *Entre el Plata y Bogotá*, quote in note 358, 220; Borrero, *La revolución quiteña*, 321–25.

35. Borja, "Pacto Solemne," 3:9–23.

36. Although much has been written about the Constitution of Quito, it is difficult to understand what occurred in that assembly. José Gabriel Navarro asserts that "upon hearing the reading of Rodríguez's Project, [Miranda] drafted one of his own that was diametrically opposed to the one by Rodríguez, that made it clear that the Kingdom belonged to Fernando VII and that it had to be governed by the Laws of Castilla and the Indies." Navarro, *La revolución de Quito*, 396–97. Navarro, along with other historians, maintains that two political groups emerged: one—led by Juan Pío Montúfar, Marqués de Selva Alegre—that preferred a monarchy, and another—led by Jacinto Sánchez de Orellana, Marqués de Villa Orellana— that preferred a republic. The sanchistas presumably favored the document written by Rodríguez while the montufaristas favored the document written by Miranda. Since the minutes of the assembly have not been found, no historian knows what occurred. Nevertheless, Alfredo Ponce Ribadeneria states: "Miranda's project was not approved, but another presented by Dr. Miguel Rodríguez, which became the constitution of the new state when it was promulgated by the congress on February 15, 1812." Ponce Ribadeneria, *Quito, 1808–1812*, 101. The majority of historians agree with that statement. Since the sanchistas were a minority group, the montufaristas without any difficulty would have been able to approve Miranda's constitution, which

was more traditional and which also favored a monarchy. On the contrary, they supposedly approved a republican charter written by Rodríguez. However, Ahmed Deidán de la Torre believes that "the congress as such did not approve any [constitution]," since the internal differences between both factions had been profound for some time. In these circumstances the sanchistas did not attend the session of February 15, the day Rodríguez's constitution was supposedly approved. In fact, the minutes of the elections of officials, which occurred on the same date, confirms that nine deputies did not attend. The legality of that approval is doubtful because the congress may have lacked a quorum. It is interesting to note that José del Carral informed President Toribio Montes that the Quito congress discussed the nature of the Patronato Real and who had the authority over it. Rodríguez's constitution does not mention the patronato while Miranda's devotes a section to it. Therefore, one may suppose that Miranda's constitution was not simply rejected. See: Deidán de la Torre, *Sovereignty and People*; Pérez Ramírez, "Autoría del Proyecto de Constitución," 75–82; Rámos Pérez, *Entre el Plata y Bogotá*, 220–22; and Morelli, *Territorio o nación*, 51–53.

37. Borrero, *La revolución quiteña*, 345–94.
38. Saint-Geours and Demélas, *Jerusalen y Babilonia*, 93.
39. López-Ocón Cabrera, "El protagonismo del clero," 124–25.
40. Rodríguez O., *"Rey, religión, yndependencia"*; "Las elecciones a las Cortes," 79–110; "Las primeras elecciones constitucionales," 3–52; "De la fidelidad a la revolución," 35–88.
41. Many curas exhorted their faithful to honor and obey the Constitution. Serafín García Cárdenas, for example, declared: "This fundamental law . . . the best combined, the most clear, just, liberal and perfect that is known, or has ever been known among the cultured nations, is no more than an immediate emanation of the principles of the divine law fortunately applied to the Spanish state." And he urged them: "Read continually and attentively this precious Code. Conserve with religious veneration this eternal monument of wisdom, justice, humanity and Spanish policy to leave as an inheritance to your children." Many curas referred to the Charter of Cádiz as "our holy Constitution." AGI: México, 1482.
42. Rodríguez O., *La revolución política*, 81–88.
43. Rodríguez O., *La revolución política*, 93–100. See also: "Plan de elecciones de Diputados en Cortes y de Provincia" in Rodríguez O., *La revolución política*, 225–35.

44. Rodríguez O., *La revolución política*, 173–86.

45. Salazar, *Actas del congreso. . . 1831*"Introducción," I-LXXXVIII; *Actas del congreso. . . 1833* "Introducción," I-LXXI; J. L. R., *Historia de la República del Ecuador*, 426–37. See also Henderson, *Gabriel García Moreno*.

4. CITIZENS OF THE SPANISH NATION

1. Benson, "The Contested Mexican Election of 1812," 336–50; Guedea, "Las primeras elecciones populares," 1–28; Guedea, "El pueblo de México," 27–61; Annino, "Prácticas criollas y liberalismo," 121–58; and Warren, "Elections and Popular Political Participation," 30–58. See also my studies: "'Ningún pueblo es superior a otro:'" 249–309; *"Rey, religión, yndepencia"*; and "Las elecciones a las Cortes," 79–110. The following are studies of the Indian communities in Mexico: Escobar Ohmstede, "Del gobierno indígena," 1–26; Ducey, "Village, Nation and Constitution," 463–93; Guardino, "'Toda libertad,'" 87–114; Guarisco, *Los indios del valle de México*, 129–92; and Guardino, *Peasants*, 85–94. The only study on the Caribbean is: Gómez Vizuete, "Los primeros ayuntamientos," 581–615. On Central America see: Avendaño Rojas, *Centroamérica*; Dym, "La soberanía de los pueblos," 309–37. On South America see: Rodríguez O., "Las primeras elecciones," 3–52; Peralta Ruiz, *En defensa de la autoridad*, 105–75; Almer, "'La confianza que han puesto en mi;'" and Rodríguez O., "La Antigua provincia de Guayaquil," 365–95 & 557–56. Federica Morelli provides a broad interpretation of the transformations that occurred in el Reino de Quito, which includes extensive discussion of elections and their impact on the Indians. See her *Territorio o nazione*, 121–76.

2. Van Young, *The Other Rebellion*.

3. Piel, "The Place of the Peasantry," 116.

4. Marie-Danielle Demélas-Bohy has studied aspects of the elections in el Reino de Quito in her "Modalidades y significación de elecciones," 291–13 and her "Microcosmos," 65–76.

5. Rodríguez O., *La independencia de la América española*, 91–94, 174–82.

6. Toribio Montes to Minister of War, Quito, April 7, 1813, AGI: Quito, Leg. 257. Reports about the publication of the Constitution in the Kingdom of Quito are found in ANHQ: PQ, vol. 477.

7. The Cortes's decree of May 23, 1812, declared: "A preparatory junta must be established in the capitals [of the provincial deputations] to facilitate the elections to deputies to the Cortes . . . ." Although the Constitution of Cádiz established provincial deputations in the kingdoms of Quito and

Charcas, the decree of the Cortes did not include the cities of Quito and Chuquisaca among the capital cities where preparatory juntas were to be established. As a result, President Toribio Montes acted in place of the preparatory junta of the Province of Quito, as the kingdom was called under the Constitution. Cortes, *Colección de decretos y órdenes*, 1:515, 508–25.

8. José Joaquín de San Clemente a Montes, Guapi, December 6, 1813, ANHQ: PQ, vol. 483, fol. 42.

9. ANHQ: PQ, vol. 491, fol. 32.

10. "Constitución política de la Monarquía Española," 64–72.

11. Dr. Salvador a Montes, Quito, October 5, 1813, ANHQ: PQ, Gobierno, Caja 63, 26-viii-1813.

12. Oberem, "Indios libres e indios sujetos," 2:106, 105–12. Oberem's calculations are based on a document that lists the tributes of 1804–1805. The document distinguishes between tributaries of "pueblos or parroquias" and those "que pertenecen a haciendas u obrajes respectivamente." Oberem, "Indios libres e indios sujetos," 2:105. Federica Morelli, who examined the "Libro de Tributarios del corregimiento de Quito" for 1784, raises the percentage of *conciertos* to 61.9 percent. See her *Territorio o nazione*, 409.

13. With an eligible population of four hundred thousand, the Province of Quito had the right to five deputies to the Cortes on the basis of one deputy for each seventy thousand inhabitants. But since fifty thousand inhabitants remained, Quito had the right to one more deputy according to Article 32 of the constitution. "Plan de elecciones de Diputados en Cortes y de Provincia," ANHQ: Gobierno, Caja 63, 26-viii-1813.

14. See "Plan de elecciones de Diputados en Cortes, y de Provincia," 35–43.

15. For a discussion of these questions, see: Chapter 1: "The Nature of Representation in New Spain."

16. General Toribio Montes' attitude illustrates that tendency. He argued that it was necessary "to establish ties among Spaniards in both hemispheres." Therefore, it was necessary for the wellbeing of the Spanish Nation, "that the Political Constitution of the Monarchy be established completely in full." AGI: Quito, Leg 258.

17. ANHQ: PQ, Gobierno, Caja 63, 26-viii-1813. The parish of Chambo received 11 compromisarios and one elector parroquial.

18. Quoted in Rodríguez O., "'Ningún pueblo es superior a otro,'" 76.

19. For examples of these practices, see: Guardino, "'Toda libertad'" and Rodríguez O., "La Antigua provincia de Guayaquil."

20. As Linda Alexander Rodríguez, writing about the post-independence period, has noted: "The concept "Indian" is alien to the indigenous people of Ecuador. Rather than a homogeneous "Indian" group, as perceived the government and the Hispanized society, Indians belong to one of hundreds of communities. They identified with individual [Indian] groups, not with a larger "Indian" society." Rodríguez, *The Search for Public Policy*, 29.

21. "Constitución Política de la Monarquía Española," 95.

22. Antonio García to Montes, Cuenca, July 14, 1813, ANHQ: PQ, vol. 478, fol. 74r-v.

23. Fernández de Córdova, Cuenca, June 14, 1813, ANHQ: PQ, vol. 477, fol. 49.

24. García to Montes, Cuenca, July 14, 1813, AHNQ: PQ, vol. 478, fol. 74r-v.

25. The Plan is reproduced in Morelli, *Territorio o Nazione*, 416–22.

26. Diego Fernández de Córdova to Montes, Cuenca, May 22, 1813, ANHQ: Gobierno, Caja 62, 2-iv-1813.

27. Montes to Fernández de Córdova, ANHQ: Gobierno, Caja 62, 2-iv-1813.

28. Oficio de Juan López Tornaleo y Contestación del Excelentísimo Señor Capital General Don Toribio Montes, ANHQ: Gobierno, Caja 62, 2-iv-1813.

29. García to Montes, Cuenca, July 14, 1813, AHNQ: PQ, vol. 478, fol. 74r-v.

30. This occurred in the Ayuntamiento de México where an Indian, Francisco Galicia of the parcialidad de San Juan, was elected regidor. See: Guedea, "Las primeras elecciones populares," 7–16.

31. García to Montes, Cuenca, July 14, 1813, AHNQ: PQ, vol. 478, fol. 74r-v.

32. García to Montes, Cuenca, July 14, 1813, ANHQ: PQ, vol. 478, fol. 72r-v.

33. García to Montes, Cuenca, July 14, 1813, AHNQ: PQ, vol. 478, fol. 74r-v.

34. Four small papers with the names of the twelve electors to be chosen are found in the pertinent legajo. The names are as follow: D. Cayetano Córdova, D. Carlos Córdova, D. José Manuel Castro, D. Pedro Peñafiel, D. José Castro, D. Francisco Zegarra, D. Maniano Yllescas, D. José Segara, D. Marcelino Peñafiel, D. Tomás Loxa, D. Juan Manuel Calle, and D. Tomás Coboa. ANHQ: PQ, vol. 590, fols. 230–32.

35. ANHQ: PQ, vol. 590, fols. 230–32.

36. ANHQ: PQ, vol. 590, fols. 230–32.

37. Guedea, "Las primeras elecciones populares," 8–16.

38. Since Quito lacked a preparatory junta to organize the elections, Superior Political Chief Montes assumed the responsibility for settling electoral issues.

39. "Sobre el despojo del Cavildo de Cuenca," ANHQ: Gobierno, caja 62, 2-iv-1813.

40. "Sobre el despojo del Cavildo de Cuenca," ANHQ: Gobierno, caja 62,
2-iv-1813.

41. Jaramillo Alvarado, *Historia de Loja*, 220–32. See also: Ynstrucción que
forma el Ylustre Cavildo de Loxa para que se dirija al Diputado Representante del Virreynato, en que se comprehende esta Provincia, y promueva
sus Artículos ante la Suprema Junta Central que govierna a number del Sr.
D. Fernando VII (que Dios no lo ha de restituir)," Archivo Histórico del
Banco Central del Ecuador: Fondo Jijón y Caamaño, 5/4, fols. 27–31 for a
description of the area's economic condition.

42. Minchom, "The Making of a White Province," 23–39.

43. José Manuel Xaramillo Celi al Fiscal, Loja, February 3, 1814, ANHQ: Gobierno, caja 64, 24-xii-1813.

44. According to the fiscal de la Audiencia: "According to the law of June
23, 1814 it is clear that the actual Corregidor [de Loja] is not, nor call he
call himself Political Chief." Dr. Salvador a Montes, Quito, March 14, 1814,
ANHQ: PQ, vol. 482, fols. 66r-v.

45. "Documentos que califican la nulidad de los electos Alcaldes y Regidores
del Cavildo Constitucional de Loja," ANHQ: Gobierno, caja 63, 7-x-1813.

46. "Expediente promovido por el Comun de la Ciudad de Loxa sobre cum-
plimiento de Constitución, e infracción de ella," ANHQ: Gobierno, caja 63,
7-x-1813; See also: ANHQ: PQ, vol. 481.

47. Quoted in Demélas-Bohy, "Modalidades y significación de elecciones," 301,
note 40.

48. "Expediente seguido sobre lo occurrido con motivo del restablecimiento
del Cavildo Constitucional de Loja," ANHQ: Gobierno, caja 64, 24-xii-1813.
See also Rodríguez O., "Las primeras elecciones constitucionales," 27–28.

49. Miguel Bello a Montes, Loja July 25, 1814, ANHQ: PQ, vol.500, fols.
137–38r-v.

50. Montes a Diputación Provincial, Quito, September 6, 1814, ANHQ: PQ, vol.
500, fol. 138r-v.

51. Chacón Zhapán, *Historia del Corregimiento de Cuenca*, 13–220.

52. Morelli, *Territorio o Nazione*, 233.

53. Agustín Padilla to Montes, Quito, January 18, 1813, ANHQ: PQ, vol. 472, fol.
167..

54. Josef, Obispo de Trujillo a Montes, Trujillo, May 14, 1814, ANHQ: PQ, vol.
498, fol. 71.

55. José Ygnacio Checa a Montes, San Felipe, May 12, 1814, ANHQ: PQ, vol. 498,
fol. 54r-v.

56. "Representación del Cura de Pimpicos al Ymo. Sor. Obispo de Trujillo," ANHQ: PQ, vol. 498, fols. 68–70.

57. In Yucatán Indian communities "were receiving regular news regarding the decisions of the Cortes." Rugely, *Yucatán's Maya Peasantry*, 39. It is probable that the Indians of Quito, like those of Yucatán, had their own sources of information.

58. "Representación del Cura de Pimpicos al Ymo. Sor. Obispo de Trujillo," ANHQ: PQ, vol. 498, fols. 68–70.

59. One official in Riobamba argued that "the Indians . . . of this Villa, misinformed about the prohibition of arresting and jailing, as decreed by the Sovereign Cortes," had given themselves over to "intensive drunkenness . . . . I believe that they do not comprehend the prohibition of arrest, nor do they understand [that they must continue] to pay their debts to the Royal Treasury, nor does a [former] vassal understand that he cannot enjoy the privileges of a citizen because of the scandal that his vice of drunkenness demonstrates." Martín Chiriboga y León to Montes, Riobamba, September 16, 1814, ANHQ: PQ, vol. 502, fol. 101r-v.

60. "Representación del Cura de Pimpicos al Ymo. Sor. Obispo de Trujillo," ANHQ: PQ, vol. 498, fols. 68–70; José Ygnacio Checa to Montes, Marañon, February 25, 1814, ANHQ: PQ, vol. 495, fols. 260–66; see also: vol. 490, fol. 127; vol. 497, fol. 133; vol. 498, fol. 54, . 68–70.

61. "Consulta del Administrador de la Fábrica de Latacunga sobre que los Yndígenas se niegan al trabajo de ella," ANHQ: Gobierno, Caja 79, 28-ix, 1822.

62. For an interpretation somewhat different than mine with respect to the political role of Indians see: Morelli, "Un neosincretismo político," 151–65.

5. THE EMANCIPATION OF AMERICA

1. In this essay, the term *monarchy* is used instead of the word *empire* for several reasons. First, monarchy is a form of government in the same manner that republic is. Second, the term empire implies a degree of subordination that did not exist at that time and which the people of those monarchies, whether in Europe or in America, did not accept. That sort of subordinate relationship was characteristic of the later European empires of the nineteenth century. Third, the term empire suggests a degree of centralization and control that did not exist at the time.

2. The Spanish Monarchy identified its component parts as kingdoms, principalities, counties, duchies, etc. The Spanish term *virreinato*, normally translated into English as *viceroyalty*, means literally vice kingdom; it was

used to refer those areas administered by a *virrey* (viceroy in French or vice king in English). The Spanish Monarchy possessed viceroyalties in Europe as well as in America. The regions of Spanish America were called *reinos* (kingdoms), and its inhabitants did not consider themselves *colonists*. See the essays in Greenglass, *Conquest and Coalescence*; and Elliott, "A Europe of Composite Monarchies," 52–69.

3. Earlier historians, such as Roger B. Merriman, understood the Spanish Monarchy as a great confederation; see his *The Rise of the Spanish Empire in the Old World and the New*. However, during nearly a century, most scholars have tended to concentrate on individual parts of that Monarchy. See, for example, Belenguer, *El imperio hispánico*, which examines only the European portion of the empire. In contrast, the recent volume by Kamen, *Empire: How Spain Became a World Power*, provides a most sophisticated explanation of the nature of the Spanish Monarchy. Most syntheses of the New World possessions no longer limit themselves to territories of the Spanish Monarchy, but discuss all of Iberoamerica; a good example is: Burkholder and Johnson, *Colonial Latin America*.

4. Although Castilian—the language that is generally called Spanish— became the dominant tongue within the Monarchy, it was not the only one spoken in the Peninsula. More importantly, Spanish scholars provided Indian languages with alphabets and grammars quite early. The first Castilian grammar was published in 1492, for example, whereas the first Nahuatl (the language of central Mexico) grammar appeared in 1531. Personal communication from Miguel León-Portilla, October 6, 1997.

5. It is often asserted that the Indians were considered minors. That is not entirely correct. Spanish law, which was based on Roman law, distinguished between two forms of legal minority. The first, *infantes* and *inpúberes*—that is, persons sixteen years and younger—lacked legal independence and were supervised by a *tutor*. The second consisted of individuals younger than twenty-five years—the age of legal maturity—and older than sixteen. They possessed the right to act independently on all legal matters, but a *curator* supervised and protected them in case others "abused their lack of experience, lack of malice or incapacity." The Indians of Spanish America were considered minors in the second sense. In their case, the king—that is, the monarch—functioned as their curator. González, *Historia del derecho mexicano*, 36.

6. Bayle, *El protector de indios*; Cutter, *The Protector of Indians*; Bonnett, *El Protector de Naturales*; and Novoa, *The Protectors of Indians*.

7. Rodríguez O., *Independence of Spanish America*, 7–11. See also MacLachlan and Rodríguez O., *The Forging of the Cosmic Race*, 196–248.

8. Morgan, *American Slavery and American Freedom*, 20.

9. Canny, "The Ideology of English Colonization," 575–98.

10. Madley, "Reexamining the American Genocide Debate," 99–100.

11. Madley, "Reexamining the American Genocide Debate," 109–10.

12. Seed, "'Are These Not Also Men?'" 651.

13. Horsman, *Race and Manifest Destiny*, 104.

14. Eccles, *France in America*, 1–221; Meyer, *Francia y América*; Seed, *Ceremonies of Possession*, 41–68.

15. Knight, "The Haitian Revolution," 108.

16. Ott, *The Haitian Revolution*, 3–21; Fick, *The Making of Haiti*, 15–28.

17. The best literature on the subject exists for Mexico. See, for example: Miranda, *Las ideas y las instituciones*; Lira, *Comunidades indígenas*; Gibson, *Aztecs Under Spanish Rule*; and Haskett, *Indigenous Rulers*.

18. Rodríguez O., *Independence of Spanish America*, 19–22, 46–49.

19. Phelan, *The People and the King*, xviii.

20. Greene, "The American Revolution," 96.

21. Gordon S. Wood, on the other hand, argues that free blacks possessed a status similar to that of white "plebeians." See his *Radicalism of the American Revolution*, 11–56.

22. Eccles, *France in America*, 158–66; Meyer, *Francia y América*.

23. Greene, "The American Revolution," 95.

24. Greene, "The American Revolution," 97.

25. MacLachlan and Rodríguez O., *The Forging of the Cosmic Race*, 144–228.

26. Quoted in Knight, "The Haitian Revolution," 107–8.

27. Knight, "The Haitian Revolution,"108.

28. Rodriguez O., *Independence of Spanish America*, 13–19; and Bernstein, *Thomas Jefferson*.

29. Rodríguez O., *Independence of Spanish America*, 47–48; and Mier, "Idea de la Constitución," 57.

30. Greene, *Understanding the American Revolution*, 74–75.

31. One explanation is offered by Maier, *From Resistance to Revolution*. Theodor Draper provides a somewhat different view in *A Struggle for Power*. See also Nelson, *The Royalist Revolution*, which asserts that the British Americans opposed the Parliament rather than the king.

32. Greene, *Understanding the American Revolution*, 72.

33. The struggle for U.S. independence is discussed in: Alden, *The American Revolution*; Higgenbotham, *The War for American Independence*; Smelser, *The Winning of Independence*; and Wallace, *Appeal to Arms*. See also Chávez, *Spain and the Independence of the United States*; Chartrand and Back, *The French Army in the American War of Independence*; and Dull, *The French Navy and American Independence*.

34. On the other hand, Wood—wrongly in my opinion—argues that the American Revolution was "as radical and social as any revolution in history." *Radicalism of the American Revolution*, 5.

35. Some Indian groups supported the British government, but no large-scale Indian movement erupted that might have threatened the British Americans.

36. See Jensen, *The Articles of Confederation*; Brown, *Redeeming the Republic*; and Bruchey, *The Roots of American Economic Growth*.

37. Greene, *Understanding the American Revolution*, 389.

38. Knight, "The Haitian Revolution" 106.

39. Knight, "The Haitian Revolution," 110.

40. The Haitian Revolution is well discussed in James's classic study *The Black Jacobins*; Ott, *The Haitian Revolution*; and Fick, *The Making of Haiti*. Two recent studies place the movement in its international context: Hernández Guerrero, *La revolución haitiana y el fin de un sueño colonial*, and Von Grafenstein Gareis, *Nueva España en el Circuncaribe*.

41. Knight, "The Haitian Revolution," 104–5.

42. This argument is developed in my book, *Independence of Spanish America*.

43. See Chapter 2 on Quito; Castro Gutierrez, *Movimientos populares en Nueva España*; Phelan, *The People and the King*; and Walker, *The Túpac Amaru Rebellion*.

44. Rodríguez O., *Independence of Spanish America*, 19–35.

45. Guedea, "The Process of Mexican Independence," 116.

46. Guedea, "The Process of Mexican Independence," 116.

47. Guedea, "The First Popular Elections in Mexico City," 39–42.

48. Quoted in Rodríguez O., *Independence of Spanish America*, 81–82.

49. Rodríguez O., *Independence of Spanish America*, 107–20.

50. Guedea, "The First Popular Elections in Mexico City," 39–63; Guedea, "El pueblo de México," 27–61; and Guedea, *En busca de un gobierno alterno*, 233–315. See also Rodríguez O., *Independence of Spanish America*, 92–103; as well as Rodríguez O., "Las primeras elecciones constitucionales," 3–52.

51. Rodríguez O., *"We Are Now the True Spaniards,"* 246–53.

52. Rodríguez O., "Transition from Colony," 97–132.

53. On this point, consult Benson, *Provincial Deputation in Mexico* and Rodríguez O., *"We Are Now the True Spaniards,"* 304–34.

54. Knight, "The Haitian Revolution," 105.

6. U.S. INDEPENDENCE

1. Armitage, *The Declaration of Independence*, 138.

2. Suárez, *Tratado de las leyes*. See also Stoetzer, *Scholastic Roots* and Quijada, "Las 'dos tradiciones,'" 61–86; and Quijada, "Sobre 'Nación', 'Pueblo', 'Soberanía,'" 19–51.

3. Herr, *Eighteenth-Century Revolution*, 172–83; Chiaramonte, "Fundamentos iusnaturalistas de los movimientos de independencia," 99–122.

4. Quoted in Polt, *Jovellanos and His English Sources*, 25.

5. Polt, *Jovellanos and His English Sources*, 15–43.

6. Archer, "Reflexiones de una edad de guerra total," 239–75. See also: Frost, "The Spanish Yoke," 33–52.

7. See also: Von Grafenstein Gareis, *Nueva España en el circuncaribe*, 113–67; and Chávez, *Spain and the Independence of the United States*.

8. See, for example, Butel-Dumont, *Historia del establecimiento y comercio de las colonias inglesas en la América Septentrional*. The volume originally appeared in French in 1755 and was published in The Hague and in London, and could be purchased in Paris.

9. García Melero, *La independencia de los Estados Unidos*, 295.

10. Alvarez, *Noticia del establecimiento y población de las colonias inglesas en la América Septentrional*.

11. Covarruvias, *Memorias históricas de la última guerra con la Gran Bretaña, desde el año de 1774*. See also García Melero, *La independencia de los Estados Unidos*; and Rodríguez, *La revolución Americana de 1776 y el mundo hispánico*.

12. Alcedo y Bexarano, *Diccionario geográfico*, 2:104–5. See also: Lerner, "The *Diccionario* of Antonio de Alcedo as a source of Enlightened Ideas," 71–93.

13. *A view of the history of Great-Britain*; *Histoire de l'administration de Lord North*; *Historia de la administración del Lord North, Primer Ministro de Inglaterra*. According to Carmen de la Guardia Herrero, "The [British] American revolution was a colonial revolution that would not impact an old metropolis such as Spain. As a result, revolutionary texts circulated in Madrid without problems. In fact, they caused a true interest in the mon-

arch [Carlos III] and his ministers.'" Guardia Herrero, "Revolución Americana," 205–18.

14. Minchom, *People of Quito*, 237.

15. On the Hispanic principles see Mónica Quijada's works: "Las dos tradiciones"; "Sobre 'nación', 'pueblo', 'soberanía'"; and "From Spain to New Spain," 185–219.

16. As Miguel Artola has observed: "The most transcendental result of the events that have occurred in all of Spain and for the Spanish protagonists is the sentiment of the reemergence of the sovereignty of the people, which is found in all the writings of the time." *La España de Fernando VII*, 68.

17. Rodríguez O, *La independencia de la América española*, 51–237.

18. See, for example: Simmons, *La revolución norteamericana* and Soto Cárdenas, *Influencia de la Independencia*.

19. Villavicencia, *Constitución de los Estados Unidos*; Simmons, *La revolución norteamericana*, 138–41.

20. Simmons, *La revolución norteamericana*, 196–201.

21. Peñalver, "Memoria presentada al Supremo Congreso de Venezuela," 5:25–39. See also: Venezuela, *Congreso Constituyente de 1811–1812*.

22. Venezuela, *Congreso Constituyente de 1811–1812* and Hébrard, "Opinión pública y representación," 196–224.

23. Benson, *The Provincial Deputation in Mexico*. See also Rodríguez O, *"We Are Now the True Spaniards,"* 268–334.

24. García de Sena, *La independencia de la Costa Firme* and *Historia de los Estados Unidos*.

25. For an interpretation different than mine see: Graces and Harkness, *Manuel García de Sena*. See also: Leal Curiel, "¿Radicales o timoratos?"

26. Quoted in Armitage, *The Declaration of Independence*, 43. The late distinguished historian Pauline Mair noted that it is "rare that men create something from nothing, particularly when they are writing documents of great importance." She indicated that Thomas Jefferson "worked from earlier models." Maier, "Independencia política," 111–31, quotes 111–12.

27. "Quando en el curso de los sucesos humanos se ve precisado un pueblo a romper los vínculos que lo ligaban a otro, es un deber de justicia, que por respeto a las opiniones de los demás hombres, se manifiesten los motivos que han conducido a esta separación. La Capital de Buenos Ayres, inseparable de las medidas de moderación que se ha propuesto, tentó todos los medios legítimos de unirse estrechamente a Montevideo." Quoted in Simmons, *La revolución norteamericana*, 191–92.

28. "Nos el Pueblo de la provincia de Texas jurando al Juez Supremo del universo la rectitud de nuestras intenciones, declaramos que los vínculos que nos mantenían bajo de la dominación de España europea están por siempre disueltos, que somos libres e independientes; que tenemos el derecho de establecer nuestro propio gobierno; y que en adelante toda autoridad legítima dimanará del pueblo, a quien solamente perteneces este derecho; que desde ahora para siempre jamás estaremos absueltos de deber y obligaciones a todo poder extranjero." Quoted in Guedea, "Autonomía e independencia," 163–64.

29. Vicente Rocafuerte initially favored the Constitution of Cádiz. But the subsequent failure of the Spanish Cortes in 1822–1823 forced him, and many others Spanish American liberals to adopt a new vision of the Spanish American community. In the process, Rocafuerte published several works praising republicanism and using Colombia and, particularly, the United States as models for the new nations. See, for example, *Ideas necesarias; Bosquejo ligerísimo*, and *Ensayo político*. After his years of experience in Britain, Rocafuerte was no longer so enamored of the United States. As he told his friend Carlos María de Bustamante: "it is necessary that you and other Mexicans open your eyes [to the idea] that the government of North America is not the enemy of Mexico." Carlos María de Bustamante, "Diario de lo especialmente occurido en México," Vázquez and Hernández Silva, eds., , April 12, 1830. See also: Rodríguez O., *The Emergence of Spanish America*.

30. Jefferson, *The Papers of Thomas Jefferson*, vol. 10.

31. Guedea and Rodríguez O., "How Relations Between Mexico and the United States Began," 17–40.

7. CAUDILLOS AND HISTORIANS

1. Moreno, "Caudillismo," 38–39.

2. The literature on caudillos is extensive; the most important texts follow. Domingo Sarmiento was among the early writers on the subject. His *Facundo: Cilización i barbarie* was published in Santigo, Chile in 1845. Kathleen Ross has published the first complete and modern translation entitled: *Facundo: Civilization and Barbarism*. Alcides Argüedas identified two types: *Los caudillos bárbaros* and *Los caudillos letrados*. Charles E. Chapman identified the age of caudillos as the post-independence period: "The Age of the Caudillos," 281–300. Francois Chevalier, however, argued that caudillaje began earlier in the antiguo régimen. "Caudilles et caciques," 30–

47. There have been a number of cultural interpretations: Bunge, *Nuestra América*, 224–48; Romero, *A History of Argentine Political Thought*; Morse, "Toward a Theory of Spanish American Government," 71–93; Dealy, *The Public Man*; Véliz, *The Centralist Tradition*. There have also been attempts by historians to study specific individuals: Haig, "The Creation and Control of a Caudillo," 481–90; Díaz Díaz, *Caudillos y caciques*; and John Lynch perhaps wrote one of the most extensive traditional works entitled *Caudillos in Spanish America*. In recent years Will Fowler has devoted his efforts to tie the caudillo with pronunciamientos. His major work glorifies the most famous Mexican caudillo in *Santa Anna of Mexico*. It is interesting to note that two distinguished historians, one a scholar of Spanish history and the other of Bolivian history, interpret the concept quite differently: see Blanco Valdéz, "Paisanos y soldados en los orígenes de la España liberal," 273–92; and Irurozqui Victoriano, "*A bala, piedra y palo.*"

3. Carr, *Spain*, 128.

4. Artola, *La España de Fernando VII*, 639–640.

5. Note 1 of Chapter 4 lists some of the most important publications on the Hispanic constitutional elections.

6. San Miguel, *Vida de D. Agustín Argüelles*, 2:62–63.

7. Warren, "The Origins," 1–20.

8. Comellas, *Los primeros pronunciamientos*, 165–86.

9. Warren, "Xavier Mina's Invasion," 52–76. Jiménez Codinach, *La Gran Bretaña*, 265–351.

10. Comellas, *Los primeros pronunciamientos*, 187–302; and Rodríguez O., *Independence of Spanish America*, 192–94.

11. Fehrenbach, "A Study of Spanish Liberalism," 73–85.

12. Alcalá Galiano, *Recuerdos de un anciano*, 91–131; and Rodríguez O., "Sobrehumano mortal," 105–31.

13. Quote in Gil Novales, *Rafael Riego*, 35.

14. Alcalá Galiano, *Recuerdos de un anciano*, 91–131; Mesonero Romanos, *Memorias de un setentón*, 97–99; Artola, *La España de Fernando VII*, 634–664; Fehrenbach, "A Study of Spanish Liberalism," 73–85.

15. Carr, *Spain*, 128–29.

16. Mesonero Romanos, *Memorias de un setentón*, 97–99; Fehrenbach, "A Study of Spanish Liberalism," 80–85. Rodríguez O., *The Emergence of Spanish America*, 22–25.

17. See, for example, Villoro, *El proceso ideológico*, 14 and his "La revolución de independencia," 2:303–56. Jaime del Arenal has recently defended Itur-

bide as a champion of the church; see his "Una nueva lectura del Plan de Iguala," and his "El Plan de Iguala y la salvación de la religion," 73–91. Canadian historian Timothy E. Anna has also joined those glorifying Iturbide. See his *The Mexican Empire of Iturbide*. I offer a different interpretation based on documentary evidence: *"We Are Now the True Spaniards,"* 253–67.

18. Benson, "The Contested Mexican Election of 1812," 336–50; *La Diputación Provincial*; "Spain's Contribution to Federalism in Mexico," 90–103 and *The Provincial Deputation in Mexico*. See also: Guedea, "Las primeras elecciones populares," 1–28; Annino, "Prácticas criollas y liberalismo," 121–58; Rodríguez O., "Las primeras elecciones constitucionales," Gortari Rabiela, "Los inicios del parlamentarismo," 255–84; and Rodríguez O., "Sobrehumano mortal," 12–132.

19. Virginia Guedea has written extensively on the topic; see: "Criollos y peninsulares en 1808"; "Las sociedades secretas," 45–62; "Las primeras elecciones populares"; "Los procesos electorales insurgentes," 201–49; "De la fidelidad a la infidencia," 95–123; *En busca de un gobierno alterno*; "El Pueblo de México," 27–61; and "Ignacio Adalid," 71–96. See also my *"We Are Now the True Spaniards,"* 35–194.

20. Rodríguez O., "The Transition from Colony to Nation: New Spain, 1820–1821," 97–132.

21. Rodríguez O., *"We Are Now the True Spaniards,"* 241–46.

22. Archer, "Where Did All the Royalists Go?" 24–43; "The Politization of the Army," 17–45; "Informe secreto de Francisco Sánchez de Tagle al Ayuntamiento Constitucional de México, 9 de enero de 1821," AGN: Ayuntamientos, vol. 178; "Informe de José Hipólito de Odoardo," 42–49.

23. Rodríguez O., *"We Are Now the True Spaniards,"* 241–46.

24. "Noticias importantes sobre nuestra independencia dadas por los S.S. Diputados a las Cortes de España," AGN: Gobernación, sin sección, caja 23; [Miguel Ramos Arizpe], *Carta escrito a un americano sobre la forma de gobierno que para hacer practicable la Constitución y las leyes, conviene establecer en Nueva España atendida a su actual situación*; D.U.L.A., *Idea general sobre la conducta*; and "Exposición presentada a las Cortes por los diputados de ultramar en la session de 25 de junio de 1821, sobre el estado actual de las provincias de que eran representantes, y medios convenientes para su definitiva pacificación; redactado por encargo de los mismos diputados por D. Lucas Alamán y D. José Mariano Michelena," V, Apéndice, 49–65.

25. Alamán, *Historia de México*, 5:33–34; Delgado, *España y México*, 1:54–59; and Rodríguez O., "Sobrehumano mortal."

26. *Carta escrita a un americano*, 3–4. Since the "carta" was published and probably circulated in Madrid, it is likely that it was intended for a European as well as for an American audience. Perhaps, it was another way to influence the European deputies who might be inclined to support American proposals. A second edition was published in San Sebastian at the Imprenta de Baroja in 1821. It concluded with the following "NOTE: The author of this letter permits its reprinting by anyone who wishes to reprint it in any part of the Spanish Monarchy," 16.

27. Alamán, *Historia de México*, 5:33–34; Delgado, *España y México*, 1:54–59. Rodríguez O., "Sobrehumano mortal."

28. Rodríguez O., *"We Are Now the True Spaniards,"* 253–63.

29. Iturbide, *Carrera militar y política*, 11.

30. Bustamante, "Copia de la Memoria de Iturbide con comentarios," Benson Latin American Collection, University of Texas, Austin (hereafter BLAC, UTA), Henández y Dávalos Papers, HD, 17–8.4255; Rodríguez O., *"We Are Now the True Spaniards,"* 256–60.

31. Alamán, *Historia de México*, 5:505–1; Rocafuerte, *Bosquejo ligerísimo*, 5–6.

32. Rocafuerte, *Bosquejo ligerísimo*, 41.

33. Rocafuerte, *Bosquejo ligerísimo*, 41–42. Iturbide's correspondence may be consulted in: Bustamante, *Cuadro histórico*, 3:117–63; Olagaray, *Colección de documentos*, 2:13–133.

34. Alamán, *Historia de México*, 5:150–290; Robertson, *Iturbide of Mexico*, 83–104; Rodríguez O., "La transición," 300–306.

35. Quoted in Benson, "Iturbide y los planes de Independencia," 442.

36. Rodríguez O., "Sobrehumano mortal"; Alamán, *Historia de México*, 5:300–326.

37. Soberana Junta, *Diario de las sesiones*, 3–6.

38. Quoted in Bustamante, *Cuadro histórico*, 3:334–36. Rodríguez O., "Sobrehumano mortal."

39. Soberana Junta, *Diario de las sesiones*, 9–11.

40. Lucas Alamán, *Historia de México*; Calcott, *Santa Anna*; González Pedrero, *País de un solo hombre*; and Fowler, *Santa Anna of Mexico*.

41. Virginia Guedea offers the most detailed account that we have of the origins of Mexican politics. See her *En busca de un gobierno alterno*, 71–91; "Las sociedades secretas"; "Las primeras elecciones populares"; "Los procesos electorales insurgentes,"; "De la fidelidad a la infidencia"; "El pueblo de México y la política capitalina,"; and "Ignacio Adalid."

42. Flores Caballero, *Counterrevolution*.

43. Rodríguez O., "The Origins of the 1832 Rebellion," 145–48. See also: Arrom, "Popular Politics in Mexico City," 245–68.

44. Alamán, *Historia de México*, 5:832–870; Bustamante, *Continuación*, 3:365–459; Costeloe, *La primera república*; and Macune, Jr., *El estado de México*, 127–72.

45. Rodríguez O., "The Origins of the 1832 Rebellion," 148–50; and Vázquez, "Los pronunciamientos de 1832," 170–86.

46. *Voz de la patria*, vol. 5, no. 22 (August 31, 1831), fols. 7–8; and *Voz de la patria*, vol. 5, suplemento no. 14 (October 18, 1831), fols. 1–8.

47. Carlos María de Bustamante, Diario histórico, vol. 19 (November 4, 1831), fol. 230, Biblioteca Pública de Zacatecas; Rocafuerte, *Observaciones*. Richard Pakenham to Henry Palmerston, Mexico City, October 6 1831, Public Record Office, Foreign Office Papers, 50/56, fols. 224–26.

48. Bustamante, Diario histórico, vol. 19 (November 30, 1831), fols. 245–46; Anthony Butler to Livinston, Mexico City, November 23, 1831, National Archives, Washington, D.C., Dispatches from United States Ministers to Mexico (hereafter NA: DUSMM); Rocafuerte, *A la nación*, 304–6; Un Español, *Dos años en México*, 110; *El Fénix de la libertad*, vol. 1, no. 1 (December 7, 1831), 1.

49. Rocafuerte, *Consideraciones generales*; Bustamante, Diario histórico, vol. 19 (December 16, 1831), fols. 299–308; *El Fénix de la libertad*, vol. 1, no. 6 (December 24, 1831), 28; *El Fénix de la libertad*, vol. 1, no. 9 (January 4, 1832), 40; *El Fénix de la libertad*, vol. 1, no. 10 (January 7, 1832), 43–44. Butler to Livingston, Mexico City, December 6, 1831, NA: DUSMM; and Andrés Quintana Roo to [Valentín Gómez Farías, México City], July 13 1832, GF 67 fol. 44A, Gómez Farías Papers, BLAC, UTA. Chust, "Armed Citizens," 235–52.

50. Rodríguez O., "The Origins of the 1832 Rebellion," 150–55. Fowler ignores the role of the political opponents of Bustamante and focus entirely on his hero *Santa Anna of Mexico*, 133–43.

51. Antonio López de Santa Anna to Anastasio Bustamante, Veracruz, January 4, 1832 (letters 1 & 2); Bustamante to Santa Anna, Mexico City, January 12, 1832; and Santa Anna to Bustamante, Veracruz, January 25, 1832, Mariano Riva Palacio Papers, BLAC, UTA; and *El Fénix de la libertad*, vol. 1, no. 19 (February 8, 1832), 82–84.

52. *El Fénix de la libertad*, vol. 1, no. 27 (March 7, 1832), 117; *El Fénix de la libertad*, vol. 1 through no. 28 (March 17, 1832), vol. 1, no. 9–40; Bustamante, Diario histórico, vol. 20 (March 11, 1832), fol. 100; and (May 25, 1832), fol.

223; *El Duende,* vol. 1, no. 16 (April 17, 1832), fol. 64; *El Duende,* vol. 1, no. 31 (April 27, 1832), 124. See also: Vázquez, "Los pronunciamientos de 1832," 163–86.

53. *El Fénix de la libertad,* vol. 1, no. 57 (June 20, 1832), fol. 239; *El Fénix de la libertad,* vol. 1, no. 67 (July 21, 1832), 278; *El Fénix de la libertad,* vol. 1, no. 72 (August 1, 1832), 299; *El Fénix de la libertad,* vol. 2, no. 16 (January 13 1833), 4; Bustamante, Diario histórico, vol. 21 (September 25, 1832), fol. 205; Bustamante, Diario histórico vol. 21 (October 12, 1832), fols. 300–301. "Convenio de armisticia entre las fuerzas del General Antonio López de Santa Anna y del General Anastasio Bustamante," December 11, 1832, Instituto Nacional de Antropología e Historia, Colección Bustamante, vol. 26, fols. 198–99; Manuel Gómez Pedraza a Gómez Farías, Puebla, December 1, 1832, GF 85, fol. 44A, Gómez Farías Papers, BLAC, UTA. Rodríguez O., "The Origins of the 1832 Rebellion," 156–67; Vázquez, "Los pronunciamientos de 1832," 182–86.

8. NEW DIRECTIONS

1. Becker, *The Heavenly City,* 29.
2. Weinberg, "The Revolution that Didn't Happen," 49.
3. Bloor, *Knowledge and Social Imagery,* 37; and Bloor, "The Strength of the Strong Programme," 199–213.
4. Novick, *That Noble Dream,* 415–68.
5. Windschuttle, *The Killing of History,* 2.
6. Skinner, *The Return of Grand Theory.*
7. Novick, *That Noble Dream.*
8. Scott, *Gender and the Politics of History,* 4.
9. Greenblatt, *New World Encounters.* He also published *Marvelous Possessions: The Wonder of the New World.*
10. Alamán, *Historia de México.*
11. Benson, "The Contested Mexican Election of 1812," 336–50.
12. Benson, *La Diputación Provincial.* An English edition appeared later: *The Provincial Deputation of Mexico: Harbinger of Provincial Autonomy, Independence and Federalism.*
13. Benson, *La Diputación Provincial,* 9.
14. See, for example, Benson, "Spain's Contribution to Federalism in Mexico," 90–103.
15. Benson, *Mexico and the Spanish Cortes.*
16. As her student I examined the 1808–1822 period but only as the introduction of my first book, *The Emergence of Spanish America,* which focused on

the next three decades. In February 1987 I invited to a conference the leading experts on the independence and early national periods. Naturally, Nettie Lee Benson was invited. The conference resulted in a volume entitled: *The Independence of Mexico and the Creating of the New Nation.*

17. Hale, *Mexican Liberalism.*

18. Joseph, "On the Trail," 293–336. Although presented initially at the University of California, Irvine symposium the essay also appeared in the *Latin American Research Review* 25:3 (1990), 7–53.

19. The most important of the volumes Joseph has coordinated include: Joseph and Nugent, *Everyday Forms of State Formation*; Salvatore, Aguirre and Joseph, *Crime and Punishment*; and Joseph, *Reclaiming the Political.* John Womack's review appeared in the *Hispanic American Historical Review* 83:2 (May 2003), 374–75.

20. Mallon, "The Promise and Dilemma," 1491–1493.

21. Mallon, *Peasant and Nation.*

22. Weinberg, "The Revolution that Didn't Happen," 49.

23. Dysen, "Clockwork Science," 42–44.

24. Sokal and Bricmont, *Fashionable Nonsense*, 1–2.

25. Sokal and Bricmont, *Fashionable Nonsense.*

26. Himmelfarb, *The New History and the Old*, 18–28.

27. Appleby, Hunt and Jacob, *Telling the Truth About History.*

28. Knight, "Subalterns, Signifiers, and Statistics," 136–58.

29. Haber, "The Worst of Both Worlds," 363–83.

30. *Hispanic American Historical Review* 79:2 (1999).

31. Rivera-Garza, "'She Neither Respected nor Obeyed Anyone,'" 656–688.

32. Peter F. Guardino's studies are excellent examples of this new work: *Peasants, Politics, and the Formation of Mexico's National State. Guerrero, 1800–1857* and *The Time of Liberty: Political Culture in Oaxaca, 1750–1850.*

BIBLIOGRAPHY

MANUSCRIPTS AND ARCHIVES

Ecuador
Archivo Nacional de Historia, Quito
    Presidencia de Quito
    Gobierno
Archivo Municipal de Quito
    Actas del Consejo
Archivo Histórico del Banco Central del Ecuador, Quito
    Fondo Jijón y Caamaño
Archivo de la Biblioteca Municipal de Guayaquil
    Actas del Cabildo Colonial de Guayaquil, 1807–1810
Mexico
Archivo General de la Nación, Mexico City
    Ayuntamientos
Biblioteca Pública de Zacatecas
    Carlos María de Bustamante *Diario histórico*
Instituto Nacional de Antropología e Historia, Mexico City
    Colección Bustamante
Spain
Archivo General de Indias, Seville
    Indiferente
    Estado
    Mexico
    Quito
United Kingdom
National Archives, London
    Foreign Office Papers
United States
Benson Latin American Collection, University of Texas, Austin
    Mariano Riva Palacio Papers
    Valentín Gómez Farías Papers
Library of Congress, Washington, DC

Agustín de Iturbide Papers
National Archives, Washington, DC
Dispatches from United States Ministers to Mexico

PUBLISHED WORKS

"Acusación del Fiscal Tomás de Aréchaga, en la causa seguida contra los Patriotas del 10 de Agosto de 1809." *Museo Histórico* 6, no. 19 (marzo de 1954): 37–65.

Adams, John. *The Works of John Adams*. Vol. 10. Boston: Little, Brown, 1850–1856.

Alamán, Lucas. *Disertaciones sobre la historia de la República Megicana*. 3 vols. Mexico City: Editorial Jus, 1942.

Alamán, Lucas, Historia de México desde los primeros movimientos que prepararon su Independencia en el año de 1808 hasta la época presente. Vol. 5 Mexico City: Fondo de Cultura de Económica,1985.

Albornoz Peralta, Oswaldo. *Páginas de la historia ecuatoriana*. Quito: Casa de Cultura Ecuatoriana, 2008.

Alcalá Galiano, Antonio. *Recuerdos de un anciano*. Madrid: Ediciones Atlas, 1955.

Alcedo y Bexarano, Antonio de. *Diccionario geográfico de las Indias Occidentales o América: es á saber, de los reynos del Perú, Nueva España, Tierra Firme, Chile y Nuevo Reyno de Grenada*. 5 vols. Madrid: Imprenta de Benito Cano, 1786–1789.

Alden, John R. *The American Revolution*. New York: Harper, 1954.

Almarza Villaloboa, Angel Rafael, and Armando Martínez Garnica, eds. *Instrucciones para los diputados del Nuevo Reino de Granada y Venezuela ante la Junta Central Gubernativa de España y las Indias*. Bucaramanga: Universidad Industrial de Santander, 2008.

Almer, Carl T. "'La confianza que han puesto en mí:' Participación local en el establecimiento de los ayuntamientos constitucionales en Venezuela." In *Revolución, independencia y las nuevas naciones de América*, edited by Jaime E. Rodríguez O., 365–95. Madrid: Fundación MAPFRE/TAVERA, 2005.

———. "The Spanish Constitution in the Eastern Provinces of Venezuela." Unpublished essay, Irvine (July 26, 2006).

Altamira, Rafael. *Historia de España y de la civilización española*. 4 vols. Barcelona: J. Gili, 1900–1911.

Alvarez, Francisco. *Noticia del establecimiento y población de las colonias inglesas en la América Septentrional: Religión, orden de gobierno, leyes y costumbres de sus naturales y habitantes; calidades de su clima, terreno, frutos, plantas y animales; y estado de su industria, artes, comercio y navegación: sacada de varios autores.* Madrid: En la oficina de Antonio Fernández, 1778.

Andrade, Roberto. *Historia del Ecuador.* 7 vols. Guayaquil: Editores Reed & Reed, n.d.

Andrien, Kenneth J. "Economic Crisis, Taxes and the Quito Insurrection of 1765." *Past and Present* 129 (November 1990): 104–20.

———. *The Kingdom of Quito, 1690–1830: The State and Regional Development.* Cambridge: Cambridge University Press, 1995.

Anna, Timothy E. *The Fall of Royal Government in Peru.* Lincoln: University of Nebraska Press, 1979.

———. *The Mexican Empire of Iturbide.* Lincoln: University of Nebraska Press, 1990.

Annino, Antonio. "Comentario." In *Le Nouveau Monde, Mondes Nouveaux: L'expérience américaine,* edited by Serge Gruzinski and Nathan Wachtel, 445–56. Paris: Editions Recherche sur les Civilisations and Editions de l'Ecole des Hautes Etudes en Sciences Sociales, 1996.

———. "Prácticas criollas y liberalismo en la crisis del espacio urbano colonial. El 29 de noviembre de 1812 en la ciudad de México." *Secuencia* 24 (September-December 1992): 121–58.

Anonymous. *A view of the history of Great-Britain, during the administration of Lord North, to the second session of the fifteenth parliament. In two parts.* Dublin: P. Byrne, 1782.

Anonymous. *Histoire de l'administration de Lord North . . . et de la guerre de l'Amérique Septentrionale jusqu'a la paix: suivie du tableau historique des finances d'Angleterre depuis Guillaume III jusqu'en 1784.* Paris: Chez l'auteur, 1784.

Anonymous. *Historia de la administración del Lord North, Primer Ministro de Inglaterra, y de la Guerra de la América Septentrional hasta la paz. Obra escrita en inglés, traducida al francés, y de este al castellano.* Madrid: La Imprenta Real, 1806.

Appleby, Joyce, Lynn Hunt, and Margaret Jacob. *Telling the Truth About History.* New York: W. W. Norton, 1994.

Archer, Christon I. "Where Did All the Royalists Go? New Light on the Military Collapse of New Spain, 1810–1821." In *The Mexican and Mexican Amer-*

ican Experience in the 19th Century, edited by Jaime E. Rodríguez O., 24–43. Tempe: Bilingual, 1989.

————. "The Politization of the Army of New Spain during the War of Independence, 1810–1821." In *The Evolution of the Mexican Political System* edited by Jaime E. Rodríguez O., 17–45. Wilmington: SR Books, 1993.

————. "Reflexiones de una edad de guerra total: El impacto de la defensa marítima de Nueva España en la época revolucionaria, 1789 a 1810." In *Por la fuerza de las armas. Ejército e independencias en España e Hispanoamerica (1750–1850),* edited by Manuel Chust and Juan Marchena, 239–75. Castelló de la Plana, Spain: Universitat Jaume I, 2008.

Arenal, Jaime del. "Una nueva lectura del Plan de Iguala." *Revista de Investigaciones Jurídicas* 18, no. 18 (1994).

————. "El Plan de Iguala y la salvación de la religión y de la Iglesia novohispana dentro de un orden constitucional." In *Historia de la iglesia en el siglo XIX* by Miguel Ramos Medina, 73–91. Mexico City: Centro de Estudios de Historia de México Condumex, 1998.

Argüedas, Alcides. *Los caudillos bárbaros.* Barcelona: Viuda de L. Tasso, 1929.

————. *Los caudillos letrados.* Barcelona: Viuda de L. Tasso, 1923.

Armitage, David. *The Declaration of Independence: A Global History.* Cambridge: Harvard University Press, 2007.

Arrom, Silvia. "Popular Politics in Mexico City: The Parian Riot, 1828." *Hispanic American Historical Review* 68 (May 1988): 245–68.

Artaza, Manuel María de. *Rey, reino y representación: La Junta General del Reino de Galicia.* Madrid: Consejo Superior de Investigaciones Científicas, 1998.

Artola, Miguel. *La España de Fernando VII.* Madrid: Espasa-Calpe, 1968.

Astuto, Philip Luis. *Eugenio Espejo. Reformador ecutoriana de la ilustración (1747–1795).* Mexico City: Fondo de Cultura Económica, 1969.

Avendaño Rojas, Xiomara. *Centroamérica entre lo antiguo y lo moderno: Institucionalidad, ciudadanía y representación política, 1810–1838.* Castelló de la Plana, Spain: Universitat Jaume I, 2009.

Bayle, Constantino. *El protector de indios.* Seville: Escuela de Estudios Hispano-Americanos, 1945.

Becker, Carl L. *The Heavenly City of the Eighteenth-Century Philosophers.* New Haven: Yale University Press, 1932.

Belenguer, Ernest. *El imperio hispánico, 1479–1665.* Barcelona: Grijalbo Mondari, 1994.

Benson, Nettie Lee. "The Contested Mexican Election of 1812." *Hispanic American Historical Review* 26, no. 3 (August 1946): 336–50.

———. *La Diputación Provincial y el federalismo mexicano.* Mexico City: El Colegio de México, 1955.

———. "The Elections of 1809: Transforming Political Culture in New Spain." *Mexican Studies/Estudios Mexicanos* 20, no 1 (Winter 2004): 1–20.

———. "Iturbide y los planes de Independencia." *Historia Mexicana* 2, no. 3 (enero-marzo 1953): 442.

———. *The Provincial Deputation in Mexico: Harbinger of Provincial Autonomy, Independence, and Federalism.* Austin: University of Texas Press, 1992.

———. "Spain's Contribution to Federalism in Mexico." In *Essays in Mexican History*, edited by Thomas E. Cotner and Carlos Castañeda, 90–103. Austin: University of Texas Press, 1958.

———. "Territorial Integrity in Mexican Politics, 1821–1833." In *The Independence of Mexico and the Creating of the New Nation*, edited by Jaime E. Rodríguez O., 275–307. Los Angeles: UCLA Latin American Center Publications, 1989.

Bernstein, Richard B, *Thomas Jefferson.* New York: Oxford University Press, 2003.

Berry, Charles R. "The Election of the Mexican Deputies to the Spanish Cortes, 1810–1822." In *Mexico and the Spanish Cortes, 1810–1822*, edited by Nettie Lee Benson, 10–16. Austin: University of Texas Press, 1966.

Betancourt, José Ramón. "Orígenes españoles del régimen autonómico." *Boletín de la Institución Libre de Enseñanza* 7, no. 164 (diciembre 1983): 360–62.

Blanco Valdéz, Roberto L. "Paisanos y soldados en los orígenes de la España liberal: Sobre revoluciones sociales, golpes de estado y pronunciamientos militares." In *Las nuevas naciones: España y México, 1800–1850*, edited by Jaime E. Rodríguez O., 173–292. Madrid: Fundación MAPFRE, 2008.

Bloor, David. *Knowledge and Social Imagery.* London: Routledge, 1976.

———. "The Strength of the Strong Programme." *Philosophy of the Social Sciences* 11 (1981): 199–213.

Blythe, James M. *Ideal Government and the Mixed Constitution in the Middle Ages.* Princeton: Princeton University Press, 1992.

Bonnett, Diana. *El protector de naturales en la Audiencia de Quito, siglos VII y XVIII.* Quito: ABYA-YALA, 1992.

Borah, Woodrow. *Justice by Insurance: The General Indian Court of Colonial Mexico and the Legal Aides of the Half-Real*. Berkeley: University of California Press, 1983.

Borchard de Moreno, Cristiana. *La Audiencia de Quito: Aspectos económicos y sociales (siglos XVI-XVIII)*. Quito: Banco Central del Ecuador y ABYA YALA, 1998.

Borja y Borja, Ramiro, ed. "Pacto Solemne de Sociedad y Unión entre las Provincias que Forman el Estado de Quito." In *Derecho constitucional ecuatoriano*. 3 vols. 3: 9–23. Madrid: Ediciones de Cultura Hispánica, 1950.

Borrero, Manuel María. *La Revolución quiteña, 1809–1812*. Quito: Editorial Espejo, 1962.

Brading, David. *The First America: The Spanish Monarchy, Creole Patriots and the Liberal State, 1492–1867*. Cambridge: Cambridge University Press, 1991.

Brett, Annabel S. *Liberty, Right and Nature: Individual Rights in Later Scholastic Thought*. Cambridge: Cambridge University Press, 1997.

Brown, Roger H. *Redeeming the Republic: Federalists, Taxation, and the Origins of the Constitution*. Baltimore: Johns Hopkins University Press, 1993.

Bruchey, Stuart. *The Roots of American Economic Growth, 1607–1861*. New York: Harper & Row, 1965.

Büchges, Christian. *Familia, honor y poder. La nobleza de la ciudad de Quito en la época colonial tardía (1765–1822)*. Quito: FONSAL Quito, 2007.

Bunge, Carlos O. *Nuestra América: Ensayo de psicología social*. 6a ed. Buenos Aires: Casa Vacarro, 1918.

Burkholder, Mark A. and Lyman L. Johnson. *Colonial Latin America*. 2nd ed. New York: Oxford University Press, 1994.

———. "Spain's America: From Kingdoms to Colonies." *Colonial Latin American Review* 25, no. 2 (2016): 1–29.

Bustamante, Carlos María de. *Continuación del cuadro histórico de la revolución mexicana*. 4 vols. Mexico City: Biblioteca Nacional & Instituto Nacional de Antropología e Historia, 1953–1963.

———. *Cuadro histórico de la revolución mexicana*. 3 vols. Mexico City: Cámara de Diputados, 1961.

———. "Diario de lo especialmente ocurido en México (12 de abril de 1830)." In *Diario histórico de México, 1822–1848*, edited by Josefina Zoraida Vázquez and Héctor Cuauhtémoc Hernández Silva. Mexico City: COLMEX/CIESAS, 2001. CD-ROM.

Butel-Dumont, George Marie. *Historia del establecimiento y comercio de las colonias inglesas en la América Septentrional: En que se da noticia del estado actual*

de su población, y algunas relaciones individuales y curiosas, acerca de la consti-
tución de su gobierno, principalmente de la Nueva Inglaterra, de la Pensilvania,
de la Carolina, y de la Georgia. Madrid: Joaquín Ibarra, 1768.

Calcott, Wilfred H. *Santa Anna: The Story of an Enigma Who Once Was Mexico.*
Norman: University of Oklahoma Press, 1936.

Cañedo, Juan de Dios. *Manifiesto a la nación española, sobre la representación de*
las provincias de ultramar en las próximas Cortes. Madrid: Imprenta de Vega,
1820.

Cañizarez-Esguerra, Jorge. *How to Write the History of the New World.* Stanford: Stanford University Press, 2001.

Canny, Nicolas P. "The Ideology of English Colonization: From Ireland to
America." *William and Mary Quarterly* 30, no. 4 (1973): 575–98.

Caplan, Karen D. "The Legal Revolution in Town Politics: Oaxaca and
Yucatán, 1812–1825." *Hispanic American Historical Review* 83, no. 2 (2003):
255–93.

Carbajal, B. Manuel. "Tesis de Filosofía." In *Pensamiento ilustrado,* edited by
Carlos Paladines Escudero, 139–56. Quito: Banco Central del Ecuador, 1981.

Cardozo Galué, Germán. *Michoacán en el siglo de las luces.* Mexico City: El
Colegio de México, 1973.

Carr, Raymond. *Spain, 1808–1975.* 2nd ed. Oxford: Clarendon Press, 1982.

Cartledge, Paul. "Greek Political Thought: The Historical Context." In *The*
Cambridge History of Greek and Roman Political Thought, edited by Christo-
pher Rowe, Malcolm Schofield, with Simon Harrison, Melissa Lane, 7-22.
Cambridge: Cambridge University Press, 2000.

Casariego, Jesús E. *El municipio y las Cortes en el Imperio español de Indias.*
Madrid: Talleres Gráficos Marsiega, 1946.

Castro Gutierrez, Felipe. *Movimientos populares en Nueva España: Michoacán,*
1766–1767. Mexico City: UNAM, 1990.

Céspedes del Castillo, Guillermo. *Lima y Buenos Aires: Repercusiones económi-*
cas y políticas de la creación del virreynato del Río de la Plata. Seville: Escuela
de Estudios Hispanoamericanos, 1949.

Chacón Zhapán, Juan. *Historia del Corregimiento de Cuenca.* Quito: Banco del
Ecuador, 1990.

———, coord. *Libro de Cabildos de Cuenca (1806–1810).* 2 vols. Cuenca:
Banco Central del Ecuador, 1991.

Chapman, Charles E. "The Age of the Caudillos: A Chapter in Hispanic American History." *Hispanic American Historical Review* 12, no. 3 (August 1932):
281–300.

Chartrand, René and Francis Back. *The French Army in the American War of Independence*. Boston: Gregg Press, 1972.

Chávez, Thomas E. *Spain and the Independence of the United States*. Albuquerque: University of New Mexico Press, 2002.

Chevalier, Francois. "Caudilles et caciques en Amerique. Contribution a l'étude de liens personnels." *Mélange offerts á Marcel Bataillon par les Hispanistes Francais* número especial de *Bulletin Hispanique* 64 (1962): 30–47.

Chiaramonte, José Carlos, "Fundamentos iusnaturalistas de los movimientos de independencia." Edited by Marta Terán & José Antonio Serrano Ortega, *Las guerras de independencia en la América Española*. Zamora: El Colegio de Michoacán, 2002, 99-122.

Chust, Manuel, ed. *1808: La eclosión juntera en el mundo hispano*. Mexico City: Fondo de Cultura Económica, 2007.

———. "Armed Citizens: The Civic Militia in the Origins of the Mexican National State, 1812–1827." In *The Divine Charter: Colonialism and Liberalism in Nineteenth-Century Mexico*, edited by Jaime E. Rodríguez O., 235–52. Boulder: Rowman & Littlefield, 2005.

Comellas, José Luis. *Los primeros pronunciamientos en España*. Madrid: Consejo Superior de Investigaciones Científicas, 1958.

Condamine, Charles Marie de la. *Diario del viaje al Ecuador*. Quito: EDIGUIAS C. LTDA, 1992.

"Confesión del Dr. Manuel Rodríguez de Quiroga, Abogado de esta Real Audiencia." *Museo Histórico* 2, núm. 5 (May 24, 1950): 18–40.

"Constitución política de la Monarquía Española." In *Leyes fundamentales de México, decimosexta edición*, edited by Felipe Tena Ramirez, 64–72. Mexico City: Editorial Porrúa, 1991.

Coronel Feijóo, Rosario. "La contra-revolución de Riobamba frente a la primera Junta de Quito de 1809." In *La independencia en los países andinos: Nuevas perspectivas*, edited by Guillermo Bustos and Armando Martínez Garnica, 105–11. Quito: Universidad Andina Simón Bolívar, 2004.

———. "Poder local en la transición de la colonia a la república: Riobamba, 1750–1820." PhD diss., Universidad Andina Simón Bolívar [Quito], 2009.

Cortes. *Colección de decretos y órdenes de las Cortes de Cádiz*. 2 vols. Madrid: Cortes Generales, 1987.

Costeloe, Michael P. *La primera república federal de México, 1824–1835*. Mexico City: Fondo de Culture Económica, 1975.

Covarruvias, José de. *Memorias históricas de la última guerra con la Gran Bretaña, desde el año de 1774: Estados Unidos de América.* Madrid: Imprenta de Antonio Ramírez, 1783.

Cushner, Nicholas P. *Farm and Factory: The Jesuits and the Development of Agrarian Capitalism in Colonial Quito, 1600–1767.* Albany: State University of New York Press, 1982.

Cutter, Charles R. *The Protector of Indians in Colonial New Mexico, 1659–1682.* Albuquerque: University of New Mexico Press, 1986.

"De los procesos seguidos contra los Patriotas del 10 de Agosto de 1809: Confesión del doctor don Juan Pablo Arenas, abogado de la Real Audiencia." *Museo Histórico* 2, núm 6 (August 10, 1950): 30–38.

Dealy, Glen C. *The Public Man: An Interpretation of Latin American and Other Catholic Countries.* Amherst: University of Massachusetts Press, 1977.

Deidán de la Torre, Ahmed. "Sovereignty and People: Conceptual Continuity and Rupture in the Kingdom of Quito 1809–1813." Honors Thesis, University of California, Los Angeles, 2014.

Delgado, Jaime. *España y México en el siglo XIX.* 3 vols. Madrid: Consejo Superior de Investigaciones Científicas, 1950.

Demélas-Bohy, Marie-Danielle. "Microcosmos. Une dispute municipale à Loja (1813–1824)." *Bulletin de l'Institut Français d'Études Andines* 13, núms. 3–4 (1984): 65–76.

———. "Modalidades y significación de elecciones generales en los pueblos andinos, 1813–1814." In *Historia de las elecciones en Iberoamérica, siglo XIX,* edited by Antonio Annino, 291–13. Buenos Aires: Fondo de Cultura Económica, 1995.

Díaz Díaz, Fernando. *Caudillos y caciques: Antonio López de Santa Anna y Juan Alvarez.* Mexico City: El Colegio de México, 1972.

Dios, Salustiano de. "Corporación y nación. De las Cortes de Castilla and las Cortes de España. In *De la Ilustración al Liberalismo,* edited by P. Cappellini, G. Cazetta, B. Clavero, P. Costa, S. De Dios, B. González Alaonzo, A. M. Hespanha, P. Grossi, C. Petit, A. Romano and F. Tomás y Valiente, 198–298. Madrid: Centro de Estudios Constitucionales, 1995.

Draper, Theodor. *A Struggle for Power: The American Revolution.* New York: Random House, 1996.

Ducey, Michael. "Village, Nation and Constitution: Insurgent Politics in Papantla, Veracruz, 1810–1821." *Hispanic American Historical Review* 79, no. 3 (August 1999): 463–49.

D.U.L.A. *Idea general de la conducta política de D. Miguel Ramos Arizpe, natural de la provincia de Coahuila, como diputado que ha sido por esta provincia en las Cortes generales y extraordinarias de la monarchía española desde el año de 1810 hasta el de 1821.* Madrid: Imprenta de Herculana de Villa, 1822.

Dull, Jonathan R. *The French Navy and American Independence: A Study of Arms and Diplomacy, 1774–1787.* Princeton: Princeton University Press, 1975.

Dym, Jordana. *From Sovereign Villages to National States: City, State, and Federation in Central America, 1759–1839.* Albuquerque: University of New Mexico Press, 2006.

———. "La soberanía de los pueblos: ciudad e independencia en Centroamérica, 1808–1823." In *Revolución, independencia y las nuevas naciones,* edited by Jaime E. Rodríguez O., 309–37. Madrid: Fundación Mapfre-Tavera, 2005.

Dysen, Freeman. "Clockwork Science." *New York Review of Books* 40, no. 17 (November 6, 2003): 42–44.

Eccles, W. J. *France in America.* Revised edition. Markham, Ontario: Fitzhenry & Whiteside, 1990.

"El Ilmo. Cuero y Caicedo Obispo de Quito en el Proceso contra los patriotas del 10 de Agosto de 1809." *Museo Histórico* 5, núm. 18 (diciembre 1953): 16–32.

Elliott, John H. "Empire and State in British and Spanish America." In *Le Nouveau Monde, Mondes Nouveaux: L'expérience américaine,* edited by Serge Gruzinski and Nathan Wachtel, 365–82. Paris: Editions Recherche sur les Civilisations and Editions de l'Ecole des Hautes Etudes en Sciences Sociales, 1996.

———. "A Europe of Composite Monarchies." *Past and Present* 137 (1992): 52–69.

Escobar Ohmstede, Antonio. "Del gobierno indígena al ayuntamiento constitucional en las Huastecas hidalguense y veracruzana, 1780–1853." *Mexican Studies/Estudios Mexicanos* 12, no. 1 (Winter 1996): 1–26.

"Estatuto de la Real Universidad de Santo Tomás de la Ciudad de Quito: 26 de octubre de 1788." In *Pensamiento universitario ecuatoriano,* edited by Hernán Malo G., 93–159. Quito: Banco Central del Ecuador & Corporación Editora Nacional, n.d.

Estupiñan Viteri, Tamara. *El mercado interno de la Audiencia de Quito.* Quito: Banco Central del Ecuador, 1997.

Fehrenbach, Charles W. "A Study of Spanish Liberalism: The Revolution of 1820." PhD diss., University of Texas, Austin, 1961.

Fernández Albaladejo, Pablo. "Católicos antes que ciudadanos: Gestación de una 'política española' en los comienzos de la edad moderna." In *La imágen de la diversidad: El mundo urbano en la corona de Castilla (siglos xvi-xvii)*. Santander: Universidad de Cantabria, 1997.

Fernández Martínez, Montserrat. *La alcabala en la Audiencia de Quito*. Cuenca: Casa de Cultura Ecuatoriana, 1984.

Fick, Carolyn E. *The Making of Haiti: The Saint Domingue Revolution from Below*. Knoxville: University of Tennessee Press, 1990.

Fiehrer, Thomas Marc. "The Baron de Carondelet as Agent of Bourbon Reform: A Study of Spanish Colonial Administration in the Years of the French Revolution." 2 vols. PhD diss., Tulane University, 1977.

Fields, W. Eugene. *King and Church: The Rise and Fall of Patronato Real*. Chicago: Loyola University Press, 1961.

Flores Caballero, Romeo. *La contrarrevolución en la independencia: Los españoles en la vida política, social y económica de México (1804–1838)*. Mexico City: El Colegio de México, 1969.

———. *Counterrevolution: The Role of Spaniards in the Independence of Mexico, 1804–1838*. Lincoln: University of Nebraska Press, 1974.

Flower, Harriet I. *Roman Republics*. Princeton: Princeton University Press, 2009.

Forment, Carlos A. *Democracy in Latin America, 1700–1900: Civic Selfhood and Public Life in Mexico and Peru*. Chicago: University of Chicago Press, 2003.

Fowler, Will. *Santa Anna of Mexico*. Lincoln: University of Nebraska Press, 2007.

Frasquet Miguel, Ivana. *Las caras del águila: Del liberalismo gaditano a la república federal mexicana (1820–1824)*. Castelló de la Plana, Spain: Universitat Jaume I, 2008.

Frost, Alan. "The Spanish Yoke: British Schemes to Revolutionize Spanish America, 1739–1807." In *Pacific Empires: Essays in Honor of Glynwr Williams*, edited by Alan Frost and Jane Samson, 33–52. Melbourne: Melbourne University Press, 1999.

García, Genaro, comp. *Documentos históricos mexicanos*. 7 vols. Mexico City: Museo Nacional de Antropología, Historia y Etnología, 1910.

García Melero, Luis Angel. *La independencia de los Estados Unidos de Norte América a través de la prensa española*. Madrid: Ministerio de Asuntos Exteriores, 1977.

García de Sena, Manuel. *Historia de los Estados Unidos desde el descubrimiento de la América hasta el año de 1807*. Philadelphia: T. & J. Palmer, 1812.

————. *La independencia de la Costa Firme justificada por Thomas Paine treinta años ha. Extracto de sus obras, traducido del inglés al español por D. Manuel García de Sena*. Philadelphia: T. & J. Palmer, 1811.

Garrido, Margarita. *Reclamos y representaciones: Variaciones sobre la política en el Nuevo Reino de Granada, 1770–1815*. Bogotá: Banco de la República, 1993.

Gibson, Charles. *The Aztecs Under Spanish Rule: A History of the Indians of the Valley of Mexico, 1519–1810*. Stanford: Stanford University Press, 1964.

Gilmore, Robert L. "The Imperial Crisis, Rebellion, and the Viceroy: Nueva Granada in 1809." *Hispanic American Historical Review* 40, no. 1 (February 1960): 8–9.

Gil Novales, Antonio, ed. *Rafael Riego: La Revolución de 1820, día a día*. Madrid: Editorial Tecnos, 1976.

Giménez Fernández, Manuel. "Hernán Cortés y su revolución comunera en la Nueva España." *Anuario de Estudios Americanos* 5 (1948): 1–144.

Gómez Vizuete, Antonio. "Los primeros ayuntamientos liberales en Puerto Rico (1812–1823)." *Anuario de Estudios Americanos* 47 (1990): 581–615.

Góngora, Mario. *El estado en el derecho indiano*. Santiago: Universidad de Chile, 1951.

González, María del Refugio, ed. *Historia del derecho mexicano*. 2nd ed. Mexico City: McGraw Hill/UNAM, 1997.

————. *Título décimo quinto. De los jueces y diputados de los reales de minas, ordenanzas de la minería de la Nueva España formadas y propuestas por su real tribunal*. Mexico City: UNAM, 1996.

González Antón, Luis. *Las Cortes en la España del Antiguo Régimen*. Madrid: Siglo XXI, 1989.

González Pedrero, Enrique. *País de un solo hombre: El México de Santa Anna*. Mexico City: Fondo de Cultura Económica, 1993.

González Suárez, Federico. *Historia general de la República del Ecuador*. 3 vols. Quito: Casa de la Cultura Ecuatoriana, 1970.

Gortari Rabiela, Hira de. "Los inicios del parlamentarismo. La Diputación Provincial de Nueva España y México, 1820–1824." In *La independencia de México y el proceso autonomista novohispano 1808–1824*, edited by Virginia Guedea, 255–84. Mexico City: UNAM, 2001.

Graces, Pedro, and Alberto Harkness. *Manuel García de Sena y la independencia de Hispanoamérica*. Caracas: Publicaciones de la Secretaría General de la Décima Conferencia Interamericana, 1953.

Greenblatt, Stephen. *Marvelous Possessions: The Wonder of the New World*. Oxford: Clarendon Press, 1991.

————, ed. *New World Encounters.* Berkeley: University of California Press, 1993.

Greene, Jack P. "The American Revolution." *American Historical Review* vol. 105, 1 (February 2000), 93–102.

————. *Understanding the American Revolution.* Charlottesville: University Press of Virginia, 1995.

Greenglass, Mark, ed. *Conquest and Coalescence: The Shaping of the State in Early Modern Europe.* New York: Routledge, Chapman & Hall, 1991.

Guardia Herrero, Carmen de la. "Revolución Americana y el primer parlamentarismo español." *Revista de Estudios Políticos* 93 (July-Sept. 1996): 205–18.

Guardino, Peter. *Peasants, Politics, and the Formation of Mexico's National State: Guerrero, 1800–1857.* Stanford: Stanford University Press, 1996.

————. *The Time of Liberty: Popular Political Culture in Oaxaca, 1750–1850.* Durham: Duke University Press, 2005.

————. "'Toda libertad para emitir sus votos': Plebeyos, campesinos, y elecciones en Oaxaca, 1808–1850." *Cuadernos del Sur* 6, núm. 15 (June 2000): 87–114.

Guarisco, Claudia. *Los indios del valle de México y la construcción de una nueva sociabilidad política, 1770–1835.* Toluca: El Colegio Mexiquense, 2003.

Guedea, Virginia. "Autonomía e independencia en la Provincia de Texas. La Junta de Gobierno de San Antonio de Béjar, 1813." In *La independencia de México y el proceso autonomista novohispano, 1808–1824,* edited by Virginia Guedea, 152–64. Mexico City: UNAM, 2001.

————. "Criollos y peninsulares en 1808: Dos puntos de vista sobre lo español." Tesis de licenciatura, Universidad Iberoamericana, 1964.

————. "De la fidelidad a la infidencia: Los gobernadores de la parcialidad de San Juan." In *Patterns of Contention in Mexican History,* edited by Jaime E. Rodríguez O., 95–123. Wilmington: SR Books, 1992.

————. *En busca de un gobierno alterno: Los Guadalupes de México.* Mexico City: UNAM, 1992, 233–315.

————. "The First Popular Elections in Mexico City, 1812–1823." In *The Origins of Mexican National Politics, 1808–1847,* edited by Jaime E. Rodríguez O., 39–63. Wilmington: SR Books, 1997.

————. "Los Guadalupes de México." *Relaciones: Estudios de Historia y Sociedad* no. 23 (1985): 71–91.

————. "Ignacio Adalid, un *equilibrista* novohispano." In *Mexico in the Age of Democratic Revolution, 1750–1850,* edited by Jaime E. Rodríguez O., 71–96. Boulder: Lynne Rienner Publishers, 1994.

———. "Las primeras elecciones populares en la ciudad de México, 1812–1813." *Mexican Studies/Estudios Mexicanos* 7, no. 1 (Winter 1991): 1–28.

———. "Los procesos electorales insurgentes." *Estudios de Historia Novohispana* no. 11 (1992): 201–49.

———. "The Process of Mexican Independence." *American Historical Review* 105, no. 1 (February 2000): 116–30.

———. "El pueblo de México y la política capitalina, 1808 y 1812." *Mexican Studies/Estudios Mexicanos* 10, no. 1 (Winter 1994): 27–61.

———. "Las sociedades secretas durante el movimiento de independencia." In *The Independence of Mexico and the Creation of the New Nation*, edited by Jaime E. Rodríguez O., 45–62. Los Angeles: UCLA Latin American Center, 1989.

Guedea, Virginia, and Jaime E. Rodríguez O. "How Relations Between Mexico and the United States Began." In *Myths, Misdeeds, and Misunderstandings*, edited by Jaime E. Rodríguez O. and Kathryn Vincent, 17–40. Wilmington: SR Books, 1997.

Guerra, Francois-Xavier. *Modernidad e independencias. Ensayos sobre las revoluciones hispánicas.* Madrid: Editorial MAPFRE, 1992.

———. "El soberano y su reino: Reflexiones sobre la génesis del ciudadano en América Latina." In *Ciudadanía política y formación de las naciones: Perspectivas históricas de América Latina*, edited by Hilda Sabato, 33-61. Mexico City: Fondo de Cultura Económica, 1999.

Haber, Stephen. "The Worst of Both Worlds: The New Cultural History of Mexico." *Mexican Studies/Estudios Mexicanos* 13, no. 2 (Summer 1997): 363–83.

Haig, Roger M. "The Creation and Control of a Caudillo." *Hispanic American Historical Review* 44, no. 4 (November 1964): 481–90.

Hale, Charles A. *Mexican Liberalism in the Age of Mora, 1821–1853.* New Haven: Yale University Press, 1968.

Hamnett, Brian. "The Appropriation of Mexican Church Wealth by the Spanish Bourbon Government: The Consolidación de Vales Reales, 1805–1809." *Journal of Latin American Studies* 1, no. 2 (1969): 85–113.

Haskett, Robert. *Indigenous Rulers: An Ethnohistory of Town Government in Colonial Cuernavaca.* Albuquerque: University of New Mexico Press, 1991.

Hébrard, Veronique. "Opinión pública y representación en el Congreso Constituyente de Venezuela (1811–1812)." In *Los espacios públicos en Iberoamérica. Ambigüedades y problemas: Siglos XVIII–XIX*, edited by

Francois-Xavier Guerra and Annick Lempériere, 163–64; 196–224. Mexico City: Fondo de Cultura Económica, 2001.

Henderson, Peter V. N. *Gabriel García Moreno and Conservative State Formation in the Andes*. Austin: University of Texas Press, 2008.

Henshall, Nicholas. "Early Modern Absolutism 1550–1700, Political Reality or Propaganda?" In *Der Absolutismus ein Mythos?: Strukturwandel monarchischer Herrschaft*, edited by Ronald G. Asch and Heinz Duchhardt, 25–53. Cologne: Böhlau Verlag, 1996.

———. *The Myth of Absolutism: Change and Continuity in Early Modern European Monarchy*. New York: Longman, 1992.

Hernández Guerrero, Dolores. *La Revolución haitiana y el fin de un sueño colonial (1791–1803)*. Mexico City: UNAM, 1997.

Herr, Richard. *The Eighteenth-Century Revolution in Spain*. Princeton: Princeton University Press, 1958.

Herzog, Tamar. *Defining Nations: Immigrants and Citizens in Early Modern Spain and Spanish America*. New Haven: Yale University Press, 2003.

———. *Upholding Justice: Society, State, and the Penal System in Quito (1650–1750)*. Ann Arbor: University of Michigan Press, 2007.

Higginbotham, Don, *The War of American Independence: Military Attitudes, Policies, and Practice, 1763-1789*. New York: McMillan, 1971.

Himmelfarb, Gertrude. *The New History and the Old*. Cambridge: Harvard University Press, 1987.

Horsman, Reginal. *Race and Manifest Destiny: The Origins of American Racial Anglo-Saxonism*. Cambridge: Cambridge University Press, 1981.

Irurozqui Victoriano, Marta. *"A bala, piedra y palo": La construcción de la ciudadanía política en Bolivia, 1826–1952*. Seville: Diputación de Sevilla, 2000.

———. "Huellas, testigos y testimonios constitucionales de Charcas a Bolivia 1810–1830." In "El laboratorio constitucional iberoamericano, 1807/08–1830," núm. 9 de la serie Estudios AHILA de Historia Latinoamericana, edited by Marcela Ternavasio and Antonio Annino, 157–78. Madrid: Iberoamericana, 2012.

Israel, Jonathan I. *The Dutch Republic: Its Rise, Greatness, and Fall, 1477–1806*. Oxford: Clarendon Press, 1995.

Iturbide, Agustín de. *Carrera militar y política de Don Agustín de Iturbide, o sea memoria que escribí en Livorna*. Mexico City: M. Ximeno, 1827.

J. L. R. *Historia de la República del Ecuador*. Tomo 1. Quito: Prensa Católica, 1920.

James, C. L. R. *The Black Jacobins: Toussaint Louverture and the San Domingo Revolution.* 3rd ed. London: Ellison & Busby, 1980.

Jaramillo Alvarado, Pío. *Historia de Loja y su provincia.* Quito: Casa de la Cultura Ecuatoriana, 1955.

Jefferson, Thomas. *The Papers of Thomas Jefferson.* 10 vols. Princeton: Princeton University Press, 1954.

Jensen, Merrill. *The Articles of Confederation.* 2nd ed. Madison: University of Wisconsin Press, 1959.

Jijón y Caamaño, Jacinto. *Influencia de Quito en la emancipación del continente americano.* Quito: Universidad Central, 1924.

Jiménez Codinach, Guadalupe. *La Gran Bretaña y la independencia de México, 1808–1821.* Mexico City: Fondo de Cultura Económica, 1991.

Joseph, Gilbert M. "On the Trail of Latin American Bandits: A Reexamination of Peasant Resistance." In *Pattern of Contention in Mexican History,* edited by Jaime E. Rodríguez O., 293–336. Wilmington: SR Books, 1992.

———, ed. *Reclaiming the Political in Latin American History: Essays from the North.* Durham: Duke University Press, 2001.

Joseph, Gilbert M., and Daniel Nugent, eds. *Everyday Forms of State Formation.* Durham: Duke University Press, 1994.

Kamen, Henry. *Empire: How Spain Became a World Power, 1492–1763.* London: Penguin Books, 2002.

Keeding, Ekkehart. *Surge la nación. La ilustración en la Audiencia de Quito.* Quito: Banco Central del Ecuador, 2005.

Kimmel, Michael. *Absolutism and its Discontents: State and Society in Seventeenth-Century France and England.* New Brunswick: Transaction Books, 1988.

Knight, Alan. "Subalterns, Signifiers, and Statistics: Perspectives on Mexican Historiography." *Latin American Research Review* 37, no. 2 (2002): 136–58.

Knight, Franklin W. "The Haitian Revolution." American Historical Review 105, no. 1 (February 2000): 103-115.

Kuethe, Allan J. *Military Reform and Society in New Granada, 1773–1808.* Gainesville: University of Florida Presses, 1978.

Ladd, Doris M. *The Making of Strike: Mexican Silver Workers' Struggles in Real del Monte, 1766–1775.* Lincoln: University of Nebraska Press, 1988.

Larrea, Carlos Manuel. *El Barón de Carondelet. XXIX Presidente de la Real Audiencia de Quito.* Quito: Corporación de Estudios y Publicaciones, n.d., 55–67.

Lavallé, Bernard. *Quito y la crisis de la alcabala, 1580–1600*. Quito: Instituto Francés de Estudios Andinos y Corporación Editora Nacional, 1997.

Lavrin, Asunción. "The Execution of the Law of Consolidation in New Spain: Economic Aims and Results." *Hispanic American Historical Review* 53, no. 1 (1973): 27–49.

Leal Curiel, Carole. "¿Radicales o timoratos? La declaración de la Independencia absoluta como una acción teórica-discursiva (1811)." *Politeia, Revista de la Facultad de Ciencias Jurídicas y Políticas de la Universidad Central de Venezuela* 31, no. 40 (2008): 15-24.

Lempériere, Annick. "La questión colonial." *Nuevo Mundo Mundos Nuevos,* núm. 4 (2004): 23-31.

————. "La representación política en el Imperio español a finales del antiguo régimen." In *Dinámicas del antiguo régimen y orden constitucional,* edited by Marco Bellingeri, 55–71. Torino: Otto Editore, 2000.

León Borja, Dora, and Adám Szászdi. "El problema jurisdiccional de Guayaquil antes de la independencia." *Cuadernos de Historia y Arqueología* 21, no. 38 (1971): 13–146.

Lerner, I. "The Diccionario of Antonio de Alcedo as a Source of Enlightened Ideas." In *The Ibero-American Enlightenment,* edited by A. Owen Aldridge, 71–93. Urbana: University of Illinois Press, 1971.

Leyes y Ordenanzas Reales de las Indias del Mar Oceano por Alonzo Zorita, 1574. Mexico City: Miguel Angel Porrúa, 1983.

Lierh, Reinhard. *Ayuntamiento y oligarquía en Puebla, 1787–1810.* 2 vols. Mexico City: Sep-Setentas, 1971.

Lira, Andrés. *Comunidades indígenas frente a la ciudad de México: Tenochtitlan y Tlatelolco.* Zamora: El Colegio de Michoacán, 1983.

Lista de los señores diputados nombrados para las Cortes del año 1820 y 1821. Mexico City: Reimpresa en la oficina de J.B. Arizpe, 1820.

Lohmann Villena, Guillermo. "Las Cortes en Indias." *Anuario de Historia del Derecho Español* 18 (1947): 650.

López-Ocón Cabrera, Leoncio. "El protagonismo del clero en la insurgencia quiteña (1809–1810)." *Revista de Indias* 46, núm. 177 (1986): 124–25.

Lucas, Stephen E. "The 'Plakkant van Verlatinge': A Neglected Model of the American Declaration of Independence." In *Connecting Cultures: The Netherlands in Five Centuries of Transatlantic Exchange,* edited by Rosemarijn Hofte and Johanna C. Kardux, 189–207. Amsterdam: V U University Press, 1994.

Lynch, John. *Caudillos in Spanish America, 1800–1850.* New York: Oxford University Press, 1992.

McFarlane, Anthony. "The 'Rebellion of the Barrios': Urban Insurrection in Bourbon Quito." *Hispanic American Historical Review* 69, no. 2 (May 1989): 283–87.

MacLachlan, Colin, *Spain's Empire in the New World: The Role of Ideas in Institutional and Social Change.* Berkeley: University of California Press, 1988.

MacLachlan, Colin M., and Jaime E. Rodríguez O. *The Forging of the Cosmic Race: A Reinterpretation of Colonial Mexico.* 2nd ed. Berkeley: University of California Press, 1990.

Macune, Jr., Charles W. *El estado de México y la federación mexicana.* Mexico City: Fondo de Cultura Económica, 1978.

Madley, Benjamin. "Reexamining the American Genocide Debate: Meaning, Historiography, and New Methods." *American Historical Review* 120, no. 1 (February 2015): 98–139.

Maier, Pauline. *From Resistance to Revolution: Colonial Radicals and the Development of American Opposition to Britain, 1765–1776.* New York: W. W. Norton, 1991.

———. "Independencia política, continuidad cultural: La Declaración de Independencia de los Estados Unidos en un contexto británico." In *Las declaraciones de independencia: Los textos fundamentales de las independencias americanas,* edited by Alfredo Ávila, Jordana Dym and Erika Pani, 111–20. Mexico City: El Colegio de Mexico, 2013.

Mallon, Florencia E. *Peasant and Nation: The Making of Postcolonial Mexico and Peru.* Berkeley: University of California Press, 1995.

———. "The Promise and Dilemma of Subaltern Studies: Perspectives from Latin American History." *American Historical Review* 99, no. 5 (1994): 1491–1493.

"Manifiesto de la Junta Suprema de Quito." In *Quito, 1809–1812, edited by* Alfredo Ponce Ribadeneira, 136–39. Madrid: Imprenta Juan Bravo, 1960.

"Manifiesto del pueblo de Quito." *Boletín de la Sociedad Ecuatoriana de Estudios Históricos Americanos* 2, no. 6 (May-June 1919): 430.

Maravall, José Antonio. *Las comunidades de Castilla. Una primera revolución moderna.* Madrid: Revista de Occidente, 1963.

Marchena Fernández, Juan. "¿Obedientes al rey y desleales a sus ideas? Los liberales españoles ante la 'reconquista de América." In *Por la fuerza de las armas. Ejército e independencias en Iberoamérica,* edited by Juan Marchena

Fernández and Manuel Chust Calero, 143–208. Castelló de la Plana, Spain: Universitat Jaume I, 2008.

Marichal, Carlos. *Bankruptcy of Empire: Mexican Silver and the Wars Between Spain, Britain, and France, 1760-1810.* New York: Cambridge University Press, 2007.

Meisel, Adolfo. "El situado de Cartagena de Indias a fines del siglo de las luces." In *El secreto del Imperio Español: Los situados coloniales en el siglo VIII,* edited by Carlos Marichal and Johanna von Grafenstein, 193–211. Mexico City: El Colegio de México/Instituto Mora, 2012.

Merriman, Roger B. *The Rise of the Spanish Empire in the Old World and the New.* 4 vols. New York: Macmillan, 1918–1934.

Mesonero Romanos, Ramón. *Memorias de un setentón.* Madrid: Ediciones Atlas, 1957.

Mexico, Ayuntamiento. *Actas del Cabildo de la ciudad de México.* Mexico City: Editorial del "Municipio Libre," 1989.

Mexico, Soberana Junta. *Diario de las sesiones de la Soberana Junta Provisional Gubernativa del Imperio Mexicano.* Mexico City: Imprenta Imperial de Alejandro Valdés, 1821.

Meyer, Jean. *Francia y América del siglo xvi al siglo xx.* Madrid: Mapfre, 1992.

Mier, Servando Teresa de. "Idea de la Constitución dada a las Américas por los reyes de España antes de la invasión del antiguo despotismo." In *Obras completas de Servando Teresa de Mier.* Vol. 4, *La formación de un republicano,* edited by Jaime E. Rodríguez O., 31–91. Mexico City: UNAM, 1988.

Minchom, Martin. "The Making of a White Province: Demographic Movement and Ethnic Transformation in the South of the Audiencia de Quito (1670–1830)." *Bulletin de L'Institut Français d'Études Andines* 12, no. 3–4 (1983): 23–39.

———. *The People of Quito, 1690–1810: Change and Unrest in the Underclass.* Boulder: Westview Press, 1994.

Miño Grijalva, Manuel. *El mundo novohispano: Población, ciudades y economía, siglos XVII y XVIII.* Mexico City: Fondo de Cultura Económica, 2001.

Miranda, José. *Las ideas y las instituciones políticas mexicanas.* 2nd ed. Mexico City: UNAM, 1978.

Mirow, Mathew C. "The Constitution of Cádiz in Florida." *Florida Journal of International Law* 24 (2012): 271–329.

Molina Martínez, Miguel. "Conflictos en la Audiencia de Quito a finales del siglo XVIII." *Anuario de Estudios Americanos* 65, núm. 1 (enero-junio 2008): 153–73.

Mora, José María Luis. "Sobre la necesidad de fijar el derecho de la ciudadanía en la república y hacerlo esencialmente afecto a la propiedad." In *Obras sueltas, 633*. Mexico City: Editorial Porrúa, 1963.

Morelli, Federica. "La revolución en Quito. El camino hacia el gobierno mixto." *Revista de Indias 62*, núm. 225 (mayo-agosto 2002): 335–56.

———. *Territorio o nación: Reforma y disolución del espacio imperial en Ecuador, 1765–1830.* Madrid: Centro de Estudios Político y Constitucionales, 2005.

———. *Territorio o nazione: Reforma e dissoluzione dello spazio imperiale in Ecuador, 1765–1830.* Soveria Mannelli: Rubbettino Editore, 2001.

———. "Un neosincretismo político. Representación, política y sociedad indígena durante el primer liberalismo hispanoamericano: el caso de la Audiencia de Quito (1813–1830)." In *Muchas Hispanoaméricas. Antropología, historia y enfoques culturales en los estudios latinoamericanistas,* edited by Thomas Krüggeler and Ulrich Mücke, 151–65. Madrid: Iberoamericana, 2001.

Moreno, Francisco José. "Caudillismo: An Interpretation of its Origins in Chile." In *Conflict and Violence in Latin American Politics,* edited by F. J. Moreno and B. Mitriani, 39–39. New York: Crowell, 1971.

Moreno, Roberto. "Instituciones de la industria minera novohispana." With the assistance of María del Refugio González. In *La minería en México,* edited by Miguel León-Portilla, 69–164. Mexico City: UNAM, 1978.

———. "Régimen de trabajo en la minería del siglo VIII." In *El trabajo y los trabajadores en la historia de México,* edited by Elsa Cecilia Frost, 242–67. Tucson: University of Arizona Press, 1979.

Moreno Yañez, Segundo E. *Sublevaciones indígenas en la Audiencia de Quito desde comienzos del siglo XVIII hasta finales de la colonia.* 4th ed. Quito: Ediciones de la Pontificia Universidad Católica del Ecuador, 1995.

Morgado García, Arturo. *Ser clérigo en la España del Antiguo Régimen.* Cádiz: Universidad de Cádiz, 2000.

Morgan, Edmund S. *American Slavery and American Freedom: The Ordeal of Colonial Virginia.* New York: W. W. Norton, 1975.

Morse, Richard M. "Toward a Theory of Spanish American Government." *Journal of the History of Ideas 15* (January 1954): 71–93.

Nader, Helen. *Liberty in Absolutist Spain: The Habsburg Sale of Towns, 1516–1700.* Baltimore: Johns Hopkins University Press, 1990.

Navarro, José Gabriel. *La revolución de Quito del 10 de agosto de 1809.* Quito: Plan Piloto del Ecuador, 1962.

Nelson, Eric. *The Royalist Revolution: Monarch and the American Founding.* Cambridge: Harvard University Press, 2014.

Novick, Peter. *That Noble Dream: The Objectivity Question and the American Historical Profession.* Cambridge: Cambridge University Press, 1988.

Novoa, Mauricio. *The Protectors of Indians in the Royal Audiencia of Lima: History, Careers and Legal Culture, 1575–1775.* Boston: Brill, 2016.

Núñez, Francisco. "La participación electoral indígena bajo la Constitución de Cádiz (1812–1814)." In *Historia de las elecciones en el Perú: Estudios sobre el gobierno representative,* edited by Cristóbal Aljovín de Losana and Sinesio López, 361–94. Lima: Instituto de Estudios Peruanos, 2005.

Oberem, Udo. "Indios libres e indios sujetos a haciendas en la sierra ecuatoriana a fines de la colonia." In *Amerikanistische Studien: Festschrift für Hermann Trimborn anlässlich seines 75. Geburtstages = Estudios americanistas: Libro jubilar en homenaje a Hermann Trimborn con motivo de su septuagésimoquinto aniversario.* 2 vols., edited by Roswith Hartmann and Udo Oberem, 2:105–12. St. Augustin: Haus Völker u. Kulturen, Anthropos-Inst., 1978–1979.

O'Callaghan, Joseph F. *The Cortes of Castile-León, 1188–1350.* Philadelphia: University of Pennsylvania Press, 1989.

Olagaray, Roberto, ed. *Colección de documentos históricos mexicanos.* 4 vols. Paris and Mexico City: Librería de la Vda. de Ch. Bouret y Antigua Imprenta Muergía-Secretaría de Guerra y Marina, 1920.

Ortiz, Sergio Elías. "Notas para la biografía del obispo José Cuero y Caicedo, prócer de la independencia." *Boletín de historia y antigüedades* 57, nos. 663, 664, and 665 (January, February and March 1970): 111–61.

Owensby, Brian. *Empire of Law and Indian Justice in Colonial Mexico.* Stanford: Stanford University Press, 2008.

Ott, Thomas O. *The Haitian Revolution, 1789–1804.* Knoxville: University of Tennessee Press, 1973.

Paladines, Carlos, ed. *Pensamiento ilustrado.* Quito: Banco Central del Ecuador y Corporación Editora Nacional, 1981.

Payne, Stanley G. *Spanish Catholicism: An Historical Overview.* Madison: University of Wisconsin Press, 1984.

Peñalver, Fernando. "Memoria presentada al Supremo Congreso de Venezuela, en que manifiesta sus opiniones sobre la necesidad de dividir la provincia de Caracas para hacer la Constitución federal permanente; y los artículos con que cree deben ligarse las provincias para formar un solo estado y soberanía." In *Academia Nacional de Historia, Pensamiento consti-*

tucional hispano-américano, 5 vols. 5: 25–39. Caracas: Academia Nacional de Historia, 1961.

Peralta Ruiz, Victor. *En defensa de la autoridad. Política y cultura bajo el gobierno del virrey Abascal, 1806–1816*. Madrid: Consejo Superior de Investigaciones Científicas, 2002.

———. *La independencia y la cultura política peruana (1808–1821)*. Lima: Instituto de Estudios Peruanos y Fundación M.J. Bustamante de la Fuente, 2010.

———. "Los inicios del sistema representative en Perú: Ayuntamientos Constitucionales y Diputaciones Provinciales (1812–1815)." In *La Mirada esquiva: Reflexiones históricas sobre la interacción del Estado y la ciudadanía en los Andes (Bolivia, Ecuador y Perú), Siglo XIX*, edited by Marta Irurozqui Victoriano, 65–92. Madrid: Consejo Superior de Investigaciones Científicas, 2005.

Pérez Prendes y Muñoz de Arracó, José Manuel. *La Monarquía Indiana y el Estado de derecho*. El Puig, Valencia: Gráficas Morverte, 1989.

Pérez Ramírez, Gustavo. "Autoría del Proyecto de Constitución." 8-29, *Constitución del Estado de Quito, 15 de febrero de 1812*. Quito: Trama Edicones, 2012.

Phelan, John L. *The People and the King: The Comunero Revolution in Colombia, 1781*. Madison: University of Wisconsin Press, 1978.

Piel, Jean. "The Place of the Peasantry in the National Life of Peru in the Nineteenth Century." *Past and Present* 46, no. 1 (February 1970): 108–33.

Polt, John. *Jovellanos and His English Sources: Economic, Philosophic, and Political Writings*. Philadelphia: Transactions of the American Philosophical Society, 1964.

Ponce, M. Clemente, ed. "Alegato de [Rodríguez de] Quiroga presentado en el primer juicio iniciado contra los próceres en febrero de 1809."*Memorias de la Academia Ecuatoriana correspondiente a la Real Española*, núm. extraordinario (1922): 62–100.

Ponce de Andrade, Andrés Quintian. *Carta del Ilmo. Sr. Don . . . , obispo de Cuenca en el Peru, al Señor Marques de Selva-Alegre*. Buenos Ayres: Imprenta de Niños Expositos, 1809.

Ponce Ribadeneira, Alfredo. *Quito, 1808–1812*. Madrid: Talleres Tipográficos del Asilo de Huérfanos del Sagrado Corazón de Jesús, 1960.

———. *Quito, 1809–1812*. Madrid: Imprenta Juan Bravo, 1960.

Porras P., María Elena. *La Gobernación y el Obispado de Mainas*. Quito: TEHIS y ABYA YALA, 1987.

Quijada, Mónica. "Las 'dos tradiciones'. Soberanía popular e imaginarios compartidos en el mundo hispánico en la época de las grandes revoluciones atlánticas." In *Revolución, independencia y las nuevas naciones de América*, edited by Jaime E. Rodriguez O., 61–86. Madrid: Fundación MAPFRE-Tavera, 2005.

———. "From Spain to New Spain: Revisiting the *potestas populi* in Hispanic Political Thought." *Mexican Studies/Estudios Mexicanos* 24, no. 2 (Summer 2008): 185–219.

———. "Sobre 'nación', 'pueblo', 'soberanía' y otros ejes de la modernidad en el mundo hispánico," In *La nuevas naciones: España y México, 1800–1850*, edited by Jaime E. Rodríguez O., 19–51. Madrid: Instituto de Cultura-Fundación MAPFRE, 2008.

Ramos, Demetrio. "Las ciudades de Indias y su asiento en Cortes de Castilla." *Revista del Instituto de Historia del Derecho Ricardo Levene* no. 18 (1967): 170–85.

[Ramos Arizpe, Miguel]. *Carta escrito a un americano sobre la forma de gobierno que para hacer practicable la Constitución y las leyes, conviene establecer en Nueva España atendida a su actual situación.* Madrid: Ibarra, Impresor de Cámara de S.M., 1821.

Ramos Gómez, Luis Javier. "La acusación contra el presidente electo don Juan José de Araujo y Río por la introducción de mercancías ilícitas a su llegada a Quito en diciembre de 1736." *Boletín de la Academia Nacional de Historia* [de Quito] 72, núm. 153/154 (1993): 249–77.

———. "La estructura social quiteña entre 1737 y 1745 según el proceso contra Don José de Araujo." *Revista de Indias* 51, núm. 91 (1991): 25–56.

———. "La pugna por el poder local en Quito entre 1737 y 1745 según el proceso contra el presidente de la Audiencia José de Araujo." *Revista Complutense de Historia de América* 18 (1992): 179–96.

Ramos Pérez, Demetrio. *Entre el Plata y Bogotá. Cuatro claves de la emancipación ecuatoriana.* Madrid: Ediciones Cultura Hispánica, 1978.

Recopilación de leyes de los Reynos de las Indias. Madrid: Consejo de la Hispanidad, Madrid, 1943.

Recopilación de leyes de los Reynos de las Indias mandadas imprimir y publicar por la Magestad Católica del Rey Don Cárlos II, Nuestro Señor. 3 vols. Madrid: Consejo de la Hispanidad, 1943.

"Relación sumaria de las dos sublevaciones de la Pleve de Quito." *Boletín de la Academia Nacional de Historia* (de Ecuador) 15, núm. 42–45 (enero-junio 1937): 102–16.

Rémond, René, ed. *Pour une histoire politique*. Paris: Editions du Senil, 1988.

Rivera-Garza, Christina. "'She Neither Respected nor Obeyed Anyone:' Inmates and the Psychiatrist Debate Gender, and Class at the General Insane Asylum La Castañeda, Mexico, 1910–1930." *Hispanic American Historical Review* 81, no. 4 (2001): 656–688.

Robertson, William S. *Iturbide of Mexico*. Durham: Duke University Press, 1952.

Rocafuerte, Vicente. *A la nación*. Quito: Tipografía de la Escuela de Artes y Oficios, 1908.

[————]. *Bosquejo ligerísimo de la revolución de Megico [sic] desde el grito de Iguala hasta la proclamación imperial de Iturbide*. Philadelphia: Imprenta de Terarouef y Naroajeb, 1822.

————. *Consideraciones generales sobre la bondad de un buen gobierno aplicadas a las actuales circunstancias de la República de México* [in three parts]. Mexico City: Imprenta de las Escalerillas, 1831.

————. *Ensayo político. El sistema colombiano, popular, electivo, y representativo, es el que más conviene a la América Independiente*. New York: Imprenta de A. Paul, 1823.

————. *Ideas necesarias a todo pueblo americano independiente que quiera ser libre*. Philadelphia: D. Huntington, 1821.

————. *Observaciones sobre la carta inserta en el Registro Oficial del 4 de octubre*. Mexico City: Imprenta de Rivera, 1831, 50/56, fols. 224–26.

Rodríguez, Linda Alexander. *The Search for Public Policy: Regional Politics and Government Finances in Ecuador, 1830–1940*. Berkeley: University of California Press, 1985.

Rodriguez, Mario. *The Cádiz Experiment in Central America, 1808 to 1826*. Berkeley: University of California Press, 1978.

————. *La revolución Americana de 1776 y el mundo hispánico: ensayos y documentos*. Madrid: Editorial Tecnos, 1976.

Rodríguez O., Jaime E. "La Antigua provincia de Guayaquil en la época de la independencia, 1809–1820." In *Revolución, independencia y las Nuevas Naciones de América*, edited by Jaime E. Rodríguez O., 511–56. Madrid: Fundación MAPFRE Tavera, 2005.

————. "Los caudillos y los historiadores: Riego, Iturbide y Santa Anna." In *La construcción del héroe en España y México (1789–1847)*, edited by Manuel Chust and Víctor Minguez, 309–35. Valencia: Universitat de Valencia, 2003.

————. "La ciudadanía y la Constitución de Cádiz." In *Bastillas, cetros y blasones: La independencia en Iberoamerica*, edited by Ivana Frasquet, 39-56. Madrid: Fundación MAPFRE-Instituto de Cultura, 2006.

————. "Las Cortes mexicanas y el congreso constituyente." In *La independencia de México y el proceso autonomista novohispano, 1808–1824*, edited by Virginia Guedea, 285–320. Mexico City: UNAM/Instituto Mora, 2001.

————. "De la fidelidad a la revolución: El proceso de la independencia de la Antigua Provincia de Guayaquil, 1809–1820." *Procesos: Revista ecuatoriana de historia* no. 21 (20 Semestre 2004): 35–88.

————. "Las elecciones a las Cortes Constituyentes Mexicanas." In *Ensayos en homenaje a José María Muriá*, edited by Louis Cardaillac and Angélica Peregrina, 79–110. Guadalajara: El Colegio de Jalisco, 2002.

————. *The Emergence of Spanish America: Vicente Rocafuerte and Spanish Americanism, 1808–1832*. Berkeley: University of California Press, 1975.

————. *The Independence of Spanish America*. Cambridge: Cambridge University Press, 1998.

————. *La independencia de la América española*. Mexico City: Fondo de Cultura Económica, 1996.

————. "Introducción a las Reales Ordenanzas de la Audiencia de Quito" *Anuario Histórico Jurídico Ecuatoriano* 4 (1976): 256–310.

————. "'Ningún pueblo es superior a otro,': Oaxaca and Mexican Federalism." In *The Divine Charter: Constitutionalism and Liberalism in Nineteenth-Century Mexico*, edited by Jaime E. Rodríguez O., 65–18. Boulder: Rowman & Littlefield, 2005.

————. "'Ningún pueblo es superior a otro:' Oaxaca y el federalismo mexicano." In *Poder y legitimidad en México, siglo xix: Instituciones y cultura política*, edited by Brian F. Connaughton, 249–309. Mexico City: Miguel Angel Porrúa, 2003.

————. "The Origins of the 1832 Rebellion." In *Patterns of Contention in Mexican History*, edited by Jaime E. Rodríguez O., 145–48. Wilmington: SR Books, 1992.

————. "Las primeras elecciones constitucionales en el Reino de Quito, 1809–1814 y 1821–1822." *Procesos: Revista ecuatoriana de historia* 14 (20 Semestre 1999): 3–52.

————. "Revolución de 1809: Cinco cartas de un realista anónimo." *ARNAHIS. Organo del Archivo Nacional de Historia* no. 19 (1973): 57–58.

―――. *La revolución política durante la época de la independencia: El Reino de Quito, 1808–1822.* Quito: Universidad Andína Simón Bolívar & Corporación Editora Nacional, 2006.

―――. *"Rey, religión, yndependencia, y unión": La independencia de Guadalajara.* Mexico City: Instituto Mora, 2003.

―――. "Sobrehumano mortal . . . que la paz nos asegura." *Memorias de la Academia Mexicana de la Historia* 54 (2013): 105–31.

―――. "The Struggle for Dominance: The Legislature Versus the Executive in Early Mexico." In *The Birth of Modern Mexico,* edited by Christon I. Archer, 205–28. Wilmington: SR Books, 2003.

―――. "The Transition from Colony to Nation: New Spain, 1820–1821." In *Mexico in the Age of Democratic Revolutions, 1750–1850,* edited by Jaime E. Rodríguez O., 97–132. Boulder: Lynne Rienner Publishers, 1994.

―――. *"We Are Now The True Spaniards": Sovereignty, Revolution, Independence, and the Emergence of the Federal Republic of Mexico, 1808–1824.* Stanford: Stanford University Press, 2012.

Roig, Arturo Andrés. *Humanismo en la segunda mitad del siglo XVIII.* Quito: Banco Central del Ecuador and Corporación Editora Nacional, 1983.

Romero, José Luis. *A History of Argentine Political Thought.* Stanford: Stanford University Press, 1963.

Rubio Fernández, María Dolores. *Elecciones en el antiguo régimen.* Alicante: Universidad de Alicante, 1989.

Rugeley, Terry, Yucatán's Maya Peasantry and the Origins of the Caste War. Austin: University of Texas Press, 1996.

Ruiz Alemán, Joaquín E. "Los municipios cubanos." *Anuario de Estudios Americanos* 29 (1972): 379–87.

Saint-Geours, Yves, and Marie-Danielle Demélas. *Jerusalen y Babilonia. Religión y política en el Ecuador, 1780–1880.* Quito: Corporación Editora Nacional, 1988.

Sala I Vila, Núria. "El Trienio liberal en el Virreinato peruano: Los ayuntamientos constitucionales de Arequipa, Cusco Y Huamanga, 1820–1824." *Revista de Indias* 71, no. 253 (September, December, 2011): 693–728.

Salazar, Francisco Ignacio. *Actas del Congreso Ecuatoriano de 1831.* Quito: Imprenta del Gobierno, 1888.

―――. *Actas del Congreso Ecuatoriano de 1833.* Quito: Imprenta del Gobierno, 1891.

Salvatore, Ricardo D., Carlos Aguirre, and Gilbert M. Joseph, eds. *Crime and Punishment in Latin America: Law and Society Since Colonial Times.* Durham: Duke University Press, 2001.

San Miguel, Evaristo. *Vida de D. Agustín Argüelles.* 4 vols. Madrid: Imprenta del Colegio de Sordo-Mudos, 1851–1852.

Sarmiento, Domingo. *Facundo: Cilización i barbarie.* Santigo, Chile: 1845.

———. *Facundo: Civilization and Barbarism.* Berkeley: University of California Press, 2003.

Scott, Joan Wallach. *Gender and the Politics of History.* New York: Columbia University Press, 1988.

Seed, Patricia. "'Are These Not Also Men?': The Indians' Humanity and Capacity for Spanish Civilization." *Journal of Latin American Studies* 25, no. 3 (October 1993): 629–652.

———. *Ceremonies of Possession in Europe's Conquest of the New World, 1492–1640.* Cambridge: Cambridge University Press, 1995.

Shafer, Robert Jones. *The Economic Societies in the Spanish World (1763–1821).* Syracuse: Syracuse University Press, 1958.

Silva y Olave, José de. *El Excelentísimo Señor doctor don . . . diputado del vireynato del Peru: A la ciudad de Quito.* Buenos Aires: n.p., 1809.

Simmons, Merle E. *La revolución norteamericana en la independencia de Hispanoamérica.* Madrid: MAPFRE, 1992.

Skinner, Quentin. *The Foundations of Modern Political Thought.* 2 vols. Cambridge: Cambridge University Press, 1978.

———, ed. *The Return of Grand Theory in the Human Sciences.* Cambridge: Cambridge University Press, 1985.

Smelser, Marshal. *The Winning of Independence.* Chicago: Quadrangle, 1972.

Sokal, Alan, and Jean Bricmont. *Fashionable Nonsense: Postmodern Intellectuals' Abuse of Science.* New York: Picador, 1998.

Solórzano Pereyra, Juan. *Política Indiana.* 3 vols. Edición de Francisco Tomás y Valiente y Ana María. Madrid: Edición Fundación José Antonio de Castro, 1996.

Soto Cárdenas, Alejandro. *Influencia de la Independencia de los Estados Unidos en la Constitución de las Naciones Latinoamericanas.* Washington: Organización de Estados Americanos, 1979.

Stevenson, William B. *Historical and Descriptive Narrative of Twenty Years' Residence in South America.* 3 vols. London: Hurst, Robinson, & Co., 1825.

Stoetzer, O. Carlos. *The Scholastic Roots of the Spanish American Revolution.* New York: Fordham University, 1979.

Suárez, Francisco. *Tratado de las leyes y de Dios legislador.* Translated by Jaime Torrubiano Ripoll. Madrid: Reus, 1918, 1979.

Taylor, William B. *Magistrates of the Sacred: Priests and Parishioners in Eighteenth-Century Mexico.* Stanford: Stanford University Press, 1996.

Terán Najas, Rosemarie. *Los proyectos del imperio borbónico en la Real Audiencia de Quito.* Quito: TEHIS and ABYA YALA, 1988.

Thompson, I. A.A. "Absolutism, Legalism and the Law in Castile 1500–1700." In *Der Absolutismus ein Mythos?: Strukturwandel monarchischer Herrschaft,* edited by Ronald G. Asch and Heinz Duchhardt, 185–228. Cologne: Böhlau Verlag, 1996.

Tobar Donoso, Julio. *La iglesia, modeladora de la nacionalidad.* Quito: "La Prensa Católica," 1953.

———. *Las instituciones del periodo hispánico, especialmente en la Presidencia de Quito.* Quito: "Editorial Ecuatoriana," n. d.

Torre Reyes, Carlos de la. *La revolución de Quito del 10 de agosto de 1809.* Quito: Ministerio de Educación, 1961.

———. *La revolución de Quito del 10 de agosto de 1809.* 2nd ed. Quito: Banco Central del Ecuador, 1990.

Tyrer, Robson B. *Historia demográfica y económica de la Audiencia de Quito. Población indígena e industria textil, 1600–1800.* Quito: Banco Central del Ecuador, 1988.

Un Español. *Dos años en México, o memorias críticas sobre los principales sucesos de la República de los Estados Unidos Mexicanos, desde la invasión de Barradas, hasta la declaración del Puerto de Tampico, contra el gobierno del grl. Bustamante.* Valencia: Imprenta de Cabrerizo, 1938.

Valencia Llano, Aloncio. "Élites, burocracia, clero y sectores populares en la Independencia Quiteña (1809–1812)." *Procesos. Revista ecuatoriana de historia* 3 (20 Semestre 1992): 82–84.

Van Gelderen, Martin. *The Political Thought of the Dutch Revolt.* Cambridge: Cambridge University Press, 1992.

———. "'So Merely Humane': Theories of Resistance in Early-Modern Europe." In *Rethinking the Foundations of Modern Political Thought,* edited by Annabel S. Brett, James Tully and Holly Hamilton-Breakly, 149–70. Cambridge: Cambridge University Press, 2006.

Van Young, Eric. "Etnia, política local e insurgencia en México, 1810–1821." In *Los colores de las independencias iberoamericanas. Liberalismo, etnia y raza*, edited by Manuel Chust and Ivana Frasquet, 143–69. Madrid: Consejo Superior de Investigaciones Científicas, 2009.

———. *The Other Rebellion: Popular Violence, Ideology, and the Mexican Struggle for Independence, 1810–1821*. Stanford: Stanford University Press, 2001.

Van Zanden, Jan Luiten, Eltjo Buringh, and Maarten Bosker. "The Rise and Decline of European Parliaments, 1188–1789." *The Economic History Review* 64, no. 1 (February 2011): 1–28.

Vázquez, Josefina Zoraida. "Los pronunciamientos de 1832: Aspirantismo político e ideología." In *Patterns of Contention in Mexican History*, edited by Jaime E. Rodríguez O., 170–86. Wilmington: SR Books, 1992.

Velasco, Juan de. *Historia del Reino de Quito en la América meridional*. In *Biblioteca Ecuatoriana Mínima, Padre Juan de Velasco S.I.* 2 vols. Puebla: Editorial Cajica, 1961.

Véliz, Claudio. *The Centralist Tradition in Latin America*. Princeton: Princeton University Press, 1980.

Venezuela. *Congreso Constituyente de 1811–1812*. Ediciones Conmemorativas del Bicentenario del Natalicio del Libertador Simón Bolívar. Caracas: Congreso de la República, 1983.

Vidaurre, Manuel de. *Manifiesto sobre la nulidad de las elecciones que a nombre de los países ultramarinos se practicaron en Madrid por algunos americanos el día de 28 y 29 de mayo del año de 1820*. Madrid: Imprenta de Vega, 1820.

Villarroel, Gaspar de. *Gobierno eclesiástico pacífico: y unión de los dos cuchillos, pontificio y regio*. 2 vols. Madrid: Domingo García Morrás, 1656–1657.

Villavicencia, Juan Manuel. *Constitución de los Estados Unidos de América. Traducida del inglés al español por don Jph. Manuel Villavicencio*. Philadelphia: Smith and M'Kenzie, 1810.

Villoro, Luis. *El proceso ideológico de la revolución de la independencia*. 2nd ed. Mexico City: UNAM, 1977.

———. "La revolución de independencia." In *Historia General de México*, 4 vols. 2: 303–56. Mexico City: El Colegio de México, 1976.

Viroli, Maurizio. *For Love of Country: An Essay on Patriotism and Nationalism*. Oxford: Oxford University Press, 1995.

Von Grafenstein Gareis, Johanna. *Nueva España en el Circuncaribe, 1779–1808: Revolución, competencia imperial y vínculos intercoloniales*. Mexico City: UNAM, 1997.

Von Wobeser, Gisela. *Dominación colonial: La consolidación de vales reales, 1804–1812.* Mexico City: UNAM, 2003.

Walker, Charles. *The Túpac Amaru Rebellion.* Cambridge: Harvard University Press, 2014.

Wallace, Willard M. *Appeal to Arms: A Military History of the American Revolution.* New York: Harper, 1951.

Warren, Harris G. "The Origins of General Mina's Invasion of Mexico." *Southwestern Historical Quarterly* 42 (July 1938): 1–20.

———. "Xavier Mina's Invasion of Mexico." *Hispanic American Historical Review* 23 (February 1943): 52–76.

Warren, Richard. "Elections and Popular Political Participation in Mexico, 1808–1836." In *Liberals, Politics & Power: State Formation in Nineteenth-Century Latin America,* edited by Vincent C. Peloso and Barbara A. Tenenbaum, 30–58. Athens: University of Georgia Press, 1996.

———. *Vagrants and Citizens: Politics and the Masses in Mexico City from Colony to Republic.* Wilmington: SR Books, 2001.

Washburn, Douglas Alan. "The Bourbon Reforms: A Social and Economic History of the Audiencia of Quito, 1760–1810." PhD diss., University of Texas, Austin, 1984.

Wiedemann, Thomas. "Reflections of Roman Political Thought." In *The Cambridge History of Greek and Roman Political Thought,* edited by Christopher Rowe and Malcolm Schofield with Simon Harrison, Melissa Lane, 517–31. Cambridge: Cambridge University Press, 2000.

Weinberg, Steven. "The Revolution that Didn't Happen." *New York Review of Books* 45, no. 15 (October 8, 1998): 49.

Windschuttle, Keith. *The Killing of History: How Literary Critics and Social Theorists Are Murdering Our Past.* San Francisco: Encounter Books, 1996.

Womack, John. "Review," *Hispanic American Historical Review* 83, no. 2 (May 2003): 374–75.

Wood, Gordon S. *The Radicalism of the American Revolution.* New York: Alfred A. Knopf, 1992.

Zavala, Silvio. "Hernán Cortés ante la justificación de su conquista de Tenochtitlan." *Revista de la Universidad de Yucatán* 26, no. 149 (January/March 1989): 39–61

Zuñiga, Neptalí. *La expedición científica de Francia del siglo XVII en la Presidencia de Quito.* Quito: Instituto Panamericano de geografía e historia, sección nacional del Ecuador, 1977.

INDEX

absolutism, 6, 7, 37–38

Der Absolutismus-ein Mythos (Asch and Duchhart), 7

Academia Pichinchense, 84

Academy of Science, 84

Act of Abjuration (1581), 4

Adams, John, 1, 82, 152

Adams-Onís Treaty (1819), 162

agriculture, 131, 145, 146

aguardiente, 54, 55, 56, 57, 58, 63, 75, 78, 83

Aguire, Juan Bautista, 86

Alamán, Lucas, 173, 175, 179, 183, 192

Alausí, 52, 83, 94

alcabala, 54, 55–56, 58, 69

Alcalá Galiano, Antonio, 164–65, 167–68

alcaldes, 38, 75, 109, 110, 113, 116

Alcedo y Bejarano, Antonio de, 152, 153

Alfonso IX, King, 3

Altamira, Rafael, 34

Althusius, Johannes, 5

Althusser, Louis, 191

Alvarez, Francisco, 152

Alvarez, Juan, 182, 185

Amati, Bernardino, 173

Ambato, 67, 79, 94, 99

American Historical Association, 197

American Historical Review, 195

American Question, 22, 23

American Revolution, 149, 153; British, 134–36, 138, 144, 151; as colonial revolution, 224n13; as radical/social revolution, 223n34

American Septentrional, 19

Andalucía, 164, 167, 168

Anderson, Perry, 6

Andrien, Kenneth, 65–66

Angostura, 18, 22

Anna, Timothy E., 228n17

Annales School, 191

Ante, Antonio, 73

antiguo régimen, 5, 6, 7–8, 111, 129, 169

Apodaca, Viceroy, 20

Appleby, Joyce, 197

Aranda, Conde de, 87

Araujo y Río, José, 53

Archive of Simancas, 34

Archivo General de Indias, 194

Archivo General de la Nación de México, 194

Archivo Nacional de Historia, 121

Aréchaga, Tomás, 79, 90

Arenas, Juan Pablo, 73, 77

Army of the Three Guarantees, 178

Arredondo, Manuel, 90

Articles of Confederation, 135, 156, 159

Artola, Miguel, 164, 165, 225n16

Ascásubi, Francisco Javier, 73

audiencia, 5, 21, 60, 61–62, 72, 74, 83, 99, 130

Audiencia de México, 47

Audiencia of Guatemala, 68

Constitution of Colombia, 122

Constitution of Quito, 214n36

Constitution of 1787, 135

Constitution of 1812. *See* Hispanic Constitution

Constitution of 1824. *See* Mexican Constitution

Consulado de México, 42

consulados, 40, 42, 64, 71

Contaduría general de Propios y Arbitrios, 40

"The Contested Mexican Election of 1812" (Benson), 193

Continental Congress (1777), 152, 156

The Copernican Revolution (Kuhn), 190

Corregimiento de Loja, 115

Corregimiento of Quito, 52, 83, 93

Cortés, Hernán, 32, 33

Cortes, 8, 20, 22, 23, 26, 31–32, 37, 113, 121, 130, 133, 135, 142, 144; abolition of, 17; concessions from, 172; convening, 3, 19, 34; Council of Regency and, 16; deputies to, 9, 10, 99, 106, 107, 143; elections for, 11, 12, 13, 14, 22, 33, 46–48, 97, 98–99, 100, 105; representation and, 7, 14, 36; true, 33–34, 35

Cortes Extraordinarias, 47

Cortes of Cadíz, 3, 12, 21, 47, 48, 95, 96, 157, 175, 178, 187, 194

Cortes of Castile, 27, 33, 35

Cortes of Madrid, 11, 12, 13, 20, 21, 22–23

Council of Regency, 16, 47, 92, 95, 140, 141, 178

Council of the Indies, 53, 64, 67, 68, 129, 130

Covarrubias, Diego de, 4

Covarruvias, José de, 152

criollos, 36, 62, 78, 115, 210n20

crisis of 1808, 8, 10, 17, 27, 28, 29, 44, 45, 72, 85, 88, 97, 139, 141, 187

Cuban Revolution, 195

Cuba with the two Floridas: constitutional order and, 11; political participation in, 20; representatives from, 10, 14, 19, 23

Cuenca, 21, 28, 51, 65, 67, 74, 78, 79, 93, 100, 104, 106, 111, 116; bishopric of, 52, 83; elections in, 75, 110, 113, 118; insurgency in, 89; parishes of, 114; partido of, 108, 109, 123; representatives from, 99; tribute for, 118, 119, 121

Cuero y Caicedo, José, 77, 88, 90, 92; election of, 94, 96; junta and, 89, 93, 95

Cuerpo y Tribunal de Minería, 42, 43

culture, 30, 196, 199; Catholic, 163, 203n1; French, 69; legal, 2, 5; Western European, 149

curas, 58, 82, 84, 97, 107, 108, 110, 111, 119, 120; elections and, 104

Cushman, Robert, 127

Cuzco, 22; constitution and, 13; representatives from, 10

Deidán de la Torre, Ahmed, 215n36

De Mann, Paul, 191

Demélas-Bohy, Marie-Danielle, 95, 96, 103, 216n4

deputies, 9, 10, 11, 19, 22, 23, 42, 45, 121, 140; civil society and, 56; election of, 12, 13, 14, 20, 21, 46, 47, 97, 98–99, 106, 107; parishes and, 61

Derrida, Jacques, 191, 192

Descartes, Rene, 84

Dessalines, Jean-Jacques, 137
Diario politico de Santafé de Bogotá, 155
Díaz de Herrera, Juan, 55, 56, 57, 59
Díaz Porlier, Juan, 166
Diccionario geográfico de las Indias Occidentales o América (Alcedo y Bejarano), 152, 153
Dios Cañedo, Juan de, 182
Dios Morales, Juan de, 73, 74, 76, 77, 90
diputaciónes, 22, 42, 99, 110, 157
La Diputación Provincial y el federalismo mexicano (Benson), 193
Dirección General de Rentas, 65, 70
divine right of princes, 3–4
División Protectora de Quito, 21
Dominicans, 82, 83, 87, 116
Draper, Theodor, 222n31

ecclesiastics, 7, 9, 10, 38, 82, 86, 87, 94, 96, 97, 99, 171, 187
economic development, 43, 126, 149, 150, 151
economic issues, 6, 10, 49, 51, 64, 72, 145, 146, 147
economic reforms, 83, 194
economic relationships, 30, 200
Ecuador, 101; martial law in, 24; militarism in, 26
elites, 53, 57, 72, 77, 199; domination by, 36
Elliott, John, 36
Enlightenment, 5, 85, 196
Escobedo, Jorge, 64
escoceses, 180–81, 183
Esmeraldas, 12, 71, 79
España, José María, 153
Espejo, Eugenio Santa Cruz y, 84, 86, 87, 153, 213n17

Espinosa de los Monteros, Juan José, 175, 176
Espiritu Santo, procurador of, 33
Espoz y Mina, Francisco, 166
estanco de aguardiente, 54, 55, 57, 58, 63
Estates General, 136
extermination, principle of, 127
Ezpeleta, José de, 86

Facio, José Antonio, 182
Fagoaga, Francisco, 173
federalism, 26, 49, 144, 147, 193
Feijóo, Benito Jerónimo, 84
Felipe II, King, 4, 157
Felipe V, King, 51, 52
El Fénix de la libertad, 183
Fernández de Córdova, Diego, 109, 113, 115
Fernando of Aragon, 31
Fernando VII, King, 8, 72, 74, 76, 81, 92, 99, 154, 168, 173, 174, 214n36; abdication of, 104; authority of, 95; Constitution of Cádiz and, 96; Hispanic Constitution and, 25; junta and, 13, 15, 93; liberals and, 18; opposition to, 165; protecting, 73; return of, 17, 142, 175; Riego revolt and, 164–65; Transcontinental Treaty and, 162
Filangieri, Gaetano, 150
Fish, Stanley, 196
Floridablanca, Conde de, 87
Forment, Carlos A., 203n1
Foucault, Michel, 191, 192
Fowler, Will, 179, 227n47, 230n50
Franciscans, 59, 82, 83
free trade, 5, 22, 136, 150
French, William, 198

Haiti, 29, 145, 146

Haitian Revolution, 136–38, 223n40

Hale, Charles A., 194

Hanoverian monarchy, 133, 134

The Heavenly City of the Eighteenth-Century Philosophers (Becker), 189

Herzog, Tamar, 81

Hidalgo, Miguel, 169

Himmelfarb, Gertrude, 197

Hispanic American Historical Review, 198

Hispanic Constitution (1812), 9, 10, 13, 31, 48, 49, 97, 99, 103, 104, 144, 164, 170, 172, 175; abolition of, 25; elections and, 12; governing institutions of, 165, 169; Indians and, 108; provincial governments and, 157, 193; representatives under, 109; restoration of, 165, 166, 168; socio-political revolution and, 121; suffrage and, 160

Historia antigua de México (Clavijero), 39, 133

Historia concisa de los Estados Unidos desde el descubrimiento de América hasta en año de 1807, 157

Historia de la administración del Lord North, Primer Ministro de Inglaterra, y de la Guerra América Septentrional hasta la paz, 153

Historia del derecho natural y de gentes, 150

Historia del establecimiento y comercio de las colonias inglesas en la América Septentrional (Butel-Dumont), 224n8

Historia del Reino de Quito (Velasco), 86

history: cultural, 30, 189, 193, 197, 198, 199; national, 199, 200; political, 163, 189; social, 191, 193, 197

Hobbes, Thomas, 4, 5

Hospital, Juan, 86

House of Representatives, 159

Humboldt, Alexander von, 70

Hunt, Lynn, 197

Hurtado de Mendoza, Oidor, 58, 59

Ibarra, 66, 67, 75, 94

Iguala, 174, 175, 176

Impostures intellectuelles (Bricmont), 197

independence, 15, 17, 21, 22, 24, 73, 74, 76, 125; Spanish American, 5, 18, 23, 138–44, 144–47, 159, 160, 169, 177–79; U.S., 8, 28, 29, 134, 135, 149, 151–52, 153, 155, 157, 160–62

La independencia de la Costa Firme justificada por Thomas Paine treinta años ha, 157

Indians, 11, 108, 115, 134; elections and, 117, 118; English Crown and, 127; extermination of, 127; mestizos and, 115; political activism of, 122; subject, 106, 126, 127; tribute and, 119, 120, 121

"Instrucción de Diputados y Personeros" (Carlos III), 40

Isabel of Castile, 31, 81

Isadoro of Seville, 32

Iturbide, Agustín de, 23, 48, 143, 164, 169–79, 228n17; abdication of, 49; analysis of, 186; independence and, 179; role of, 30; strategies of, 176

Iturrigaray, José de, 44, 175

Jacob, Margaret, 197

Miranda, Calixto, 88, 95, 96, 99; constitution by, 97, 214–15n36

Miranda, José, 33

miscegenation, 115, 126, 129

Mississippi River, 131, 161

Moctezuma, Francisco, 185

Molina, Joaquín, 118

Molina, Luis de, 4

monarchy, 1, 147; constitutional, 23, 103, 172; term, 220n1. *See also* Spanish Monarchy

Monteagudo, Matías, 175, 176

Montenegro, Bishop, 58

Montes, Toribio, 12, 110, 112, 115, 118, 215n36, 217n7, 218n38; *blancos hidoneos* and, 117; elections and, 104, 105; Junta of Quito and, 104; regime of, 97–100; tribute and, 119, 120; triumph of, 95

Montesclaros, Viceroy Marqués de, 34

Montevideo, 158; representatives from, 14

Montúfar, Carlos, 92, 93, 94

Montúfar, Javier, 78

Montúfar, Pedro de, 73, 75, 93

Montúfar, Xavier, 67

montúfaristas, 95, 214n36

Montúfar y Larrea, Juan Pío de, 66, 70, 75, 86, 93, 214n36

Mon y Velaverde, Juan Antonio de, 68

Mora, José María Luis, 49, 194

Morelos y Pavón, José María, 166

Moreno, Francisco José, 163

Moreno, Mariano, 158

mulattos, 108, 114, 129

Muñoz, Pedro, 76

Muslims, 2, 5, 31, 81, 125, 126, 212n1

Múzquiz, Melchor, 184

Napoleon Bonaparte, 8, 29, 72–73, 74, 137; Louisiana Purchase and, 161; Portugal and, 154; Spanish world and, 14–15

Nariño, Antonio, 153

natural-law theory, 4, 150

Navarro, José Gabriel, 211n44, 214n36

Navarro, Juan Romualdo, 58, 59

Navigation Act, 134

New Galicia, 176; representatives from, 10

New Granada, 12, 17, 18, 22, 28, 45, 51, 52, 54, 57, 63, 70, 71; assault in, 89; autonomy movement in, 15, 79, 142; constitutional order and, 11; elections in, 75; junta in, 47; militarism in, 26; representatives from, 10, 14, 19; revolt in, 67, 139; separatists and, 24

New Historicism, 192

The New History and the Old (Himmelfarb), 197

New Spain, 9, 23, 24, 25, 27, 33, 37, 39, 45, 65, 68; access to, 161; autonomy movement in, 15, 142, 170; constitutional system and, 11, 143, 172; elections in, 46, 170; finances of, 43; independence for, 178; political evolution of, 35; political participation in, 20; population of, 132; provinces of, 161; reforms in, 40; regencies for, 174; representatives from, 10, 14, 19, 46, 48, 172; royal army in, 135; unrest in, 139, 141

New World, 5, 8, 14, 18, 19, 22, 31, 32, 38, 39, 88, 96, 107; assemblies in, 33–34; balance of power in, 134; conflict in, 17, 23, 154; consensus in, 36, 37; cultural/biological integration of, 126; elections in, 45, 47; improvements in, 23; kingdoms of, 129; legal systems of, 126; representation from, 27; royal authority in, 142; Spanish Monarchy and, 139–40, 221n3; ties to, 15–16

New World Encounters (Greenblatt), 192

Nicaragua, 11; representatives from, 10

Notes on the State of Virginia (Jefferson), 133

Nouvelle Histoire Politique, 26

Novikc, Peter, 191–92

novohispanos, 11, 24, 49, 96, 176, 193; aspirations of, 174; politically active, 170–71

Oberem, Udo, 106, 217n12

O'Donnell, Enrique, 167

O'Donojú, Juan, 173, 177, 178, 179; Great Masonic Plot and, 168; novohispanos and, 174

Olañeta, Pedro Antonio, 25

oligarchy, 1, 26, 135, 136, 199

Olmedo, José Joaquín, 21

Ordenanzas de Monzón de Aragón, 5, 204n17

Ordinary Cortes, 11, 14

Otavalo, 78, 94, 99

Owensby, Brian, 37

Pacheco Leál, Antonio, 182, 183

Padilla, Agustín, 118, 119

Paine, Thomas, 157

País de un solo hombre: El México de Santa Anna (González Pedrero), 179

Panama, 12, 71, 79; proprietary deputies from, 23; representatives from, 14

parlements, creation of, 3, 150

partido, 47, 105, 108, 110

Partido of Cuenca, 108, 109; region of, 123

Partido of Loja, 108, 115, 117, 119, 124

Partido of Riobamba y Macas, 107

Pasto, 12, 93, 99; elections in, 75

patria, 3, 51, 73, 74, 78, 93, 134

Paul, Fermín, 173

Peasant and Nation: The Making of Postcolonial Mexico and Peru (Mallon), 195, 197

Peñalver, Fernando, 156

Peña, Nicolás de la, 73, 74

Pérez, Antonio Joaquín, 175

Pérez Calama, José, 85, 86, 87

Pérez de Billups, Mariano, 61

Peru, 15, 22, 28, 45, 52, 65, 71, 86, 172; assault in, 89; autonomy movement and, 79; constitutional order and, 11; cortes *indianas* and, 34; representatives from, 10, 14, 19

petits blancs, 128, 136, 137

Phelan, John, 37–38, 130

Philippines, 45, 146; representatives from, 10, 19

Philosophes, 189

Pichincha, battle of, 24, 122

Piel, Jean, 103, 206n62

Plan of Iguala, 169, 174, 176, 177

Plan of Veracruz, 179, 184

Plaza Mayor, 58, 61, 210n23

Política indiana (Solórzano Pereira), 38

Political Constitution of the Spanish Monarchy, 105, 178

political culture, 15, 27, 30, 189; challenging, 36–37; shared, 1–7

political issues, 6, 23, 49, 51, 144, 145, 146, 171

Ruiz de Castilla, President, 72, 74, 77, 89, 90–91, 92, 93, 94, 211n44, 213n23; French rule and, 75; reinstating, 79; removing, 73, 76

Ruiz de Quevedo, Tomás, 116, 117

Saint Domingue, 128, 132, 134, 145; revolution in, 136; white population of, 137

Saint-Geours, Yves, 96

Salinas, Juan, 73, 74, 76, 77, 90

San Agustin, church of, 92

San Blas, 55, 59, 60, 76, 77

Sánchez, José, 78

Sánchez de Orellana, Jacinto, Marqués de Villa Orellana, 59, 66, 76, 78, 94, 214n36

Sánchez de Orellana, Joaquín, 66

Sánchez de Tagle, Regidor, 178

Sánchez Osorio, Corregidor, 59–60

Sandinistas, 195

San Felipe, 122

San Felipe Neri, 175

San Juan del Valle, 112, 113, 116, 117, 124

San Juan Tenochtitlan, 129

San Luis, procurador of, 33

San Luis Potosí, 10, 41

San Martín, José de, 18, 22, 24–25, 142

San Miguel, Evaristo, 165

San Roque, 55, 57, 59, 61, 76, 77; unrest in, 58, 60

San Sebastián, 55, 57, 59, 61, 76, 77, 116, 229n26; compromisarios from, 124; parish of, 117; protests in, 58, 60

Santa Anna, Antonio López de, 164, 179–86; analysis of, 186; Plan de Veracruz and, 179; role of, 30

Santa Anna of Mexico (Fowler), 179, 227n2

Santa Anna: The Story of an Enigma Who Once Was Mexico (Calcott), 179

Santa Cruz y Centeno, Luis de, 56, 62

Santa Cruz y Espejo, Francisco de, 70

Santa Fé, 52, 54, 55, 56, 70, 71, 79, 86, 90, 93; elites in, 53

Santa Fé de Bogotá, 12, 16, 93

Santiago: electors from, 124; federalism and, 26; junta in, 32

Santiago Tlatelolco, 129

Santo Domingo, 137; constitutional order and, 11; political participation in, 20; representatives from, 10, 14, 19

School of Salamanca, 3–4

Schwartz, Steward, 198

Scott, Joan, 192

self-government, 31, 38, 43, 129, 130, 168, 169, 170

Selva Alegre, Marqués de, 66, 67, 70, 71, 73, 74, 76–79, 86, 89, 92, 93; election of, 94; sanchistas and, 95

Selva Florida, Conde de, 58, 60, 61, 66

Sendero Luminoso, 195

Septimo, Fernando, 73

Serna, Joaquín de la, 25

Seven Years' War (1756–1763), 29, 127, 134, 151, 152

Sicilia Americana, 71

Sigüenza y Góngora, Carlos, 35

Silva y Olave, José de, 89–90

silver, production of, 42, 132

Skinner, Quentin, 4, 5, 191

slaves, 29, 128, 135, 136–37, 138

Smith, Adam, 150

social compact, 26, 128–30

"social contract" theories, 4
social issues, 54, 144
social mobility, 115, 126
social relationships, 30, 200
social revolution, 135, 172
social structure, 30, 125, 128, 151, 190, 196
Social Text (journal), 196
Sociedad Económica de Amigos del
  País, 70, 86–87
Socolow, Susan, 198
Sokal, Alan, 196, 197
Solanda, Marqués de, 76
Solemn Pact of Association and Union
  Among the Provinces the State of
  Quito (Rodríguez), 95
Solórzano Pereira, Juan de, 38, 56,
  209n13
Sosaya, Juan de, 53
Sovereign Governing Junta, 177, 178
sovereignty, 2, 8, 15, 39, 97, 100;
  divided, 49; king, 73, 74; legislative, 178; popular, 3, 4, 5, 32, 44,
  139, 141, 149–50, 154, 187, 225n16
Spanish America: Bourbon reforms
  and, 138; independence of, 5, 29,
  138–44, 146, 155, 159, 160, 162; nations
  of, 160, 161; reconquering, 165
Spanish Americans, 7, 44, 142; Indian
  heritage of, 134; locality/history
  and, 39
Spanish Monarchy, 1, 7, 9, 23, 29, 31,
  47, 74, 75, 87, 88, 96; absolutism of,
  37–38; American Revolution and,
  153; Catholicism and, 81, 82, 161,
  163; confederation of, 125, 221n3;
  crisis of, 27, 28, 45, 85, 139; dissolution of, 8, 27, 29, 44, 138, 142,
  170, 172; extermination and, 127;

French domination of, 69, 153, 154,
  157; independence from, 100, 142,
  158, 160; New World and, 139–40;
  overseas possessions of, 146; political revolution and, 147; political
  system of, 1, 7, 15; reform and, 150;
  religious unity by, 126; repres-
  sion by, 17–18; restoration of, 99;
  Spanish America and, 20, 151, 165;
  structure of, 128, 129; unrest and,
  139; wars for, 151
Spanish Nation, 8, 78, 217n16
Spanish War of Independence, 166
Stamp Act, 134, 152
States-General, 3
Stevenson, William B., 213n23, 214n28
Structure of Scientific Revolutions
  (Kuhn), 190
Suárez, Francisco, 4, 149
Sucre, Antonio José de, 24, 25, 100
suffrage, 10, 41, 48, 49, 135, 160
Sugar Act, 152
Superior Junta, 92, 93
suplentes, 12, 13, 14, 18, 19, 22, 23, 99, 106
Supreme Central and Governing
  Junta of the Kingdom, 74

Tamaulipas, unrest at, 185
Tampico, battle at, 185
taxes, 55–56, 138–39; collecting, 62;
  liquor, 54; property, 78; resisting
  unjust, 35; unwarranted, 36; war, 171
Tea Act, 134
Te Deum, 88, 99, 104
Telling the Truth About History
  (Appleby, Hunt, and Jacob), 197
Teresa de Mier, Servando, 5–6, 38,
  159, 166